PRODUCT
DEVELOPMENT

Product Development shares a specialist's perspectives and ideas, and develops concepts and methods. The result is a comprehensive overview of the main theoretical and empirical research work being undertaken by product development specialist – from a marketing perspective.

Margaret Bruce and Wim Biemans have brought together a team of specialists who have been working on product development within a European framework for many years.

The book is divided into sections dealing with:

- ***The Marketing Perspective*** the impact of technology and the needs of the business

- ***The Design–Marketing Interface*** design management from concept to market and interfaces between design and other key functions

- ***Networks and Relationships*** Managing collaboration and developing capabilities for innovation

- ***Launch Strategies*** managing product announcements and devising launch strategies

- ***Adoption and Diffusion*** impact in consumer and business-to-business markets

- ***Contemporary Issues*** environmentally responsible new products and product liability issues

All of these points are vividly illustrated throughout the book.

All in all, ***Product Development*** shows how to manage the process so that products can be brought to the market-place quickly and at a competitive price that appeals to a global market.

PRODUCT DEVELOPMENT

Meeting the Challenge of the Design–Marketing Interface

Edited by

Margaret Bruce
UMIST, UK

and

Wim G. Biemans
University of Groningen, The Netherlands

JOHN WILEY & SONS

Chichester · New York · Brisbane · Toronto · Singapore

Other Wiley Editorial Offices

John Wiley & Sons, Inc., 605 Third Avenue,
New York, NY 10158-0012, USA

Jacaranda Wiley Ltd, 33 Park Road, Milton,
Queensland 4064, Australia

John Wiley & Sons (Canada) Ltd, 22 Worcester Road,
Rexdale, Ontario M9W 1L1, Canada

John Wiley & Sons (SEA) Pte Ltd, 37 Jalan Pemimpin #05-04,
Block B, Union Industrial Building, Singapore 2057

Library of Congress Cataloging-in-Publication Data

Product development : meeting the challenge of the design–marketing
    interface / edited by Margaret Bruce and Wim G. Biemans.
        p.   cm.
    Includes bibliographical references and index.
    ISBN 0-471-95353-9
        1. Product management.   2. New products—Marketing.   3. Design,
    Industrial.   I. Bruce, Margaret.   II. Biemans, Wim G., *1960–*   .
    HF5415.15.P762   1995
    658.5'75—dc20   94–41380
                                                                    CIP

British Library Cataloguing in Publication Data

A catalogue record for this book is available from the British Library

ISBN 0-471-95353-9

Typeset in 10/12pt Times by Dorwyn Ltd, Rowlands Castle, Hants
Printed and bound in Great Britain by Bookcraft (Bath) Ltd

This book is printed on acid-free paper responsibly manufactured from
sustainable forestation, for which at least two trees are planted for each one
used for paper production.

CONTENTS

ABOUT THE EDITORS

Margaret Bruce

Manchester School of Management, University of Manchester Institute of Science and Technology (UMIST), PO Box 88, Manchester M60 1QD, UK
Dr Margaret Bruce is a senior lecturer in design management and marketing at Manchester School of Management, UMIST. Over the past 10 years, she has carried out major research programmes in the area of design management, all of which have been independently funded by the Economic and Social Research Council (ESRC). Three books and major reports and a number of publications have arisen from the research, including *Winning by Design* (co-authored with Vivien Walsh, Robin Roy and Stephen Potter), Basil Blackwell (1992).

Dr Bruce received a Fulbright Scholarship in 1992 and was a senior visiting research fellow at the Design Management Institute, Boston, and Harvard Business School.

Wim G. Biemans

Faculty of Management and Organisation, University of Groningen, PO Box 88, 9700 AV Groningen, The Netherlands
Dr Wim Biemans is associate professor of marketing at the Faculty of Management and Organisation of the University of Groningen. His research centres on product development, collaboration, strategic alliances and industrial marketing. He has published extensively on product development, and is the author of *Managing Innovation with Networks* (Routledge, 1992). Current research projects concern the management of new product announcements, the 'grey area' between industrial and consumer marketing, and the implementation of market-oriented product development.

CONTRIBUTORS

Contributors are drawn from a wide range of Universities and Business Schools in Europe. Their breadth and depth of experience provides an unrivalled perspective on product development. The strength of Product Development is that this perspective is coordinated and organised into themes which will be of great practical use to everyone whether their interest is as an academic or as a practioner.

Rachel Davies-Cooper
Research Unit, Adelphi House, University College Salford, Peru Street, The Crescent, Salford M6 6PU, UK
Dr Rachel Davies-Cooper is a research fellow and head of the Research Unit at University College Salford, as well as a senior research fellow of the Design Management Institute and an associate member of the Design Innovation Group. Trained as a graphic designer, she has worked as a design consultant and lecturer in design, design management and marketing for over ten years. Dr Davies-Cooper has completed research projects in design management for the Department of Trade and Industry (DTI) and the Council for National and Academic Awards (CNAA), and is currently funded by the Marketing Science Institute to research the design/marketing relationship in new product development, and by the Engineering and Physical Sciences Research Council to study market research techniques for identifying and translating end-user requirements into new product design briefs. She is also working on research with the Universities of Michigan and Alabama. Dr Cooper has written three books and over twenty articles on design, design management, design research and psychology, and has worked with such major companies as GPT Ltd, Motorola and Pacific Bell.

Janine Dermody

University of Greenwich Business School, University of Greenwich, Wellington Street, Woolwich, London SE18 6PF, UK.

Janine Dermody is a lecturer in marketing at the University of Greenwich Business School. She holds a first degree in psychology and law, and a postgraduate marketing diploma. She worked in market research for several years before joining Bristol Business School to read for her PhD. Her current areas of research are in environmental issues and marketing, and she also lectures in market research and consumer behaviour.

Gordon R. Foxall

Director, Research Centre for Consumer Behaviour, University of Birmingham, PO Box 363, Edgbaston, Birmingham B15 2TT, UK

Gordon Foxall is professor of consumer research at the University of Birmingham, where he is also director of the Research Centre for Consumer Behaviour at the Birmingham Business School. He holds doctorates from the University of Birmingham (in industrial economics and business studies) and from the University of Strathclyde (in psychology). Gordon Foxall is the author of a dozen books, including *Consumer Psychology in Behavioural Perspective*, described by one reviewer as a 'landmark monograph' and by another as 'one of the best, if not the best, books in its field to date'. He also recently co-authored a consumer behaviour text, *Consumer Psychology for Marketing* (with Ron Goldsmith), and has written well over 100 refereed papers and articles on consumer behaviour, marketing and related themes. His research interests are in consumer theory and innovativeness.

Ruud T. Frambach

Department of Business Administration, Tilburg University, PO Box 90153, 5000 LE Tilburg, The Netherlands

Ruud Frambach received his PhD in 1993 from the Faculty of Economics at Tilburg University, The Netherlands, where he is currently assistant professor in the department of business administration. His dissertation was on the diffusion of innovations in the industrial market. His current research interests include the adoption and diffusion of innovations, and the formulation and implementation of marketing strategy.

Stuart Hanmer-Lloyd

Bristol Business School, University of the West of England, Frenchay Campus, Coldharbour Lane, Bristol BS16 1QY, UK

Stuart Hanmer-Lloyd is a senior lecturer at Bristol Business School, University of the West of England. He holds a first degree from City University, London, an MBA from Birmingham University and a PhD from Cranfield School of Management. After an early career in marketing, he became a self-employed marketing consultant, and in 1983 he joined Bristol Business School. He is involved in a variety of research projects, mainly in relation to the health market.

Susan Hart

Heriot-Watt Business School, Department of Business Administration, Heriot-Watt University, PO Box 807, Riccarton, Edinburgh EH14 4AS, UK
Susan Hart is a professor in the department of business organisation at Heriot-Watt University, teaching marketing strategy and new product development. After working in industry in France and the UK, she joined the University of Strathclyde as a researcher. She completed her doctoral degree on the subject of product management, and worked on research projects examining the contribution of marketing to competitive success and new product design and development in manufacturing industry, funded by the ESRC, the Chartered Institute of Marketing and the Design Council. She has worked with several companies in teaching company schemes and has held visiting professorships in Europe and the USA. Her current research interests are in the development of new products and innovation, the contribution of marketing to company success and product deletion.

Erik Jan Hultink

Delft University of Technology, Jaffalaan, No. 9, 2628 BX Delft, The Netherlands
Erik Jan Hultink is assistant professor of marketing at the Faculty of Industrial Design Engineering, Delft University of Technology. He received his MSc in economics from the University of Amsterdam in The Netherlands. His PhD research concentrates on launch strategies and new product success measures. Other current research interests include high-technology marketing and marketing planning for new products.

Birgit Helene Jevnaker

Centre for Research in Economics and Business Administration, Breviken 2, N-5035 Bergen, Sandviken, Norway
Birgit Helene Jevnaker has an economics degree and examinations from the doctoral programme in administration from the Norwegian School of Economics and Business Administration. She studies public administration and organisation theory and psychology at the University of Bergen.

She has sixteen years of applied research experience, mainly for the Institute of Industrial Economics and the Foundation for Research in Economics and Business Administration in Bergen. She has specialised in strategic management and design, and is currently conducting a study on design expertise and industry commissioned by the Norwegian Design Council. She also teaches design and management courses for industrial design students at the Royal College of Art and Design, Oslo.

Axel Johne

Director, Innovation Research Unit, City University Business School, Frobisher Crescent, Barbican Centre, London EC2Y 8HB, UK

Axel Johne is professor of marketing and director of the Innovation Research Unit at City University Business School, London. His research interests are focused on product and business development. He has conducted empirical studies examining product development success in manufacturing companies. His current work concentrates on product development in financial services companies.

Axel Johne was born in Germany in 1940, but received all of his formal education in Britain. Prior to entering university teaching he worked with ICI, Britain's largest chemical company, in market research, product development and marketing management. He has published three books concerned with market-led innovation and new product development, as well as over forty research papers in journals such as *International Journal of Research in Marketing, Industrial Marketing Management* and *Journal of Product Innovation Management*.

Tim Jones

Research Unit, Adelphi House, University College Salford, Peru Street, The Crescent, Salford M6 6PU, UK

Tim Jones, currently a research fellow at the Centre for Design, Manufacture and Technology, University College Salford, graduated from the University of Cambridge with an honours degree in engineering. He worked as a design engineer, before reading for his PhD in new product development at the University of Salford. He has worked on an international programme aimed at resolving conflict between the different functions involved in the development process, and on an EPSRC-funded project to identify best practice in market research and specification generation in high technology industries. He has presented several papers at international conferences.

Fiona Leverick

Manchester School of Management, University of Manchester Institute of Science and Technology (UMIST), PO Box 88, Manchester M60 1QD, UK

Fiona Leverick is a research associate at the Manchester School of Management. She graduated from Lancaster University with a first class honours degree in marketing, and since then has been pursuing research interests in the areas of new product development, strategic marketing in new technology based sectors, and consumer behaviour in relation to innovative products.

Dale Littler
Manchester School of Management, University of Manchester Institute of Science and Technology (UMIST), PO Box 88, Manchester M60 1QD, UK
Dale Litter is professor of marketing at the Manchester School of Management. He has undertaken wide-ranging research on marketing and technological innovation, including aspects of new product development, the marketing of innovative consumer products, strategic marketing in new technology sectors and adoption and diffusion with particular regard to ICTs. He is the author of many articles and several books, including *Marketing and Product Development* and *Technological Development*.

Gerard H. Loosschilder
Delft University of Technology, Jaffalaan, No. 9, 2628 BX Delft, The Netherlands
Gerard H. Loosschilder is assistant professor of consumer research, at the School of Industrial Design Engineering, Delft University of Technology, The Netherlands. He holds a degree in mass communication from the Catholic University of Nijmegen, The Netherlands. He has worked as a project manager at a market research agency (Centrum voor Marketing Analyses, Amsterdam). His current research and teaching focus primarily upon methodological and application-orientated issues in qualitative and quantitative consumer research in industrial design engineering, particularly the design process. His current area of interest concerns the application of computer-aided design and computer graphics in consumer research.

Barny Morris
Manchester School of Management, University of Manchester Institute of Science and Technology (UMIST), PO Box 88, Manchester M60 1QD, UK
Barny Morris is a research associate for the Manchester School of Management, UMIST, from which he recently graduated with an MSc in marketing. Originally a product designer with two years' industrial experience and a degree in three-dimensional design, he now researches design management as a member of the Design Innovation Group (DIG).

Arie P. Nagel
Eindhoven University of Technology, PO Box 513, 5600 MB Eindhoven, The Netherlands
Arie Nagel studied mechanical and industrial engineering and management science. After having worked with Hoogovens, Ahold, Shell and Philips, he is now a part-time assistant professor at the Eindhoven University of Technology. In 1992 he was awarded his doctorate with a dissertation on 'Increasing the potential for strategic product innovation'. In 1994 he was elected president of the International Society for Professional Innovation Management (ISPIM).

Henk Ritsema

Faculty of Management and Organisation, University of Groningen, PO Box 88, 9700 AV Groningen, The Netherlands

Henk Ritsema studied economics and law at the University of Groningen. He is currently an assistant professor at the Faculty of Management and Organisation there. His teaching and research interests are in the areas of international management and international commercial law. He has co-authored books on Dutch company law and on product liability. He is also the (co-)author of various articles on product liability issues, international management and strategic management.

Henry S.J. Robben

Delft University of Technology, Jaffalaan, No. 9, 2628 BX Delft, The Netherlands

Henry Robben is associate professor of marketing at the Faculty of Industrial Design Engineering, Delft University of Technology. He received a BA in psychology and an MA in economic psychology from Tilburg University, and his PhD in psychology from Erasmus University, both in The Netherlands. He has published on business management simulations, marketing effects of scarcity, and the effectiveness of marketing communications.

Jan P.L. Schoormans

Delft University of Technology, Jaffalaan, No. 9, 2628 BX Delft, The Netherlands

Jan Schoormans is associate professor of consumer research at the School of Industrial Design Engineering, Delft University of Technology. He received his MA in economic psychology and his PhD in psychology from Tilburg University in the Netherlands. He has published on consumer behaviour and on consumer research in product development.

Henriette J. Setz

c/o Professor Wim Biemans, Faculty of Management and Organisation, University of Groningen, PO Box 88, 9700 AV Groningen, The Netherlands

Henriette Setz studied management science at the Faculty of Technology of the Enschede Polytechnic, from 1987 to 1991. From 1991 to 1994, she studied business administration at the Faculty of Management and Organisation of the University of Groningen, and conducted a study of product development processes and the announcement of new products in the telecommunications industry. In 1994 she joined Quest International, a Unilever subsidiary, as marketing support manager.

PREFACE

The book has arisen out of two highly successful workshops, 'Meeting the Challenges of New Product Development', held in 1993 at the University of Groningen, The Netherlands and in 1994 at UMIST, UK. The participants of both workshops were European academics specialising in the area of product development and marketing. The idea behind both workshops was to have a small, informal group of invited scholars to share and exchange ideas and to develop conceptual themes and methodological approaches. This book provides a comprehensive overview of the main theoretical and empirical work being undertaken by European researchers in the field of product development, from a marketing perspective. As such, it is a valuable collection that reflects the range and quality of research that is being undertaken.

Margaret Bruce
Wim G. Biemans
July 1994

ACKNOWLEDGEMENTS

We are indebted to two colleagues, Dale Littler, professor of marketing, UMIST, and Fiona Leverick, research associate, CROMTEC, UMIST, for their support and encouragement. Their pertinent comments, boundless energy and enthusiasm have culminated in the successful UMIST–Groningen Workshop, 'Meeting the Challenges of New Product Development', and in this collection of papers. We wish to thank all of the authors for their contributions. Thanks must go to Michelle Tierney of UMIST, who word-processed the material, and to Diane Taylor and Claire Plimmer of John Wiley & Sons.

THE ROLE OF MARKETING IN PRODUCT DEVELOPMENT
Margaret Bruce and Wim G. Biemans

Product development is fundamental to stimulating and supporting economic growth for organisations and for wealth generation in many industrialised nations. Product development is a strategic process and product development and design activities are powerful corporate tools.

Products are the lifeblood of organisations. They are the public face of a corporation. The style, quality and ingenuity of the company's image are represented through its products. BMW cars denote quality engineering, as well as status, while Volvo cars are renowned for safety; both are sought after throughout the world. Levi jeans mean style, sex appeal and a Western life-style. Body Shop cosmetics reinforce the company's mission; that is, 'to be the honest cosmetic company' with its use of environmental packaging and non-animal tested products. The ability to differentiate one's products in an increasingly competitive and crowded market-place and to meet the needs of the main target markets are the cornerstones of success. A sense of urgency to develop new products and to reduce 'time to market' are affected by the competitive nature of the market-place.

A critical facet of product development is marketing. No matter how technology is acquired, it has to be used in products that customers need and want, and products have to be positioned and competitively priced to meet market

Product Development: Meeting the Challenge of the Design–Marketing Interface.
Edited by M. Bruce and W.G. Biemans.   © 1995 John Wiley & Sons Ltd.

needs and expectations. Without effective marketing, products may be over-engineered or too highly priced. It is the combination of marketing with design and development activities that requires effective management.

Designing and developing products that are appropriate for market needs is not easy; market demands and user needs are unstable and constantly open to change. For example, 'environmental' issues are a major selling point for some consumer goods, such as washing machines, and affect consumer choice in the mass market. Companies have to be able to anticipate and identify new consumer demands, in the abstract, and ahead of potential competitors.

A number of factors have been identified as particularly affecting the product development process. The rapid pace of technological change, the high cost of product development, the need for correct market timing and ever increasing competition are among these factors. Uncertainty is another dimension governing the product development process. The effects of both market uncertainty (What are the target markets? What price would they be willing to pay? etc.) and technological uncertainty (What will be the dominant standard? What are the optimum design features? etc.) make it problematic for companies to gauge the appropriate technology path and, within this, the optimum design for given market segments. The more radical the development, the greater the difficulty in making, *ex ante*, assessments of the technical and market opportunities and problems that are likely to arise.

Essentially, product development is the process that transforms technical ideas or market needs and opportunities into a new or modified product that is launched onto the market.

A variety of ways of developing effective products quickly – however 'effective' is assessed – exist. Current 'best practice' indicates that multidisciplinary teams that are process-orientated rather than function-orientated, and co-located and embedded in a culture that fosters innovativeness and some degree of risk taking are likely to be effective. A major implication of this approach to managing the product development process is that marketing and design interfaces are critical, and good communication between these aspects of product development is essential.

Collaboration in product development to reduce the risks and costs of product development is increasingly commonplace, so much so that a collaborative approach is part of the 'received wisdom' of various industries, notably biotechnology and information technology. The collaboration has to be managed, and this can absorb a great deal of management time and effort, and needs top level support and an equitable contribution, if it is to work to the mutual satisfaction/

benefit of all parties concerned. One implication is that of managing the tension and potential conflict between, on the one hand, being open and sharing knowledge between different companies, who may be competitors in other product markets, and on the other, ensuring that proprietary knowledge remains secure. A major risk of collaborative ventures for product development is that so much effort is put into maintaining the relationship that changes to the external environment may be neglected, so that the product fails to meet market needs.

Outsourcing of expertise and skills pertinent to product development is evident, rather than all of the relevant skills and expertise being located in-house. What is the likelihood of losing core competencies from within the firm in order to outsource, which, once lost, may be difficult to replace? The main implication for management practice is a shift from the management of in-house product development teams to the establishment of relationships with external suppliers.

This book looks at product development from a marketing perspective, and discusses a number of relevant marketing issues, ranging from defining product development within a broader context to the use of conjoint analysis for the evaluation of launch strategies. In this introductory chapter we will integrate the various marketing perspectives presented by discussing the major themes of the book.

STRUCTURE AND ORGANISATION OF THE BOOK

This book is divided into six sections, each of which addresses a separate theme in product development. The sections and chapters are briefly introduced here, before a discussion of the major integrating themes of the book.

Section 1 provides an overview of the main conceptual themes in the marketing literature that addresses the product development process. Hart reviews the main themes, which consider product development from a strategic point of view to a tactical level, and covers different approaches to the management of the product development process. Finally, she provides a critique of the literature and argues that a perspective taking account of the complex information flows involved in the product development process is that of networks. Hart ends by providing a model – the multiple convergent approach – for examining the product development process.

Johne places product development within a broader business context and examines ways of integrating product development with business objectives. From this broader perspective, he discusses the evaluation of product success.

Technology has a critical role to play in the product development process. Nagel provides a framework technology strategy to assist smaller companies, in particular, to integrate technology into their strategic plans.

After this overview, more specific themes are examined in detail. The second section focuses on the management of the design and marketing interface. Eliciting communication problems between different functions involved in the product development process is dealt with by Davies-Cooper and Jones. They have developed and implemented a diagnostic tool to help companies to improve the design–marketing interface. Bruce and Morris consider the issue of outsourcing of design expertise, and question the basis on which the decision to outsource is made: are companies in danger of losing their core design competencies? Different cases are presented to explore this issue.

Testing design concepts with potential end users so as to provide the design team with precise information about consumer attitudes and perceptions is addressed by Loosschilder and Schoormans. They describe a study they have carried out using a means–end chain approach.

Section 3 introduces the theme of networks and relationships. Biemans argues that companies need to integrate external and internal networks to manage the product development process effectively.

Bruce, Leverick and Littler consider the risks and rewards of collaborative product development based on a major survey of UK companies. A framework to assist in the management of collaborative product development is presented.

Jevnaker examines the process by which new design ideas are accepted by senior executives. She documents the case of a Norwegian furniture company that worked closely with an external designer to devise and market a radically new seating concept, the Balans chair. For Jevnaker, 'inaugurative learning' is the key to the acceptance of new ideas.

Section 4 considers a neglected area in product development, that of companies' strategies for launching new products. Biemans and Setz consider both internal and external launch strategies for a number of telecommunications products. Hultink and Robben identify the main variables affecting product launch strategies, and recommend an approach to improve these, based on conjoint analysis.

Adoption and diffusion is the theme of Section 5. Frambach focuses on business-to-business markets. He critically appraises the literature and suggests that the role of suppliers needs to be considered in the diffusion process. Foxall considers the features of adoptors and maintains that the needs of early innovators have been neglected. He presents empirical evidence to support his argument.

Issues that are particularly acute to the product development process are discussed in Section 6. Dermody and Hanmer-Lloyd investigate the extent to which companies are taking account of environmental issues in product planning, and they examine how the product development process can take account of environmental issues. Ritsema demonstrates the role of product liability and the implications for product development.

MAJOR INTEGRATING THEMES OF THE BOOK

Taking a closer look at the various contributions presented in this book, five integrating themes emerge:

- product development in a broader context
- use of innovative theoretical perspectives and techniques
- relevance of relationships and networking
- improvement of specific product development activities
- influence of specific issues on product development

Each of these integrating themes is discussed briefly below.

PRODUCT DEVELOPMENT IN A BROADER CONTEXT

The main thrust for this theme comes from Johne's chapter on the evaluation of product development success. Johne makes a convincing case for viewing product development within the broader context of business development, which can be pursued by four types of supporting development:

- product development
- market development
- product positioning development
- supply development

The emphasis placed on each of these activities may depend on the company and industry concerned. By making this distinction, Johne effectively integrates the development of the physical product with, for example, that of the supporting marketing mix; a sensible approach, as many companies have experienced in practice.

By discussing adoption and diffusion theory (Frambach) and the characteristics of early innovators and late adopters (Foxall), the process of product development is explicitly linked to market acceptance. Far too often, the development of new products is regarded in isolation from adoption of the product by the market. Companies can increase their chances of successful product development by integrating both processes, for instance by developing a continuous dialogue with potential product users.

Naturally, defining product development in a broader context has consequences for the way in which companies should evaluate new product success. For instance, Johne argues that companies should evaluate the success of their new products against market potentials rather than against internal corporate objectives.

USE OF INNOVATIVE THEORETICAL PERSPECTIVES AND TECHNIQUES

Both Hart and Biemans argue that a new theoretical perspective might prove to be fruitful for improving product development research and practice. In summing up her extensive review of the product development literature, Hart concludes that new product development is not a linear process, and may involve a number of different functions and external parties, all of which share information and need to be integrated. To accommodate for these observations, she proposes a multiple convergent process model and suggests that network analysis provides the right tools to study the interaction processes that are central to product development practice. This observation is also taken up by Biemans, who distinguishes between internal and external networks, and strongly advocates the integration of both.

In addition to these suggestions, at a conceptual level, several authors argue in favour of specific techniques that may be applied during product development. For instance, Hultink and Robben suggest the use of conjoint analysis to evaluate launch strategies, while Loosschilder and Schoormans describe their approach to testing concepts with potential end users and then feeding this market research information directly to the design team. More precise design specifications limited to user needs can be developed.

RELEVANCE OF RELATIONSHIPS AND NETWORKING

Many chapters mention the relevance of relationships and networking. Jevnaker describes long-term relationships between designers and clients, and the influence of designers on the design philosophy of the client firm. Similarly, Bruce and Morris analyse the increasing outsourcing of design expertise and different approaches taken to manage external design expertise. Bruce, Leverick and Littler discuss collaborative product development and highlight the risks and rewards of such ventures. Davies-Cooper and Jones focus on collaboration within the firm by investigating the interfaces between design and other key functions. Biemans and Hart make a case for integrating both external and internal networks.

Indeed, collaboration, interaction and networks seem to be key words describing new product development. Whether the discussion is about reducing time to market or improving the quality of new products, the emphasis is put onto collaboration and networking. As Tom Peters (1994) put it recently, 'Networking is life itself for many leading-edge firms. For MCI, as for Apple, the ability to create – then manage and then disintegrate – networks of assorted sizes and flavours is arguably core competence No.1'.

IMPROVEMENT OF SPECIFIC PRODUCT DEVELOPMENT ACTIVITIES

Page (1993) considers the 'execution of activities within the new product development process' to be the most important obstacle to successful new product development. The various chapters in this book provide useful suggestions to improve specific new product development activities, as follows:

- Loosschilder and Schoormans argue that the value of concept testing is largely determined by the nature and quality of the information included in the concept. They provide a theoretical base for concept testing and propose that firms can improve their concept testing by using the means–end chain model.
- Biemans and Setz investigate new product announcements in the Dutch telecommunications industry and offer detailed guidelines that firms can use to improve their management of new product announcements, thus increasing their chances of successful new product launches.
- Hultink and Robben explore the variables influencing new product launch strategies and illustrate how companies may use conjoint analysis to improve their launch strategies.

INFLUENCE OF SPECIFIC ISSUES ON PRODUCT DEVELOPMENT

Throughout the book, there are a number of specific issues that clearly affect the management of the product development process. For instance, there is the growing interest in design. With products becoming more and more similar in appearance, function and performance, many companies find that design can be used as a competitive advantage, clearly distinguishing their products from the competition. However, design involves much more than just the aesthetic aspects of the product, and is closely related to development and production (design for assembly, ease of production, recycling, etc.). A number of chapters illustrate various aspects of the management of design, such as:

- the interfaces between design and other key functions in new product development (Davies-Cooper and Jones)
- the outsourcing and management of external design expertise (Bruce and Morris)
- the influence of external design consultants on a client's design philosophy (Jevnaker)

In addition, the book contains two chapters on contemporary issues that influence the product development process. Dermody and Hanmer-Lloyd focus on environmental aspects, and discusses how firms can integrate environmental responsibility into their new product development process. Ritsema discusses the issue of product liability and argues that this kind of legal matter should be reflected in the management and execution of product development. Naturally, these are just a sample of the various specific issues that may affect the management of new product development. For instance, with the increasing use of collaborative product development, firms will find the issue of patents and patent protection becoming increasingly relevant.

Product development is central to wealth generation, and effective product design combined with product and process innovation is critical to long-term competitiveness. Marketing has a key role to play throughout the process of product development, to ensure that creative ideas and new technologies that fulfil changing market needs are exploited commercially. This edited collection is intended to provide some conceptual and practical guidelines for those attempting to improve the management and practice of product development from a marketing perspective.

REFERENCES

Page, A.L. (1993). Assessing new product development practices and performance: Establishing crucial norms, *Journal of Product Innovation Management*, **10**, 273–290.

Peters, T. (1994). *The Tom Peters Seminar – Crazy Times Call for Crazy Organizations*, Vintage Books, New York.

PRODUCT DEVELOPMENT: A MARKETING PERSPECTIVE

INTRODUCTION

Margaret Bruce

The central role of product development in a business context is discussed in this section. By critically appraising major conceptual themes in the field of product development, new directions, which may provide further insights into the management of product development, are presented and discussed.

One of the prevalent themes of product development is that of identifying critical success factors, so Hart claims in her review of the conceptual evolution of the field. Attempts to isolate critical success factors have meant that product development has been considered in terms of strategy, organisation and management practice, as well as people, process and information. Essentially, the main issues of product development relate to the need for interdisciplinary inputs, for quality inputs and for speed in the process. One area that is neglected is that of harnessing the internal and external networks that are extensively involved in product development. Building on her comprehensive literature review, Hart elaborates a framework for product development, which she refers to as 'the multiple convergent approach'.

The conceptual difficulties of measuring product development success are discussed by Johne in Chapter 2. He places product development in the broader context of business development, and assesses its role. Both objective and subjective measures are commonly used, and there is no consensus as to which measures – for example, market, financial, product objectives, etc. – are the most effective. Hence, different studies draw upon different measures of success, thus precluding the possibility of comparative analysis. Johne focuses on one factor that is regarded as being an indicator of success, namely, 'listening to the market'. He reviews various 'styles of listening to the market' and pinpoints the most effective ones.

Product development is usually closely related to technological development. The thrust of Nagel's chapter serves to put technology at the forefront of the product development process. He suggests that product development practice is unduly governed by short-termism, and fears that 'me-too' products will emerge at the expense of radical innovations, which require a longer term vision and commitment. Nagel presents a framework for a technology strategy, and demonstrates its applicability for small and medium-sized companies.

CHAPTER ONE

WHERE WE'VE BEEN AND WHERE WE'RE GOING IN NEW PRODUCT DEVELOPMENT RESEARCH

Susan Hart

'New product development' is a topic that continues to exercise the minds of researchers across the gamut of academic disciplines. From economics to engineering, manufacturing to marketing sciences, organisational behaviour to operations research, a plethora of studies cover a huge variety of issues whose identity of interest lies within the quest for improving new product development in companies. This chapter considers the research in these disciplines that has specifically focused on the critical success factors in new product development, and, based on the research findings, proposes an alternative model of the new product development process and suggests that this process be examined by means of network analysis.

INTRODUCTION

Recognition of the importance of new product developments to corporate and economic prosperity, coupled with the high risk of failure in such endeavours, has triggered considerable research interest in the dynamics of new product development (NPD). The research, from a variety of domains including marketing, management, engineering, R&D and economics, has been widely reported in a number of journals and has created a large and complex body of literature relating to the various elements involved in NPD.

Product Development: Meeting the Challenge of the Design–Marketing Interface.
Edited by M. Bruce and W.G. Biemans.   © 1995 John Wiley & Sons Ltd.

This chapter reviews the literature that examines the critical success factors in NPD and attempts to draw some conclusions and make suggestions for future directions.

The chapter uses the term 'new product development' to cover the process by which new products are developed in companies. However, NPD is not the only term used to describe this process. In fact, the particular terminology employed depends very much on the domain in which it is used. 'NPD' tends to be the label used by those in marketing and management (Cooper 1979); those in the R&D domain invariably refer to 'innovation' (Rothwell 1977; Rothwell et al. 1974); those from the sphere of engineering use the term 'design'; and those from a 'design' background – in the widest sense of the word – may prefer to see 'new product design' as a specific stage in the process of developing new products. However, this categorisation is not always clear cut, and writers from marketing and management also use the terms 'design' and 'innovation' (Johne and Snelson 1988a, 1988b; Ughanwa and Baker 1989). In this chapter the terms are used interchangeably, reflecting the inter-disciplinary nature of NPD.

This chapter does not attempt an exhaustive review of NPD literature. Indeed, attempting such a feat across the salient disciplines would be an onerous task. Rather, it focuses on the themes that research has shown to have an impact on the success rates of NPD, and further examines two of these themes, namely, the NPD *process* itself, and the *people* responsible for its implementation. These two, it is argued, are central to the future of NPD research, not because they matter uniquely, but because they can help to bridge the cross-disciplinary gap, which is currently holding back NPD research, and because they relate to the most frequently cited reasons for NPD success. In addition, they are linked not only to each other, but also to the other themes important to the 'success' literature, and therefore serve as convenient summary issues, preserving the scientific demands of parsimony. Following these central themes, an NPD process model is proposed that takes cognisance of contemporary issues in NPD, such as time-based competition, integration of markets and technologies, and closer horizontal interfirm alliances of the kind described by Rothwell (1991) and Biemans (1992) (see also Biemans, Chapter 7, this volume).

MAJOR THEMES IN THE NPD SUCCESS LITERATURE

A previous review of the literature (Craig and Hart 1992) has, using content analysis, identified key themes in the NPD literature as being crucial to the

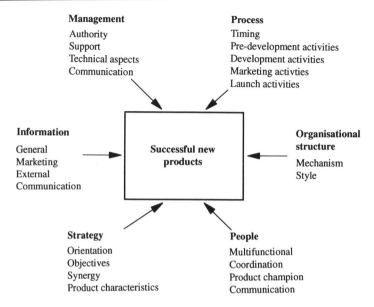

Figure 1.1 Key themes from the product development literature

success of NPD activities. Figure 1.1 presents the following themes, which capture the similarities between the variety of factors cited, while highlighting the differences between particular areas of interest:

- NPD process
- management
- information
- strategy
- people
- structure

These themes are detected at two different organisational levels: (i) relating to the specific NPD project, i.e. the way in which individual products are developed, and (ii) relating to the way in which the innovating company approaches the development of new products in general. The latter are called 'strategic' and the former 'project' level issues. The 'strategic' issues operate at the organisational level. They are not particular to one project, but instead exert an influence over every project.

STRATEGIC THEMES

The three themes of strategy, NPD management and organisational structure are closely interrelated. Top management has responsibility for developing strategy and the organisational structure. At the same time, the strategy and organisational structure are inextricably linked, a change in one automatically triggering a change in the other. Each of the three strategic themes is discussed in turn in the following sections.

Strategy

The strategy of a company dictates how it will operate internally and how it will approach the outside world. According to the literature, the relationship between the corporate strategy and the NPD activity, and the strategic orientation within the innovating company, including the fit between new and existing activities, will influence the outcome of the NPD.

Linking NPD to Corporate Strategy

A number of papers argue that NPD must be guided by the corporate goals of the company, or, in other words, derived from the corporate strategy (Cooper 1984, 1987; Goltz 1986; Kortge and Okonkwo 1989), and therefore, that there is a need to set clearly defined objectives for NPD projects (Larson and Gobeli 1989). A number of authors have sought to guide managers in how best to *link* NPD to corporate strategy. A new product strategy ensures that product innovations become a central facet of corporate strategies (Cooper 1984), that objectives are set and that the 'right' areas of business are developed (Cooper 1987).

Strategic Orientation

While it is clear that NPDs should be guided by a new product strategy, it is important that the strategy is not so prescriptive as to restrict or stifle the creativity necessary for NPD. To this end, some papers reflect on the most appropriate strategic orientations, which should be reflected in the new product strategy document.

Technology and marketing. One of the most prevalent themes that runs throughout the contributions on strategic orientations is the merging of the technical and marketing strategic thrust. The emphasis on a balance between the technological and the marketing orientations in the strategy literature reflects an overall trend away from arguing the benefits of one orientation above the other, and towards an acceptance that there should be a *fusion* between technology-led and market-led innovations at the strategic level (Dougherty 1992; Johne and Snelson 1988b; Nagel, Chapter 3, this volume).

Proaction. Another major element of the new product strategy stressed in the literature is the importance of 'proaction', rather than reaction, especially in turbulent and uncertain environments (Cooper 1984; Goltz 1986; Nystrom 1985).

Product differentiation. Thirdly, the literature refers to new product strategies that emphasise the search for a differential advantage, through the product itself (Cooper 1984). Specific reference is made to technical superiority (Myers and Marquis 1969; National Industrial Conference Board 1964), product quality (Cooper 1979; Link 1987), product uniqueness and novelty (Cooper 1979), product attractiveness (Link 1987) and high performance to cost ratio (Maidique and Zirger 1984).

Synergy. A fourth consideration, identified in the literature, for those developing new product strategies is the relationship between the NPD and existing activities, known as the synergy with existing activities (Cooper and Kleinschmidt 1987; Davies-Cooper and Jones, Chapter 4, this volume; Johne and Snelson 1989; Link 1987; Maidique and Zirger 1984; Rothwell 1972; Rothwell et al. 1974).

Risk acceptance. Finally, the creation of an internal orientation or climate which accepts risk is highlighted as a major role for the new product strategy (Cooper 1984; Gupta and Wilemon 1988; Lowe and Hunter 1991).

NPD Management

Some research attention has focused on the role of top management in the eventual success of NPD. The themes are summarised below.

Top Management

While Maidique and Zirger (1984) found new product successes to be characterised by a high level of top management support, Cooper and Kleinschmidt (1987) found less proof of top management influence, discovering new product failure to have as much top management support as success. Among the 'top management' issues covered by the literature are managerial orientation, involvement of top management and top management roles.

Managerial orientation. Hart and Service (1988) report on the attitudes and opinions of company managers to product design, and identify the managerial orientations that are most consistent with successful performance. A 'balanced' managerial orientation that combines technical commitment with marketing inputs is found to be most closely associated with superior competitive performance.

Involvement of top management. In considering how best to get top managers involved in NPD, Ramanjam and Mensch (1985) found that by approaching innovations as strategic choices, top and middle management become directly involved in setting goals and allocating resources.

Top management roles. One of the most important roles that top management has to fill is that of climate setting by signalling the nature of the corporate culture to the rest of the organisation (Goltz 1986; Gupta, Raj and Wilemon 1985; Gupta and Wilemon 1988; McDonough 1986). Closely aligned to the notion of climate creation is the responsibility that top management has for the overall organisational structure, which is a research theme in its own right and will be discussed later. However, few studies have examined, in an integrative way, the relationship between top management's role and structure.

Organisational Structure

As with new product management, the structure of the organisation operates at two levels – the overall organisational structure and the structure of particular projects. Many of the contributors to this field include the question of organisational style alongside that of structure. Moreover, the issue of which organisational level is treated by any particular study is rarely addressed. This gives rise to the tendency to oversimplify the extent to which various important factors interplay. The overall company structure may well be a function of style (and therefore related to top management issues) but the operational structures – be they teams or new product champions – have a style and dynamism of their own. These latter factors are considered under the heading 'People' on p. 27.

Bentley (1990) presents the findings of an empirical study based on the hypothesis that the structure and style adopted by a company are closely related to its ability to connect with its market, and, since proximity to the market is a determinant of new product success, that the organisational structure and style are important issues. Bentley advocates a flexible structure and style that support the ability of individuals to behave innovatively, thus echoing, in terms of organisation structure, the issues raised by the section on strategic orientation (p. 18). Similarly, in considering organisational styles, Rothwell and Whiston (1990) lean towards flexibility, advocating an organic style of organisation which:

- is free from rigid rules
- is participative and informal
- has many views aired and considered
- has face to face communication and little 'red tape'
- has interdisciplinary teams and breaks down departmental barriers
- puts emphasis on creative interaction and aims

- is outward looking and willing to take on external ideas
- has flexibility with respect to changing needs, threats and opportunities
- is non-hierarchical
- has information flowing downwards as well as upwards

PROJECT THEMES

As with the strategic themes in the NPD literature, the project themes of process, people and information are closely interrelated, which will become apparent as the discussion of the themes unfolds.

NPD Process

The process of NPD involves the activities and decisions from the time when an idea is generated (from whatever source) until the product is commercialised (i.e. launched onto the market). A number of studies have identified the efficient execution of the development process, or particular activities within the development process, as critical to new product success (Cooper 1979, 1980; Cooper and Kleinschmidt 1987; Maidique and Zirger 1984; National Industrial Conference Board 1964; Rothwell 1972; Rothwell et al. 1974). The process of NPD cannot be neatly separated from the people who undertake the activities within the process. In fact, the writings in NPD often talk about these two themes as though they were indeed one, especially when the simultaneous nature of process activities and the coordination of those in NPD is being discussed (Takeuchi and Nonaka 1986). Nevertheless, in the interests of clarity, this chapter considers the particular research under two discrete banners – NPD process and the people involved in the process – while highlighting the links that arise between the two themes, and between these and key strategic themes.

NPD Process Activities

There have been many commentators, from the domains of marketing, management, design and engineering, who have developed normative and descriptive models of the NPD process, and a selection of these are reproduced in Figures 1.2 to 1.5 (British Standards Institution 1989; Kotler 1980; Pahl and Beitz 1984; Pugh 1983).

Marketing Activities

A number of studies emphasise the importance of the marketing activities within the NPD process (Cooper 1979; Maidique and Zirger 1984; National

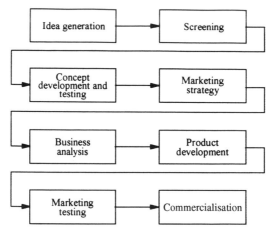

Figure 1.2   Major stages in new product development (reproduced from Kotler 1980 by permission of Prentice-Hall)

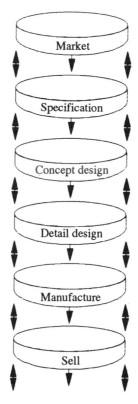

Figure 1.3   Design activity model (reproduced from Pugh 1983 by permission of EDC Loughborough University)

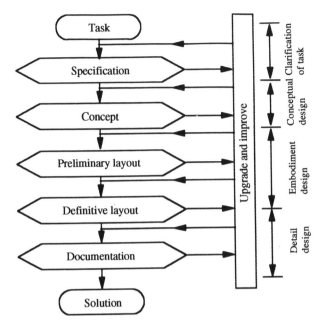

Figure 1.4   Model of the design process (reproduced from Pahl and Beitz 1984 by permission of the Design Council, London)

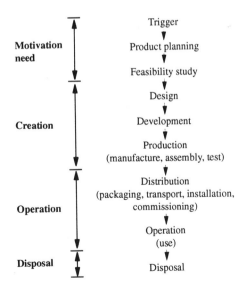

Figure 1.5   Idealised product evolution (reproduced by permission from British Standards Institution 1989)

Industrial Conference Board 1964; Rothwell 1972; Rothwell et al. 1974) and there is a small body of research that concentrates on the marketing activities within the NPD process. As the result of their research findings, Johne and Snelson (1988b) advise companies to be novel in their market research approaches as well as to seek emerging new product opportunities and to offer more applications advice to customers, so that they can create different ways of using products. Wind and Mahajan (1987) present a conceptual argument in which they identify a key role for marketing in what they call 'marketing hype'. Marketing hype is a pre-launch activity encompassing concept testing, product testing and new product forecasting models (see Biemans and Setz, Chapter 10, this volume).

The importance of the market research activities in the NPD process is highlighted by Cooper and Kleinschmidt (1986, 1987, 1990). Hill (1988) argues that market appraisals are crucial to a clear understanding of the market. Much of the extensive research of the Design Innovation Group has concentrated on the importance of good market research (Bruce 1994, Walsh et al. 1992).

However, an opposing view cites the well-known example of the Sony Walkman product development, in which the company entrepreneurs doggedly ignored the limiting factor of current demand patterns (Walsh et al. 1992). In the case of true innovations the role of traditional marketing and market research may be less useful, as Lowe and Hunter (1991, p. 1152) note: 'the end user cannot possibly express a useful opinion about a totally new product before s/he has a chance to see it'. However, these comments do not remove the importance of marketing's role in NPD. Instead, the nature of the marketing role is shifted away from the traditional 'exchange' philosophy of marketing, towards a 'matching' philosophy, and, in so doing, the 'organisation goes out into the market and finds customers who agree with their already developed product' (Lowe and Hunter 1991, p. 1155) rather than developing the product around users' needs. A less substantial shift may be attained by changing the marketing techniques (Johne and Snelson 1988b).

Completion of the NPD Process Activities

The models of NPD processes tend to be idealised and, for this reason, may be quite far removed from reality. A number of authors have researched to what extent the prescriptive activities of the NPD process take place. In 1986, Cooper and Kleinschmidt used a 'skeleton' of the process taken from a variety of normative and empirically based prescriptive processes developed by other authors (Booz, Allen and Hamilton 1982; Cooper 1983; Little 1970; Myers and Marquis 1969; Utterback 1971), which has thirteen activities, as detailed below:

- initial screening
- preliminary market assessment
- preliminary technical assessment
- detailed market study/market research
- business/financial analysis
- product development
- in-house product testing
- customer tests of product
- test market/trial sell
- trial production
- precommercialisation business analysis
- production start-up
- market launch

They found that there is a greater probability of commercial success if all of the process activities are completed. This finding is confirmed in another study replicating the investigation in Australian companies (Dwyer and Mellor 1991). Unfortunately, Cooper and Kleinschmidt (1986) also found that very few of the companies in the survey carried out all thirteen activities, and those that were carried out were done so only superficially.

That said, while it may be desirable to have a complete process of NPD, each additional activity extends the overall development time and may lead to late market introduction. There can be a price to pay for this (Cordero 1991; Davis 1988; Gehani 1992; Johne and Snelson 1987; Trygg 1992). Evans (1990) has quantified the consequences of extending the development time: delaying launch by 6 months can equal a loss of 33% in profits over 5 years. Therefore, a trade-off has to be made between completing all of the suggested activities in the NPD process and the time that these activities take.

Simultaneity of the NPD Process Activities

In recognition of the time pressures facing those developing new products, Cooper (1988a, p. 246) suggests that there should be 'parallel processing'. Parallel processing means that the NPD activities are performed parallel in time. Takeuchi and Nonaka (1986) refer to this as the 'holistic' or 'rugby' approach to NPD, as opposed to the traditional 'linear' or 'relay race' approach. In this method of NPD the stages of the process overlap, rather than being carried out sequentially. The difference between the sequential and simultaneous methods is well represented in the diagram presented in Takeuchi and Nonaka (1986) and reproduced in Figure 1.6.

The benefits of the parallel approach are the reduction of time to market (Cooper 1988b), a smoother transition between phases (thus avoiding the

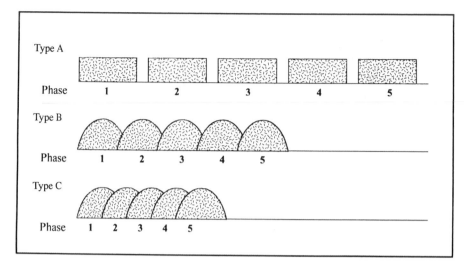

Figure 1.6   Sequential (A) versus overlapping (B and C) phases of development
(reproduced by permission of Harvard Business School Press, Boston, MA, from
H. Takeuchi and I. Nonaka, 1986. The new product development game, *Harvard Business
Review*, **64**, 137–146. Copyright © 1986 by the President and Fellows of Harvard College)

bottlenecks that often occur in a sequential process; Takeuchi and Nonaka
(1986)), and a number of 'soft' advantages relating to those who are involved,
such as shared responsibility, cooperation, involvement, commitment, sharp-
ened problem solving focus, initiative, diversified skills and heightened sen-
sitivity towards market conditions.

It should be mentioned that a substantial amount of what has been written
about the concept of parallel processing is in the engineering domain. (For
further reading, see Finger and Dixon 1989; Murrin 1990; Stoll 1986.) A
theoretical and empirical contribution is needed from researchers in marketing, because – although greater integration through parallel processing is
being attempted by various technical disciplines such as manufacturing and
engineering – the market perspective is still apparently being 'tacked on' and
reduced to sales and promotional activities. More profound again is the level
of complexity in business-to-business marketing, which has shown the importance of networks in NPD (see Biemans, Chapter 7, this volume). Unfortunately, parallel processing, derived from the manufacturer-active
perspective ignores the insights to be gained from the network literature.
Furthermore, there is a need for research to tackle *how* simultaneous processing can be achieved, and in what circumstances, thus moving on from research
that, at present, is largely at the level of truism. The final section of the
chapter discusses this more fully.

While the above discussion relates to the research focusing on the particular *activities* of the development process – the construction of models, the proficiency of companies in carrying out these activities and investigating how the different stages may best be integrated – there is another body of research that focuses on the integration of the *people*, or *functions*, within the process. This second body of research is addressed in the following section.

People

The people involved in the NPD process and the way in which these people are organised are critical factors in the outcome of NPDs (Maidique and Zirger 1984; Myers and Marquis 1969; Voss 1985). A substantial section of the literature has concentrated on the people theme in NPD, focusing on functional coordination, especially of the R&D and marketing functions, the importance of information and the way it is communicated, project organisation structure, project management and the skills needed for successful developments. Each of these particular issues is considered below.

Functional Coordination

Maidique and Zirger (1984) identified functional coordination as a critical factor contributing to the development of *successful* new products. Support for the importance of functional coordination is to be found in the paper by Pinto and Pinto (1990), who found that the higher the level of cross-functional cooperation, the more successful the outcome of NPD. The close relationship between functional coordination and an integrated set of NPD activities has already been emphasised, and the benefits of functional coordination are similar to those associated with an integrated process, including the reduction of the development cycle time, cost savings and effective communication so that potential problems are detected early in the process (Larson 1988).

This part of the literature is confusing, not only because of the variety of aspects of functional coordination that have been investigated, but also because of the variety of terms used to refer to what this paper calls 'functional coordination' (Maidique and Zirger 1984). The recent review of the literature by Craig and Hart (1992) uses the work of Pinto and Pinto (1990) to construct a table of relevant definitions.

While the degree of closeness between functions may differ among the different terms and definitions, the underlying concept is of *individuals working together to achieve a common task*, which in this case is the development of a new product. Nevertheless, the move towards integration is not absolute, and both Moenaert and Souder (1990) and Rothwell and Whiston (1990) suggest that some degree of differentiation should be preserved. While integration serves 'to bridge the differentiated parties', differentiation enables 'the organisation to optimise the separate tasks to be accomplished' (Moenaert and Souder 1990, p. 93). This allows for inputs to the process to be of high quality, derived from the differentiated, professional experience.

Turning attention towards the particular aspects of the research into functional coordination, the remainder of this section is split into four areas reflecting the particular areas of interest found in the literature: R&D/ marketing coordination, project organisational structures, project management and roles.

R&D/Marketing coordination. In the period since 1983 much has been written about the nature of integration of R&D and marketing in the NPD process, overcoming the criticisms made by Wind and Robertson (1983) and Hutt and Speh (1984), who observed the lack of research attention given to the inter-relationships between marketing and the other business functions. Indeed, the large majority of studies in the area of functional coordination have concentrated on the relations between R&D and marketing. This concentration of research appears to be based on the recognition of the need to integrate the market and technology perspectives in NPD. While some of the earliest researchers in NPD (Myers and Marquis 1969) found market-pull products more likely to succeed, Cooper (1979) and Brockhoff and Chakrabarti (1988) found technology-push *and* market-pull products equally likely to be commercially successful. This observation led Johne and Snelson (1989) to call for a 'fusion' between technology-push and market-pull perspectives. Recognising the need for a fusion of technology and market perspectives calls attention towards integrating the functions involved with these perspectives – that is, R&D and marketing – from the outset of the NPD process.

A host of issues mentioned in the literature relate to the integration of the R&D and marketing functions. These include the organisational climate (Gupta, Raj and Wilemon 1985), and the need for R&D and marketing personnel to be more adaptive to each other (Lucas and Bush 1988), for which 'role swopping' may play an important part (Souder 1988). The key notion within all of the methods of achieving R&D/marketing integration is that R&D and marketing managers must work together to solve the disharmony in their relations. An interesting contribution from Souder (1988) presents seven ways in which managers should try to achieve integration:

- make personnel aware that interface problems occur naturally
- make personnel sensitive to the characteristics of disharmony
- give equal praise to both functions

- continuously reinforce their desire for R&D and marketing collaboration
- use teams of R&D and marketing personnel at every opportunity
- solve personality clashes as soon as possible
- avoid complacency – too much harmony is a bad thing

Project organisational structure. There is a debate as to which – if indeed any – organisational structure is more appropriate to successful project outcomes. A number of alternative project organisational structures exist and they can be classified on a continuum from 'boundary spanning' to 'boundary eliminating' (Moenaert and Souder 1990, p. 94). The former grouping of structures preserve functional differentiation, while the latter emphasise self-containment, If, as Moenaert and Souder (1990) and Rothwell and Whiston (1990) advocate, some degree of differentiation should be maintained then the 'boundary spanning' structures will be more appropriate.

However, as Van de Ven (1986) argues, 'requisite variety', which means reflecting the complexity of the environment into an autonomous (say, NPD) unit, would assert that personnel within the innovation unit should 'understand and have access to each of the key environmental stakeholder groups or issues that affect that innovation's development' (p. 600).

A number of authors refer to 'project teams', where those involved in NPD are dedicated to NPD activities on a full-time basis, as the most appropriate structures (Larson 1988; Thamhain 1990). Larson and Gobeli (1989) make an important contribution to the debate on project structures by considering a variety of possible project organisational designs, which are explained in Craig and Hart (1992). Their work suggests that managers may be best advised to take a contingency perspective, selecting a structure on the basis of the project and organisation at hand. That said, the research carried out thus far into appropriate mechanisms has been too idiosyncratic to have given any real insights as to the more effective methods of organising NPD activity. In particular, these studies have done very little to take account of different types of product development. Specifically, we ask the question: 'should different types of innovation not require different organisational mechanisms?'

Project management. As already discussed, top management within the innovating organisation has an important contribution to make in NPD. At the same time, an even more significant role is played by those who are in charge of managing the day-to-day operations of the NPD project, namely the *project managers.* The organisational structure overall and at the project level will greatly determine the role that project managers can play in managing project activities, and the project manager will have lesser, or greater, degrees of authority and control depending on the type of project structure.

A number of studies have considered the style, roles and skills that project managers must assume to be successful in project management (Barczak and Wilemon 1989; McDonough 1986; McDonough and Leifer 1986; Meyers and Wilemon 1989; Takeuchi and Nonaka 1986; Voss 1985). Each of these project management issues is explained in detail in Craig and Hart (1992).

Roles. A few of the 'people' related studies have investigated the particular roles that must be fulfilled within the NPD process and the skills that the people within the process should, ideally, possess. These studies are similar to the ones that investigate the most appropriate roles and skills of project managers.

By assessing the activities carried out within the innovation process, Roberts and Fusfield (1991) were able to identify five major work roles critical to innovation:

- idea generating
- entrepreneuring and championing
- project leading
- gatekeeping
- sponsoring and coaching

The authors emphasise that different types of people will fulfil each role, although it is not impossible for one person to take on more than one role. Therefore, the people who fulfil different roles will have to be recruited, managed and supported in different ways. It is possibly the 'entrepreneuring and championing' role that has been given the most attention in the NPD literature (Roberts and Burke 1974; Roberts and Fusfield 1991; Voss 1985).

In summary, the literature has shown that the people who are involved in the NPD process, from a variety of functions, must work together if developments are to be successful (see Davies-Cooper and Jones, Chapter 4, this volume). However, achieving functional integration (especially of the R&D and marketing functions) is a difficult issue to resolve. The sharing of information, the organisation of functions into teams and effective leadership have been suggested as ways in which this problem could be tackled.

Information

The role that information can play in facilitating an efficient NPD *process* and achieving *functional coordination* is emphasised throughout the literature.

The Role of Information in the NPD Process

The notion of reducing uncertainty as the main objective of project development activities is reiterated throughout the literature (Bonnet 1986; Goltz 1986; Moenaert and Souder 1990). Thus, project activities 'can be considered as discrete information processing activities aimed at reducing uncertainty' (Moenaert and Souder 1990, p. 92). The evaluation activities within the process are extremely important (Cooper and Kleinschmidt 1986, 1987, 1990). These include gathering and disseminating information and making decisions based upon this information. The main point made by the writers who consider the importance of information processing, or evaluation, activities is that they must include evaluations of both the market *and* technical aspects.

As well as reducing uncertainty, the transfer of information between the two functions is perceived by both sides to be a key area for establishing *credibility* (Gupta, Raj and Wilemon 1985; Gupta and Wilemon 1988). In recognition of the importance of information in establishing and maintaining a credible relationship between R&D and marketing, marketing managers are advised to consider carefully the nature of the information they provide to R&D (Gupta, Raj and Wilemon 1985) and to ensure that it is realistic, well analysed, well presented, consistent, complete and useful (Gupta and Wilemon 1988).

The Role of Information in Functional Coordination

In order to reduce uncertainty, it is not sufficient that information be processed; it also has to be transferred between different functions (Bonnet 1986; Moenaert and Souder 1990). In this way the uncertainty perceived by particular functions can be reduced. At the same time, the efficient transfer of quality information between different functions encourages their coordination (Moenaert and Souder 1990).

Information, therefore, is a base currency of the NPD process; evaluative information is crucial and must be efficiently disseminated to facilitate communication. However, far less is known about *how* the information is generated and what contingencies might affect this.

CRITIQUE AND SYNTHESIS

This review of the literature does not claim to be exhaustive, but it does give a flavour of the variety of issues and disciplines central to furthering the understanding of the processes of innovation and NPD. Disciplines such as engineering, design, marketing, organisational behaviour, human resource management, economics, psychology and operations management all have important potential inputs to the development of NPD, given the range of issues outlined in the preceding section: organisational roles, managerial style, market information, organisational mechanisms, communication and information use, interfunctional integration, decision making processes, strategy and so on. Indeed, one of the problems researchers face in dealing with the multiplicity of issues stems from the diversity of 'base disciplines' from which these issues come. Specifically, writing within disciplines tends to be rather insular, which has led to the parallel development of terms for phenomena and concepts that are similar and common. Thus, issues in design management, NPD and innovation may be closely related in a conceptual sense, but have different labels, rendering cross-disciplinary research that bit less accessible. It follows, then, that literature in this field has tended to be guilty of 're-inventing the wheel' when viewed as a totality, rather than from the perspective of any one discipline. However, it can be argued that two of the areas outlined in the previous section are of value in bridging the cross-disciplinary gaps in NPD research: process and people. Nearly all contributions to the literature in NPD, irrespective of the base discipline of the author, will touch on aspects of either the process of development or the people responsible for carrying out the process. These two, therefore, might be fruitfully used as a 'common currency' across disciplinary borders. They are particularly useful for three further reasons:

1. 'People' and 'process' are inextricably linked: the process cannot unfold without the appropriate people, nor can the process be organised to facilitate cross-functional inputs without reference to the people involved. Although so apparent as to appear something of a truism, the linkage between the process – its tasks and decisions – and people – their skills and organisation – has been widely ignored by researchers in most of the single disciplinary research. As a result, these important concepts remain blurred, as, for example, in the work of Van de Ven (1986) and Dougherty (1992). Both start with the proposition that the NPD *process* cannot be linear, that the integration of the market and technological perspectives is required by the *process*, but end up discussing, at length, the organisational *mechanisms* required to facilitate the fusion of these perspectives. While there is nothing flawed with this approach *per se*, the ensuing discussion of organisation does rather leave the issue of how the process unfolds to chance. What is required of researchers is a search for how the two may be linked – conceptually and in practice.

2. 'People' and 'process' encapsulate other important themes, for example, the role of information in promoting cross-functional integration, and sharing a link between the themes of 'people' and 'information'. In addition, 'people' as a theme is clearly connected by 'organisational structure and style'.

Similarly, the theme of the 'process' is related to that of 'information', because the NPD process can be viewed as one of information processing (see Snelson and Hart 1991). Top management and strategy are linked with 'people' as a theme, as these two set the context for the nature of the process itself. If these linkages are accepted, focusing on 'process' and 'people' allows access to many of the other salient variables in NPD research.

3. 'People' and 'process' relate to the most commonly cited reasons for NPD success:

   – The need for interdisciplinary inputs. In order to combine technical and marketing expertise, a number of company functions have to be involved: R&D, manufacturing, engineering, marketing and sales. As the development of a new product may be the only purpose for which these people meet professionally, it is important that the NPD process adopted ensures that they work well and effectively together. Linked to this is the need for the voice of the customer to be heard, as well as that of suppliers, where changes to supply may be required or advantageous.

   – The need for quality inputs to the process. Both technical and marketing information, which are building blocks of NPD, have to be both accurate and timely, and must be constantly reworked in the light of changing circumstances during the course of the development.

   – The need for speed in the process. The NPD process has to be managed in such a way as to be quick enough to capitalise on the new product opportunity before competitors. The value of being first into the market with a new product is often significant, and the window of opportunity for a new development may be open only fleetingly. The speedy undertaking of the complex and intricate product development task will require careful consideration.

A final shortcoming of the literature reviewed above is its tendency to view NPD from the manufacturer-active paradigm. Apart from the work of von Hippel (1988), which tends to be cited as evidence of the need for market inputs to NPD, the considerable advances in business-to-business marketing made by those adopting the network approach (De Bresson and Amesse 1991) has been largely ignored. A special issue of *Research Policy* with notable contributions by Freeman (1991) and Lawton-Smith, Dickson and Lloyd-Smith (1991) has addressed this, as has the research by Biemans (1992) on the functioning of networks in the development of new products (see Chapter 7, this volume).

THE MULTIPLE CONVERGENT APPROACH

In suggesting a way forward in NPD research that takes account of the lessons to be learned from the success literature and the importance of networks in

NPD, and that attempts to break down research discipline boundaries, an alternative *process* model has been forwarded, which has direct and explicit consequences for *people* as a theme, namely the 'multiple convergent process'. This model is conceptually derived from the idea of parallel processing.

Dictionary definitions of 'parallel' refer to 'separated by an equal distance at every point' or 'never touching or intersecting', and, while there are references to simultaneity, it is a somewhat troublesome notion that suggests functional separation, when all of the performance indicators in NPD point to the need for functional integration. On the other hand, 'to converge' is defined as 'to move or cause to move towards the same point' or to 'tend towards a common conclusion or result', and is therefore, a more precise indicator of what is required of NPD management.

Realising, however, that there are still functionally distinct tasks that must be carried out at specific points throughout the NPD process, it is clear that the tasks will be carried out simultaneously at some juncture and that the results must *converge*. Due to the iterations in the process, this convergence is likely to happen several times, culminating at the time of product launch. As mentioned previously, the process is a series of information gathering and evaluating activities, and as the new product develops from idea to concept to prototype and so on, the information gathered becomes more precise and reliable, and the decisions are made with greater certainty. Therefore, as the development project progresses, there are a number of natural points of evaluation and a number of types of evaluation (market, functional) that need to be carried out in an integrated fashion. Hence, there are multiple convergent points. An example of the early stages of the multiple convergent process is shown in Figure 1.7.

The advantages of viewing the process in this way are:

1. Iterations among participants within stages are allowed for in the convergent points and the horizontal communication system they embrace.
2. The framework can easily accommodate third parties.
3. Mechanisms for real integration throughout the process among different functions are set in the convergent points.

While the first two advantages compensate for the problems of linear models, the third deals with some of the disadvantages forwarded by Biemans (1992) regarding the management of NPD in networks. In his analysis of 22 NPDs, Biemans noted the extent of user involvement and gave ample evidence on the functioning of networks in the development of new products. Indeed, at

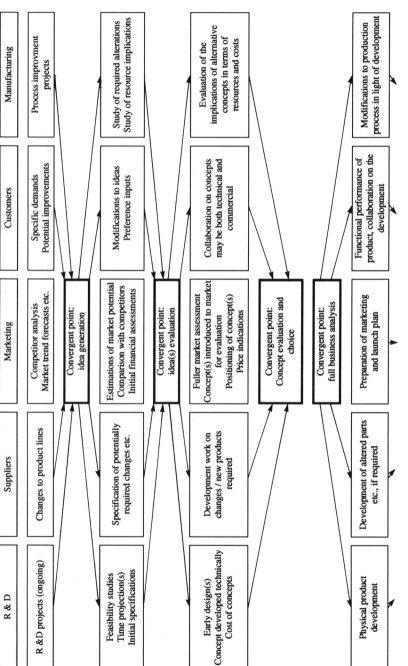

Figure 1.7 The early stages of the multiple convergent process

several points in the work, the problems associated with manufacturer-active models of the NPD process are explained and concur largely with the thread of argument presented in this chapter. However, a key problem associated with developing products within networks is also tackled, namely the now familiar issue of integration of marketing and R&D activities.

Only two of the companies in the study by Biemans (1992) characterised their NPD process as being a balanced mixture between marketing and R&D, yet this is a fundamental element of the success literature.

In Biemans' study, most of the companies showed an understanding of the need to integrate R&D and marketing activities, *although the desirability of this is not considered to be automatic*, based on the evidence of the companies surveyed. A key element in integration is the amount of information sharing, and the multiple convergent process provides the opportunity for information sharing which is neglected by other models.

FUTURE RESEARCH METHODS

In analysing the cases under study, Biemans suggested that networks in NPD could and should be considered at two different levels: external and internal (Chapter 7 elaborates on this notion). He argues that, although part of a wide network of different organisations, each of the major parties in the network has, in turn, its own internal network. However, this aspect of networking has been largely neglected by the literature on NPD and networks, despite the fact that 'the functioning of the internal networks directly influences the efficiency and efficacy of the external network' (Biemans 1992, p. 176). On the other hand, research that has been focusing on the interactions between R&D and marketing from the perspective of survey research within the manufacturer-active paradigm, has had limited success in explaining the nature of the interaction because of the linearity of the models and an incomplete view of the role of information in integration. According to Gupta, Raj and Wilemon (1986), integration is comprised of information sharing, decision-making agreement and decision-making authority agreement. However, beyond stating the need for information sharing between marketing and R&D throughout the process, very little is said regarding how this might be researched, and nothing is said about the integration of other parties in the process. However, from a network perspective, it is possible to find a framework for research that takes account of this issue.

External networks are based on exchange among various firms whose aim is to pool different resources and competencies. A key resource in a network is

Table 1.1   Analytical dimensions of networks

Size	The number of functions/outside parties in the network
Density	The number of linkages among functions and parties
Diversity	Linkage: the number of different types of linkages in the network
	Organisational: the number of different types of functions and outside parties in the network
Reachability	The number of links separating the different functions and parties
Stability	Linkage: whether the network remains the same throughout the NPD process
	Organisational: whether the actors in the functions and outside parties remain the same throughout the NPD process
	The frequency of change in linkages or organisation
	The magnitude of change in linkages or organisation
Stars	The number of functions and outside parties with greater than x number of ties
Isolates	The number of functions and third parties with no linkages to others
Linking pins	Functions or outside functions with extensive and overlapping ties to different parts of a network

often information, and nowhere is this more so than in the case of NPD (Imai, Nonaka and Takeuchi 1985; Kenney and Nonaka 1989; von Hippel 1988). Indeed, a recent article by Campbell (1991) underlines the importance of information in Japanese multinationals, where collecting and analysing information is part of everyone's duty and where interaction between all levels of the organisation is required, and listening to all external actors is encouraged. The author appears to suggest that the importance of information and the way in which Japanese companies use networks of independent firms, and the separation of manufacturing and marketing are mutually reinforcing aspects of organisational design. Thus, the extent of information sharing and the involvement of several parties are issues inherent to network analysis. The appropriateness of network analysis is further justified due to its grounding in the theories of exchange, power and resource dependence (Aldrich 1979; Aldrich and Whetten 1981; Auster 1990), which have been only partially included in studies of integration in NPD to date.

The tools of network analysis, however, provide a framework for mapping the nature of the internal and external networks within NPD. These tools, as summarised by Auster (1990) are shown in Table 1.1. Using this format, the changing roles of the actors and the structure of the network can be mapped as the new product evolves. The advantage of using the multiple convergent process as the level of analysis is that greater understanding of the dynamic forces at play is afforded than by using the company as the investigative level. Furthermore, as a basic tenet of networks is their dynamism, the extent to which they change as the NPD process unfolds can be monitored.

Finally, although networks are more than a series of interactive relationships, the latter are the basic building blocks. Here, too, the well-developed analytical frameworks might be applied in order to provide insights into the key linkages ('stars', see Table 1.1), that are critical in reducing the duration of the process. Biemans (1992) distinguishes five characteristics of interaction:

- type of interaction (vertical/horizontal, competitive/complementary)
- purpose of interaction (task performance or task stimulation)
- intensity of interaction
- duration of interaction
- formalisation of interaction

By combining these two analytical frameworks to study the nature of the relationships throughout a set of specific tasks, the scope for understanding why some NPD processes are effective and efficient has greater potential than research based on the traditional manufacturer-active paradigm, which tends to ignore iteration and multiple inputs in the NPD process.

SUMMARY AND CONCLUSION

This chapter essentially discusses the status of research into NPD and syn-thesises the insights gained via research into success and failure into a pre-scriptive view of the decision making process. This research highlights the development of successful new products as essentially a task of cross-functional information management and decision making. Integrating the contributions that have been forwarded by those studying NPD in networks, it is argued that a new model of 'multiple convergent processing' provides a dynamic and cross-functional context in which to examine and advance the practice of NPD. The multiple-convergent processing model overcomes the manufacturer-active paradigm that dominates 'mainstream' research into NPD, but by focusing on networks internal to the company also tackles some of the shortcomings of analysing NPD solely externally. It is hoped that this greater synthesis of two powerful research traditions will bring more insight-ful, relevant and ultimately beneficial comments to bear on the way in which companies advance new products from ideas to commercialisation.

REFERENCES

Aldrich, H. (1979). *Organisations and Environments*, Prentice Hall, Englewood Cliffs, NJ.

Aldrich, H. and Whetten, D. (1981). Organisation-sets, action-sets and networks: Mak-ing the most of simplicity, in Nystrom, P.C. and Starbuch, W. (eds), *Handbook of Organisational Design*, Vol. 1, Oxford University Press, London, pp. 385–408.

Auster, E.R. (1990). The interorganisational environment, in Williams, F. and Gibson, D.V. (eds), *Technology Transfer: A Communication Perspective*, Sage, London.
Barczak, G. and Wilemon, D. (1989). Leadership differences in new product development teams, *Journal of Product Innovation Management*, **6**(4), 259–267.
Bentley, K. (1990). A discussion of the link between one organisation's style and structure and its connections with its market, *Journal of Product Innovation Management*, **7**, 19–34.
Biemans, W.G. (1992). *Managing Innovations within Networks*, Routledge, London.
Bonnet, D.C.L. (1986). Nature of the R&D/marketing co-operation in the design of technologically advanced new industrial products, *R&D Management*, **16**(2), 117–126.
Booz, Allen and Hamilton (1982). *New Products Management for the 1980s*, Booz, Allen and Hamilton Inc., New York.
Brockhoff, K. and Chakrabarti, A.K. (1988). R&D/marketing linkage and innovation strategy: Some West German experience, *IEEE Transactions on Engineering Management*, **35**(3), 167–174.
British Standards Institution (1989). *Guide to Managing Product Design, BS 7000*, BSI, Milton Keynes.
Bruce, M. (1994). Managing the interface of marketing and design, in Saunders, J. (ed.), *The Marketing Initiative: ESRC Studies into British Marketing*, Prentice-Hall, London.
Campbell, N. (1991). The borderless company: Networking in the Japanese multinational, presented at the 7th IMP conference, Uppsala, Sweden, September.
Cooper, R.G. (1979). The dimensions of industrial new product success and failure, *Journal of Marketing*, **43**, 93–103.
Cooper, R.G. (1980). How to identify potential new product winners, *Research Management*, **4**, 277–292.
Cooper, R.G. (1983). A process model for industrial new product development, *IEEE Transactions on Engineering Management*, **30**(1), 2–11.
Cooper, R.G. (1984). The strategy–performance link in product innovation, *R&D Management*, **14**(4), 247–267.
Cooper, R.G. (1987). Defining the new product strategy, *IEEE Transactions on Engineering Management*, **34**(3), 184–193.
Cooper, R.G. (1988a). The new product process: A decision guide for management, *Journal of Marketing Management*, **3**(3), 238–255.
Cooper, R.G. (1988b). Predevelopment activities determine new product success, *Industrial Marketing Management*, **17**, 237–247.
Cooper, R.G. and Kleinschmidt, E.J. (1986). An investigation into the new product process: Steps, deficiencies and impact, *Journal of Product Innovation Management*, **3**, 71–85.
Cooper, R.G. and Kleinschmidt, E.J. (1987). New products: What separates winners from losers? *Journal of Product Innovation Management*, **4**(3), 169–184.
Cooper, R.G. and Kleinschmidt, E.J. (1990). New product success factors: A comparison of 'kills' versus successes and failures, *R&D Management*, **20**(1), 169–184.
Cordero, R. (1991). Managing for speed to avoid product obsolescence: A survey of techniques, *Journal of Product Innovation Management*, **8**, 283–294.
Craig, A. and Hart, S. (1992). Where to now in new product development research? *European Journal of Marketing*, **26**(11), 2–49.
Davis, J.S. (1988). New product success and failure: Three case studies, *Industrial Marketing Management*, **17**(2), 103–109.
De Bresson, C. and Amesse, F. (1991). Networks of innovators: A review and introduction to the issue, *Research Policy*, **20**(5), 363–379.

Dougherty, D. (1992). A practice-centered model of organizational renewal through product innovation, *Strategic Management Journal*, **13**, 77–92.

Dwyer, L. and Mellor, R. (1991). Organisational environment, new product process activities and project outcomes, *Journal of Product Innovation Management*, **8**, 39–48.

Evans, S. (1990). Implementation framework for integrated design teams, *Journal of Engineering Design*, **1**(4), 355–363.

Finger, S. and Dixon, J.R. (1989). A review of research in mechanical engineering design. Part II: Representations, analysis and design for the life cycle, *Research in Engineering Design*, **1**, 121–137.

Freeman, C. (1991). Networks of innovators: A synthesis of research issues, *Research Policy*, **20**(5), 499–514.

Gehani, R.F. (1992). Concurrent product development for fast-track corporations, *Long Range Planning*, **25**(6), 40–47.

Goltz, G.E. (1986). A guide to development, *R&D Management*, **16**, 243–249.

Gupta, A.K. and Wilemon, D. (1988). The credibility–cooperation connection at the R&D–marketing interface, *Journal of Product Innovation Management*, **5**, 20–31.

Gupta, A.K., Raj, S.P. and Wilemon, D. (1985). The R&D–marketing interface in high-technology firms, *Journal of Product Innovation Management*, **2**, 12–24.

Gupta, A.K., Raj, S.P. and Wilemon, D. (1986). A model for studying the R&D–marketing interface in the product innovation process, *Journal of Marketing*, **50**, 7–17.

Hart, S.J. and Service, L.M. (1988). The effects of managerial attitudes to design on company performance, *Journal of Marketing Management*, **4**(2), 217–229.

Hill, P. (1988). The market research contribution to new product failure and success, *Journal of Marketing Management*, **4**(3), 269–277.

Hutt, M.D. and Speh, T.W. (1984). The marketing strategy centre: Diagnosing the industrial marketer's interdisciplinary role, *Journal of Marketing*, **48**, 53–61.

Imai, H., Nonaka, I. and Takeuchi, H. (1985). Managing the new product development process: How Japanese companies learn and unlearn, in Clark, K., Hayes, R. and Lorenz, C. (eds), *The Uneasy Alliance*, Harvard Business School, Boston, MA.

Johne, F.A. and Snelson, P.A. (1987). Innovate or die, *Management Today*, November, 133–138.

Johne, F.A. and Snelson, P.A. (1988a). Success factors in product innovation: A selective review of the literature, *Journal of Product Innovation Management*, **5**(2), 114–128.

Johne, F.A. and Snelson, P.A. (1988b). Marketing's role in successful product development, *Journal of Marketing Management*, **4**(3), 256–268.

Johne, F.A. and Snelson, P.A. (1989). Product development approaches in established firms, *Industrial Marketing Management*, **8**(2), 113–124.

Kenney, M. and Nonaka, I. (1989). Innovation as an organizational information creation process, discussion paper, Hitotsubashi University.

Kortge, D.G. and Okonkwo, P.A. (1989). Simultaneous new product development: Reducing the new product failure rate, *Industrial Marketing Management*, **18**, 301–306.

Kotler, P. (1980). *Principles of Marketing*, Prentice Hall, Englewood Cliffs, NJ.

Larson, C. (1988). Team tactics can cut development costs, *Journal of Business Strategy*, **9**(5), 22–25.

Larson, E.W. and Gobeli, D.H. (1989). Significance of project management structure on development success, *IEEE Transactions on Engineering Management*, **36**(2), 119–125.

Lawton-Smith, H., Dickson, K. and Lloyd Smith, S. (1991). There are two sides to every story: Innovation and collaboration within networks of large and small firms, *Research Policy*, **20**(5), 457–469.

Link, P.L. (1987). Keys to new product success and failure, *Industrial Marketing Management*, **16**, 109–118.

Little, B. (1970). Characterising the new product for better evaluation and planning, working paper series, No. 21, University of Western Ontario, London, Canada.

Lowe, A. and Hunter, R.B. (1991). The role of design and marketing management in the culture of innovation, presented at the EMAC conference.

Lucas, G.H., Jr and Bush, A.J. (1988). The marketing–R&D interface: Do personality factors have an impact? *Journal of Product Innovation Management*, **5**(4), 257–268.

Maidique, M.A. and Zirger, B.J. (1984). A study of success and failure in product innovation: The case of the US electronics industry, *IEEE Transactions on Engineering Management*, **31**(4), 192–203.

McDonough, E.F., III (1986). Matching management control systems to product strategies, *R&D Management*, **16**(2), 141–149.

McDonough, E.F., III and Leifer, R.P. (1986). Effective control of new product projects: The integration of organisation, culture and project leadership, *Journal of Product Innovation Management*, **3**(3), 149–157.

Meyers, P.W. and Wilemon, D. (1989). Learning in new technology development teams, *Journal of Product Innovation Management*, **6**(2), 79–88.

Moenaert, R.K. and Souder, W.E. (1990). An information transfer model for integrating marketing and R&D personnel in new product development projects, *Journal of Product Innovation Management*, **7**(2), 91–107.

Murrin, T.J. (1990). Design for manufacturing: An imperative for US global competitiveness, *Design Management Journal*, **1**(2), 37–41.

Myers, S. and Marquis, D.G. (1969). *Successful Industrial Innovations*, National Science Foundation, Washington, DC, pp. 69–17.

National Industrial Conference Board (1964). Why new products fail, *The Conference Board Record*, NICB, New York.

Nystrom, H. (1985). Product development strategy: An integration of technology and marketing, *Journal of Product Innovation Management*, **2**, 25–33.

Pahl, G. and Beitz, W. (1984). *Engineering Design*, The Design Council, London.

Pinto, M.B. and Pinto, J.K. (1990). Project team communication and cross functional cooperation in new program development, *Journal of Product Innovation Management*, **7**, 200–212.

Pugh, S. (1983). *Design Activity Model*, Engineering Design Centre, Loughborough University of Technology, pp. 28–32.

Ramanjam, V. and Mensch, G.O. (1985). Improving the strategy–innovation link, *Journal of Product Innovation Management*, **2**(4), 213–223.

Roberts, E.B. and Fusfield, A.R. (1991). Staffing the innovative technology based organisation, *Sloan Management Review*, **22**, 19–34.

Roberts, R.W. and Burke, J.E. (1974). Six new products – What made them successful? *Research Management*, **17**, 21–24.

Rothwell, R. (1972). Factors for success in industrial innovations: Project SAPPHO – A comparative study of success and failure in industrial innovations, Science Policy Research Unit, University of Sussex, Brighton.

Rothwell, R. (1977). The characteristics of successful innovations and technically progressive firms (with some comments on innovation research), *R&D Management*, **7**(3), 191–206.

Rothwell, R. (1991). External networking and innovations in small and medium-sized manufacturing firms in Europe, in networks of innovators – an international and inter-disciplinary workshop, Montreal, *TechnoVation*.

Rothwell, R. and Whiston, T.G. (1990). Design, innovation and corporate integration, *R&D Management*, **20**(3), 193–201.

Rothwell, R., Freeman, C., Horsley, A., Jervis, V.T.P., Robertson, A.B. and Towns-end, J. (1974). SAPPHO updated – Project SAPPHO phase II, *Research Policy*, **3**, 258–292.

Snelson, P.A. and Hart, S.J. (1991). Product policy: Perspectives on success, in Baker, M.J. (ed.), *Perspectives on Marketing Management*, Vol. 1, pp. 193–225.

Souder, W.E. (1988). Managing relations between R&D and marketing in new product development projects, *Journal of Product Innovation Management*, **5**(1), 6–19.

Stoll, H.W. (1986). Design for manufacture: An overview, *Applied Mechanics Reviews*, **39**(9), 1356–1364.

Takeuchi, H. and Nonaka, I. (1986). The new product development game, *Harvard Business Review*, **64**(1), 137–146.

Thamhain, H.J. (1990). Managing technologically innovative team efforts toward new product success, *Journal of Product Innovation Management*, **7**, 5–18.

Trygg, L. (1992). Simultaneous engineering: A movement or an activity of the few? presented at the EISAM conference on international product development – new approaches to development and engineering, Brussels, May.

Ughanwa, D.O. and Baker, M.J. (1989). *The Role of Design in International Competitiveness*, Routledge, London.

Utterback, J.M. (1971). The process of technological innovation within the firm, *Academy of Management Journal*, March, 75–88.

Van de Ven, A. (1986). Central problems in the management of innovation, *Management Science*, **32**(4), 590–607.

von Hippel, E. (1988). *The Sources of Innovation*, Oxford University Press, Oxford.

Voss, C.A. (1985). Determinants of success in the development of applications software, *Journal of Product Innovation Management*, **2**(2), 122–129.

Walsh, V., Roy, R., Bruce, M. and Potter, S. (1992). *Winning by Design*, Basil Blackwell, Oxford.

Wind, Y. and Mahajan, V. (1987). Marketing hype: A new perspective for new product research and introduction, *Journal of Product Innovation Management*, **4**(1), 43–49.

Wind, Y. and Robertson, T.S. (1983). Marketing strategy: New directions for theory and research, *Journal of Marketing*, **47**, 12–25.

CHAPTER TWO

EVALUATING PRODUCT DEVELOPMENT SUCCESS WITHIN A BUSINESS DEVELOPMENT CONTEXT

Axel Johne

Product development is presented in the context of organic business development, which consists of four interrelated processes: product development, supply development, product positioning development, and market development. In addition, concepts and criteria used by analysts and by practitioners in evaluating product development success are discussed, and the question of why it is difficult to measure product development success in a way that is useful to all interested parties is explored. Suggestions are made on how present methods of measuring success might be strengthened to provide more realistic insights.

INTRODUCTION

It is necessary to start with a caveat. This chapter is not a listing of factors that have been identified as contributing to product development success. That task has been undertaken skilfully by analysts whose work is discussed later. This chapter invites the reader to stand back and reflect on the limitations of studies of product development success. Following a conceptual reappraisal, suggestions are made on how future investigations might be designed so as to provide better insights. For illustrative purposes, this chapter focuses on one universally acclaimed factor underpinning product development success:

Product Development: Meeting the Challenge of the Design–Marketing Interface.
Edited by M. Bruce and W.G. Biemans.   © 1995 John Wiley & Sons Ltd.

listening to the market. Different styles of listening to the market are identified and some are shown to be better suited for certain purposes than others. There is nothing startlingly new in this contingency approach to managing product development. It is suggested that the greatest payoff in the study of product development will come not from more and more studies that identify the importance of fairly obvious input factors, but from studies that provide detailed guidance on how particular inputs are best operationalised. A framework is advanced that can be used for this purpose.

Few analysts doubt that product development can be good for companies. Without a stream of new products, or at least a healthy trickle of product updates, a supplier is seen to be vulnerable to more innovative competitors. However, many managers see this activity differently for personal reasons. Because of high failure rates, product development is often regarded as a high-risk activity which is best avoided in favour of more exciting alternative methods for safeguarding the future of a business. Such alternatives include growth through acquisition or merger, which typically involve taking joint decisions with colleagues. Although such alternatives are potentially even more vulnerable to failure, the dilution of personal risks often makes them more attractive.

The arguments advanced in this chapter are developed in the context of organic business development. It is incumbent upon top management of a business, sometimes with the support of corporate management, to decide how much importance to attach to organic development. In some businesses top management regards organic growth as being of secondary importance to growth by acquisition or joint ventures. When this is the case, activities such as product development do not necessarily stop. Despite shallow interest on the part of top management, middle-level managers may even in such circumstances pursue product development to gain personal professional satisfaction. Burgelman (1986) refers to this phenomenon as 'autonomous innovation', as opposed to innovation programmed by top management.

It is, however, the need on the part of managers to avoid product development failures that has been the cause of a thriving industry of advisers, comprising consultants, academics and government agencies. A growing body of academic researchers is now applying itself with great vigour to exploring and quantifying factors that contribute to success. An overview of relevant studies is to be found in the literature reviews undertaken by Griffin and Page (1993), Hart and Craig (1993), Hauschildt (1991) and Johne and Snelson (1988). Indeed, the study of effective and efficient new product development has become a major area of specialisation within the marketing discipline. This is not surprising, given the gratifying revelation, in study after study, that marketing inputs matter a lot in achieving product development success.

BUSINESS DEVELOPMENT

Product development is potentially very important for business development purposes. Along with other forms of development described later – market development, product positioning development and supply development – product development can contribute to the attainment of key business objectives. One of the most important objectives for a business is to increase profitability over the longer run. While this objective can be contributed to by organic product development, it is rarely explained how this can be made to occur. It is, however, widely asserted that organic product development lends support to three important activities which, over time, can contribute to increased business profitability. These activities are:

1. building competitive advantage in target markets
2. increasing market shares in target markets
3. building reputation for technical excellence in target markets

PRODUCT DEVELOPMENT

Product development is an umbrella term embracing improvements and also radical alterations to the performance attributes of the supplied merchandise or service. Booz, Allen and Hamilton (1982) have suggested six main types of product developments. Four are typified by varying forms of newness, in terms of their operational newness to the supplier and also in terms of the newness of the customer base to the supplier:

1. Improvements and revisions to existing products: new products that provide improved performance and so replace existing products in served markets.
2. New product lines: new products that allow a business to enter a market segment for the first time – even though other suppliers may already be active in it.
3. Additions to existing product lines: new products that supplement a company's established product lines, so making the whole product mix more competitive in selected markets.
4. New-to-the-world products: new products that create an entirely new market, which has not been developed successfully before.

Table 2.1   Main types of product development

	Newness of the customer base (from the viewpoint of the supplier)	
	Low	**High**
High Operational newness (from the viewpoint of the supplier) **Low**	Radical product development: aimed at the existing customer base 'new-product lines'	New style product development: aimed at a new customer 'new-to-the world products'
	Routine product development: aimed at the existing customer base 'improvements and revisions'	Extended product development: aimed at a new customer base 'additions to existing lines'

Source: Based on Booz, Allen and Hamilton (1982) and Cardozo et al. (1993)

Although Booz, Allen and Hamilton (1982) refer to all of the above four types as 'new' products, it is obvious that some are newer to the supplying company than others. It is for this reason that many analysts have divided product development simply into 'old product development', representing product improvements, and 'new product development', representing products that pose greater development challenges. This distinction was made originally by Kraushar (1985), and has subsequently been built on in many studies of product development. Table 2.1 shows the four types of product developments suggested by Booz, Allen and Hamilton (1982), subdivided according to the level of newness of the challenge to the supplier, as well as the newness of the customer base to that supplier.

Booz, Allen and Hamilton (1982) suggest two other types of product developments. We shall argue, however, that these are not distinct types in their own right. The two additional variants are:

5. Cost reductions: new products that provide similar performance at a lower cost of supply.
6. Repositionings: existing products that are targeted to new markets or market segments.

Both cost reduction and repositioning are possible for all of the first mentioned types of product developments. Cost reductions and repositionings are, however, not distinct types of product developments in their own right. For reasons that are now explained, cost reduction is henceforth referred to as 'supply development', and repositioning as 'product positioning development'.

SUPPLY DEVELOPMENT

All four product development types in Table 2.1 can benefit from supply development in the form of reductions in cost. An efficient supplier who keeps working on productivity can expect, over time, to develop products that offer the same or even improved performance at a lower cost. Such cost reductions may or may not be passed on to customers in the form of lower prices.

Rarely does a supplier not have to concern himself with cost reductions, even for new products. This does, however, happen in very fast-moving markets, such as electronic components, in which an early market launch will commonly generate more profit than a later market entry made with a product for which costs of production have been trimmed through learning and economies of scale (Dumaine 1989).

Supply development is particularly important in the case of service product development. For example, in the government-supported British betting market, computing advances have made possible quite new mechanisms for placing bets at the last moment. This form of supply development has greatly increased possibilities for the four types of product development.

PRODUCT POSITIONING DEVELOPMENT

Just as cost reduction is not a separate category of product development, this is also the case with repositioning. Like cost reduction, repositioning is possible for all four types of product developments. Repositioning involves making changes to the way in which newly developed product or service features are advertised or offered to customers. It is for this reason that we refer to repositioning as 'product positioning development'.

Product positioning development is important operationally because the same newly developed product can be offered with more or less support to different market segments. An appropriate premium price can normally be charged when support is given, which can lead to higher profit margins. Product positioning development relies on accurately interpreting and acting upon customers' preferences for promotional, distribution and technical support. This form of development represents a particularly powerful lever for gaining competitive advantage, because skilful manipulation of support variables allows the same core attributes to be sold at different prices to distinct customer groups.

Product positioning development is closely linked with product development. If a narrow definition of product development is used, product development is considered to be concerned solely with performance attributes – what some analysts have referred to as the 'merchandise' (Mathur 1992). When a wider definition of product development is used, positioning development is implicitly included – it being assumed that what is offered embraces both core performance attributes and the way in which these are presented.

Surprisingly, product positioning development is rarely discussed explicitly in its own right as an activity lending critical support to product development. Product positioning development is, however, of great importance. For example, a newly developed product may be offered as a commodity, which means that it is distinguished from competitive offerings chiefly on the basis of price. This is frequently the case in new service development, where innovative developments are quickly copied. Alternatively, a newly developed product can be offered with superior support (through advertising to inform and to build an appropriate image, through distribution facilities, and through technical support services), for which a higher price can usually be charged.

Product positioning development is often as critical to market acceptance as are the performance attributes of the core product. Only in comparatively rare circumstances do customers choose a new product solely on the basis of performance features and price. In most buying situations it is the complete marketing mix that determines a target market's response. From the supplier's viewpoint the competitive process begins with the selection of target markets (market development). Selected markets are then served with marketing mixes comprising the new product's performance features (product development), its price (facilitated by supply development), and the support given in the form of promotional, distribution and technical support (product positioning development).

There is strong empirical evidence that reinforces the importance of product positioning development. For example, Cooper and Kleinschmidt (1987) have shown that the provision of appropriate support is important in achieving product superiority in the eyes of customers, and have identified this as a key factor determining product development success. Similarly, in a study of successful consumer financial services product development, Easingwood and Storey (1993) found that product advantage on its own is relatively unimportant in differentiating between success and failure, it being variations in the nature and level of support that explain most of the differences between success and failure.

MARKET DEVELOPMENT

Market development is often undertaken in parallel with other forms of development. Market development is concerned with improving the mix of target markets into which a newly developed product can be sold (Baker 1983). It is likely to be the most important type of development to be addressed initially if the aim is to develop the profitability of a business to the full. Sloppy market development will almost certainly result in an unwise mix of target markets. When this is the case, skilled efforts at product development, product positioning development and supply development are likely to fail in achieving their full potential.

Market development is concerned with changing the customer base. New products may be aimed at the existing customer base or at new customer groups. Market development thus provides a rationale for different types of product developments, as was shown in Table 2.1. Interestingly, Cooper and Kleinschmidt (1993), in reporting on product development success factors in the chemical industry, found choice of customer groups to be unimportant for explaining success. However, in the fast-moving 1990s, choice of target markets is likely to become far more important, certainly more important than it was in the 1980s, when markets were much more stable than they are now.

MEASURING BUSINESS DEVELOPMENT SUCCESS

We have so far argued that organic business development can be pursued by means of four types of supporting development: market development, product development, product positioning development and supply development. In practice, these activities are likely to be undertaken in parallel, but with differing emphasis on each. In predominantly technology-driven companies, the greatest emphasis is likely to be placed on product, rather than market, development. On the other hand, in predominantly marketing-driven companies, the greatest emphasis is likely to be placed on market and product positioning development. In companies supplying services the situation is often different again, with greater emphasis often being placed on supply development. The relationship between the four main ways of developing a business is shown in Figure 2.1.

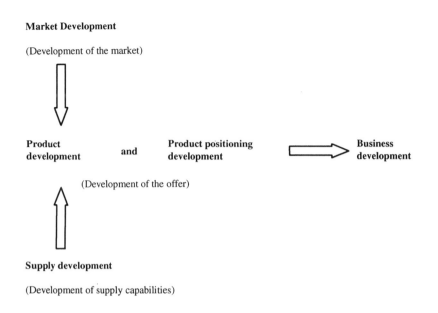

Figure 2.1   Main types of development that support organic business development

Because the four types of development are in practice closely interrelated, it is very difficult to evaluate the precise contribution of any one to the development of the total business operation. What we can say, however, is that weaknesses in one are likely to affect the others. The development of the Philips V2000 video system illustrates this. Despite the fact that the V2000 system was widely acknowledged to be technologically superior as a core product development to the competitive Japanese VHS and Beta formats, it failed. It failed because Philips was unable to commercialise the new core product effectively. Within the company, there was no shortage of theories to explain the failure of what was widely recognised as being an excellent new product (Bartlett and Ghosal 1988). Some managers suggested that those who developed the product were too distant from the market. Others in the company felt that the barriers between research, development, manufacturing and marketing led to delays and cost overruns. Another group pointed to the fact that worldwide subsidiaries were uninvolved in the project and were therefore not committed to making it succeed – through appropriate product positioning development – in the key markets that mattered. Irrespective of exactly what happened, the example illustrates starkly that developing superior core product attributes is insufficient for achieving business success.

MEASURING PRODUCT DEVELOPMENT SUCCESS

Ideally, top management should shoulder the responsibility for steering each of the four types of development. There is, however, abundant anecdotal and empirical evidence suggesting that top management in many businesses does not take full responsibility for doing this. In many firms product development has become the responsibility of lower level managers charged with product updating and with identifying the occasional new product breakthrough (Johne and Snelson 1990). A recent review of success factors in product development (Griffin and Page 1993) is insightful as far as managerial requirements are concerned. It shows that most middle level product development managers are interested in a distinctly different type of product development success from that focused on by academic researchers and by top corporate level executives. Product development managers are reported, first and foremost, as wanting to avoid development failures.

Academic researchers, as well as top corporate level executives – those concerned with comparing the performance of constituent businesses – are, however, showing increasing interest in studying factors associated with continuous product development success; that is to say, programme success. The reason for the interest in programme rather than project success is because even businesses with a poor overall record of success can occasionally produce a one-off product success, quite possibly by chance. Hence, the established research practice of asking middle level managerial respondents to nominate a successful product development, which is then compared with an unsuccessful one, is flawed on methodological grounds. At best, the results of this type of research yield broad generalisations; at worst, the results have emphasised factors that are inappropriate in specific situations.

Undue focus on project success in the product development literature has resulted in neglect of wider strategic considerations. Most effort has been directed at overcoming internal operating problems – avoiding product development failures – rather than at exploiting external market opportunities. Focusing on failure represents a limited and, as we shall argue, dangerously restricted approach to competitive strategy formulation. The traditional research approach fails to consider adequately the full span of ways in which product development can contribute to business development.

While in the past there was far less need in businesses to understand the levers for their further development, the situation is different today. Until the 1980s many industry players stuck to well-known rules of competitive engagement. The much publicised generic strategies of analysts like Porter (1985) served most businesses well. Businesses found that they could perform satisfactorily if they concentrated either on low costs of production or on differentiating themselves in the market-place. Today, however, increasing numbers of businesses are pursuing different strategies simultaneously. Indeed, in today's more turbulent circumstances, managers who pin their hopes on one so-called 'generic' approach constrain their options (Mathur 1992). The result is lack of attention on targeting market segments precisely, often because undue attention is focused on capitalising on supply-side synergies.

In the same way as using a generic competitive strategy is now very limiting for business development purposes, so is the use of a generic way for developing new products, as we show below. Each separate input factor needs to be managed appropriately for the purpose in hand. We now describe what is involved in doing this as far as one such factor is concerned – listening to the voice of the market.

LISTENING TO THE VOICE OF THE MARKET SELECTIVELY

With respect to listening to customers, a rich literature now exists which indicates the potential advantages of acting on such information for product development purposes (Foxall and Johnston 1987; Parkinson 1982; Simonson 1993; von Hippel 1988; Voss 1985). It is important to emphasise that studies of successful practice in American and British companies have indicated that product development success results from proactive market interpretation, rather than from lamely following the suggestions of key customers. Although meeting customers' needs is a prerequisite for successful product change, the danger exists that a business may end up acting as nothing more than a subcontractor for key customers. When this happens, a business risks losing control over its own destiny.

While listening to the voice of the external market, and also to the voice of the internal market (Piercy and Morgan 1991), is potentially one of the most important marketing inputs, it requires little stretch of the imagination to realise that such listening is likely to be more important for some business purposes than for others. For example, market share can normally always be increased in the short run by pandering to the precise wishes of customers, whereas building a reputation for technical excellence is often achieved on the basis of making independent scientific breakthroughs, which could not have been envisaged by even the most forward-looking customers. In this chapter, it is shown why distinctly different styles of listening to the market are needed for particular business activities. Three business activities are considered in turn:

1. building competitive advantage
2. increasing market share
3. building reputation for technical excellence

It is argued that, because each of these three business activities is served by different mixes of product developments, care needs to be exercised in order that a type of market listening is selected that is appropriate to the type of product development being undertaken.

Building Competitive Advantage in Target Markets

Building competitive advantage is an important business objective served by product development. This objective is concerned with building long-term advantages over competitors through leveraging market and supply-side factors. Guidance on how much *routine product development* (see Table 2.1) is required for this purpose will come from feedback from the external market in the form of representatives' reports, and also internally from technical specialists responsible for applying the latest product technology. However, listening and reacting passively to the voice of the external market will not be sufficient in the long run. The reason for this is that product development is not the sole ingredient for achieving competitive advantage. Supply development and, particularly, product positioning development may be equally or even more important. Indeed, the message from listening to the voice of the market may be to throttle back on routine product development in favour of other forms of product development.

Radical product development is particularly popular for the purpose of building competitive advantage. This form of product development is concerned with products with completely new attributes, aimed at existing market segments. It is the type of product development on which most academic product innovation research claims to focus. However, because few checks are normally undertaken on how radical a new product development is to both customers and suppliers, the danger exists of supposedly radical product developments being lumped together for analysis purposes. As this has been common practice in empirical studies, it is not surprising that research findings conflict, particularly with respect to listening to the voice of the market. This is illustrated in the apparent conflict between the 'customer-active' paradigm of product development propounded by von Hippel (1988) and the 'manufacturer-active' paradigm propounded by Foxall and Johnson (1987).

Listening to the market is also critically important in the case of *extended product development*. If the hoped-for market is either not present or not captured, this type of product development will prove unnecessarily costly.

Listening to the external market will allow a business to identify market potentials. However, the extent to which market potentials can be realised in the face of competitive offerings will also depend on listening to the internal market. This is particularly critical in the case of service product line extensions, where product proliferation can create multiple tensions between marketing and operations. However, the guiding light for successful extended product development is focusing on likely market demand. Practised skilfully, extended product development demonstrates a new approach. Routine product development and radical product development, being traditional forms of product development, are typically judged against internal hurdles, such as target rates of return and avoiding flops. Extended product development, on the other hand, is now increasingly judged against external performance criteria. This is so particularly in businesses that recognise that the traditional approach to product development is flawed when – as so often happens – hurdles set for internal performance ignore market potentials; that is to say, what might have been achieved.

The last main type of product development – *new style product development* (see Table 2.1) – illustrates a new approach to building competitive advantage. New style product development is concerned with the development of new products for gaining access to quite new customer groups. As in the case of extended product development, the success of new style product development is best measured in terms of market success. What distinguishes new style product development is that it involves taking a long and hard look to see how a new market can be shaped with new products (Johne 1994).

Examples of new style product developments are Canon copiers sold via office retailers, Direct Line telephone insurance, First Direct telephone banking, credit card telephone dating (now estimated to be a £30 000 000 industry in Britain) and mall-type second-hand car selling. Each of these new style product developments was successful because an existing market was turned into a new market. Success was achieved not by narrowly defined product development, but by a skilful combination of market and product development supported by product positioning development and supply development. It was achieved as a result of listening to each link in external and internal markets to indicate the precise mix of developments needed for serving distinct target markets. In the case of Canon copiers, international market research teams reported back at regular intervals to headquarters in Japan to exchange information and gain commitment from those involved.

Increasing Market Share in Target Markets

Market share is a popular type of business objective that many managers aim for, despite the fact that it might not serve the longer term aims of the business. Listening to the voice of the market is again of considerable potential importance for each of the four main types of product developments which can be invoked for this purpose. For reasons of space, we shall not review each type here. It is enough to say that market share can, in the short run, be improved by listening reactively to the voice of the external market. For longer run increases in market share, proactive listening will be needed, so that product developments are made for those customers who will still be in a strong demand position tomorrow. New style product development is particularly useful for increasing market share. For example, Direct Line insurance increased its customer base from nil to 1 500 000 customers in eight years, making it the largest insurer of private cars in the UK (Gapper 1993).

Building Reputation for Technical Excellence in Target Markets

Listening to the internal market over the external market has typically been the case in companies intent on building a reputation for technical excellence. This, however, represents an old approach to product development. More and more companies, including IBM, Mercedes-Benz and even Rolls-Royce, have reappraised the merit of building a reputation for technological excellence *per se*. While not denying the need to be technically excellent, today's successful modern businesses increasingly consider supply capabilities after having reflected on market possibilities, or at the very least they consider supply strategies simultaneously with market strategies. Obviously, listening to the voice of the market is important for the purpose of building a reputation for technical excellence, but, as in the case of the two previous business activities, different types of market listening will best serve the product development types invoked for the purpose.

LISTENING SELECTIVELY IS IMPORTANT BUT INSUFFICIENT

It has been shown that different types of listening are required for (i) specific business purposes and (ii) specific types of product developments. The lesson to be drawn from the above exposition is that great care is needed in applying the findings of empirical studies on factors underpinning product development success. There is no doubt that market listening is an important factor. However, while engaging in 'market listening' is important, the precise type of listening needs to be spelt out. This is also likely to be the case with other important factors contributing to product development success. For example, as with market listening, engaging in market research is important. What is, however, critically important is to engage in the type of market research that is appropriate for the product development being undertaken. Here empirical findings have identified the usefulness of engaging in conventional market research for product updating purposes and the usefulness of in-depth qualitative market research for examining radical product development concepts (Johne and Snelson 1990).

ASSESSING PRODUCT DEVELOPMENT SUCCESS AGAINST POTENTIALS

It has already been stressed that managers commonly regard a product development as successful if it does not fail. This is not only a negative, but is also a dangerous way of measuring success. It is dangerous because it fails to consider stretching objectives. An alternative way is to assess product developments against market potentials; that is to say, what might be achieved. It is a sad fact, however, that many product development managers continue to undertake their duties in a constrained way, paying the scantiest attention to the broader business development picture. The complexity of organic business development will only be addressed realistically when managers are routinely required to consider their specialist inputs within a broader framework. Doing this requires considerable reorientation and reorganisation. Businesses that have been restructured on a business basis are very likely to have in place criteria of performance that require product development contributions to be assessed against a wider background (Meyer 1994).

There are considerable advantages in measuring success against market potentials rather than against limited internal objectives. However, even today, many companies continue to measure product development performance in this way. This poses a dilemma for researchers. Should researchers help managers to reach the objectives they set themselves, no matter how limiting these might be, or should they admonish them for not using more stretching objectives? From an analytic perspective, it is clear what advice should be provided. Managers, however, are more concerned with what can be made to happen than with what might conceivably be achieved. Their interest is on what will work in some circumstances, but will not work in others. The reasons for this are not hard to find. Many managers are risk-averse. Others thrive on entrepreneurial challenges. The payoff from telling managers what they should do is limited when, as is so often the case, managers steer into the future on the basis of their past experiences; that is to say, they change by looking in, not out (Martin 1993).

In practical terms, there are likely to be many different views concerning how a business is to be developed. Some managers will favour the longer term over the shorter term; some will favour risk-taking over building up reserves. But perhaps the biggest potential for conflict is the type of development to be favoured in driving a business forward. As has been shown, four main types of development can be used for this purpose: market, product, product positioning and supply development. Selection of one or more of these types of development will be tempered by managers' views of the costs and benefits involved. Both task and non-task considerations will come into play. When a business is not under severe competitive pressures – a state that many managers seek to attain and retain – we can expect personal considerations to play a dominant role. Researchers have a responsibility to analyse these hidden motives, so that they can move away from ascribing unrealistic criteria for success.

CONCLUSION

A schema has been presented in this chapter for conceptualising the activities underpinning business development. The purpose of the schema is to aid understanding of how product development can help in the pursuit of business development. There are two operational approaches to product development: active and passive. The passive approach is commonly invoked by middle-level managers. It focuses on avoiding product development failure. The active approach focuses on exploiting market potentials as fully as possible. The active approach is as yet poorly understood and so, not surprisingly, applied unevenly.

If one accepts that an effective way of measuring product development success is to do so within a business context, then one needs to select, in empirical studies, the focus that best serves this purpose. Focusing at the product level is problematical. It is, however, the most commonly used focus at the present time. However, at the product level so many different objectives are normally in play that it is most unlikely that we can control for each within businesses, let alone across different businesses. An alternative focus is provided by programme performance. Analysis at this level is concerned with the way in which product development is routinely undertaken. This provides a powerful alternative way of assessing business success. It is not, however, without attendant problems. Importantly, very careful control needs to be exercised over the types of markets chosen by businesses for self-development purposes.

Last, but not least, it is necessary to stress again that in today's fast-moving market environments, getting core product attributes right is a necessary but, on its own, insufficient requirement for business success. It is important for those involved in product development processes to recognise and act upon this uncomfortable fact. For example, the present spate of product developments in the automobile industry may well represent a 'side-show' activity in an industry afflicted by overcapacity. In future, more effective business development may be achieved by automobile suppliers not so much through product development, but through product positioning development. One example is the innovative ways of selling cars through networks of personal contacts, rather than through conventional car showrooms; or leasing them, rather than relying on cash purchasers. Customers rarely buy solely on the basis of only one of the marketing-mix elements. Success is likely to come from targeting customers with a package of benefits suited to their purposes, and one that is superior in this respect to that offered by competitors. Doing this successfully requires not only effective product development, but also supporting product positioning development, as well as market and supply development.

REFERENCES

Baker, M.J. (1983). *Market Management*, Penguin, Harmondsworth.

Bartlett, C.A. and Ghosal, S. (1988). Organizing for worldwide effectiveness: The transnational solution, *California Management Review*, **31**(1), 54–74.

Booz, Allen and Hamilton (1982). *New Products Management for the 1980s*, Booz, Allen and Hamilton Inc., New York.

Burgelman, R.A. (1986). Designs for corporate entrepreneurship in established firms, *California Management Review*, **26**(3), 154–166.

Cardoza, R., McLaughlin, K., Harmon, B., Reynolds, P. and Miller, B. (1993). Product-market choices and growth of new business, *Journal of Product Innovation Management*, **10**(4), 331–340.

Cooper, R.G. and Kleinschmidt, E.J. (1987). New products: What separates winners from losers? *Journal of Product Innovation Management*, **4**(3), 169–184.

Cooper, R.G. and Kleinschmidt, E.J. (1993). Major new products: What distinguishes the winners in the chemical industry? *Journal of Product Innovation Management*, **10**(2), 90–111.

Dumaine, B. (1989). How managers can succeed through speed. *Fortune International*, February 13, 30–35.

Easingwood, C.J. and Storey, C. (1993). Marketplace success factors for new financial services, *Journal of Services Marketing*, **7**(1), 41–54.

Foxall, G.R. and Johnston, B. (1987). Strategies of user-initiated product innovation, *TechnoVation*, **6**(1), 77–102.

Gapper, J. (1993). Next target: High risk homes and drivers, *The Financial Times*, 26 November, 23.

Griffin, A.J. and Page, A.L. (1993). An interim report on measuring new product development success and failure, *Journal of Product Innovation Management*, **10**(4), 281–308.

Hart, S. and Craig, A. (1993). Dimensions of success in new product development, in Baker, M.J. (ed.), *Perspectives on Marketing Management*, Vol. 3, John Wiley & Sons, Chichester.

Hauschildt, J. (1991). Zur Messung des Innovationserfolgs, *Zeitschrift für Betriebswirtschaft*, **61**, 451–476.

Johne, F.A. (1994). New style product development: The essential ingredients, in Saunders, J. (ed.), *ESRC Studies into British Marketing*, Prentice Hall, London.

Johne, F.A. and Snelson, P.A. (1988). Success factors in product innovation: A selective review of the literature, *Journal of Product Innovation Management*, **5**(2), 114–128.

Johne, F.A. and Snelson, P.A. (1990). Successful product innovation in UK and US firms, *European Journal of Marketing*, **24**(12), 7–21.

Kraushar, P. (1985). *Practical Business Development*, Holt, Rhinehart and Winston, London.

Martin, R. (1993). Changing the mind of the corporation, *Harvard Business Review*, **71**(6), 81–94.

Mathur, S.S. (1992). Talking straight about competitive strategy, *Journal of Marketing Management*, **8**(3), 199–217.

Meyer, C. (1994). How the tight measures help teams excel, *Harvard Business Review*, **72**(3), 95–103.

Parkinson, S.T. (1982). The role of the user in successful new product development, *R&D Management*, **12**(3), 123–131.

Piercy, N. and Morgan, N. (1991). Internal marketing – The missing half of the marketing programme, *Long Range Planning*, **24**(2), 82–93.

Porter, M. (1985). *Competitive Advantage: Creating and Sustaining Superior Performance*, Free Press, New York.

Simonson, I. (1993). Get closer to your customers by understanding how they make choices, *California Management Review*, **35**(4), 68–84.

von Hippel, E. (1988). *The Sources of Innovation*, Oxford University Press, Oxford.

Voss, C.A. (1985). The role of users in the development of applications software, *Journal of Product Innovation Management*, **2**(2), 113–121.

CHAPTER THREE

A FRAMEWORK FOR TECHNOLOGY STRATEGY

Arie P. Nagel

This chapter deals with the small and medium sized industrial firm that chooses to develop, produce and market new products on a regular basis. It elaborates on the importance of technology in strategic decision making, both in theory and in practice. A seven-step framework for the development of a technology strategy is briefly discussed. The chapter concludes by describing how a number of Dutch firms have implemented the framework in practice.

INTRODUCTION

Technology is a vital and strategic resource for companies. The technology of an industrial firm can be defined as the know-how, skills and experience needed to design and produce new products and product updates. Core technology refers to those technologies that are essential to the firm's competitiveness and that prove necessary for its product designs and/or production processes.

Technology and strategy interlace, at the firm level, in at least three important ways. Firstly, a major strategic issue concerns the acquisition of know-how and skills to develop, produce and market products and to continue to do so over the long term. Secondly, product innovation contributes to the firm's business performance, and this contribution is achieved by possessing appropriate know-how and skills. Finally, firms have to focus not just on present market needs but also on future ones, so they must be ready and prepared to

Product Development: Meeting the Challenge of the Design–Marketing Interface.
Edited by M. Bruce and W.G. Biemans.   © 1995 John Wiley & Sons Ltd.

meet potential new market demands. Corporate strategy that takes account of technological change can help the firm to survive changing market demands. This chapter focuses on the issue of linking technology and strategy. For this purpose, it describes a seven-step framework and illustrates its use by Dutch firms.

LINKING TECHNOLOGY AND STRATEGY

One source of difficulty for companies appears to be the linking of technological innovation to their strategies. Capon and Glazer (1987) suggest that the sustainability of a firm's competitive position depends on its ability to control its technological assets. Burgelman and Maidique (1988) point out that technology strategy is an important, but often neglected, part of the strategy formulation process. The development of a precisely defined and consistent policy with regard to technology is crucial for firms, especially for those that compete in industries characterised by rapid technological change, such as biotechnology, telecommunications, and so on. Frambach, Nijssen and De Freytas (1989) suggest that the problem with most strategic considerations concerning technology is that they focus on the technology itself and fail to incorporate technological issues conceptually into a strategic and marketing perspective.

Considering the strategic plans of small firms, it was noticed in a study of Dutch companies that strategic decisions hardly take account of technology (Nagel 1992). Even high-tech firms describe their analyses, objectives, strategy and action plans in product/market and/or financial terms (market segments, regions, market shares and so on). Where attention is paid to technology in the companies' strategic plans, this is with regard to one product group and not to the underlying knowledge and skills of the firm as a whole.

Another difficulty in linking strategy and technology may be due to over-emphasis on market-demand or market-pull factors – What does the customer want? What business are we in? – rather than technology-push – What are we able to do? What do we want to do? For example, in a medium sized, high-tech firm (Nagel 1992), management attention and improvement actions were based on the following assessment by a consulting firm: 'You are already excelling in technology, so let's concentrate on marketing'. The firm acted as it was advised and marketing received much attention, while the technology side was neglected. For the next 10 years synergy between the different technologies that the company was using was purely accidental. This occurred despite the fact that the R&D managers were involved in strategic planning.

But as the R&D director stated, 'We tried to be loyal and contribute to the strategic thinking, although we never understood what it had to do with our work, i.e. the decisions we had to make in the field of R&D'.

Overemphasis on marketing and/or the financial future can lead to a technology policy that is short termist. Business plans often have a two- to three-year time horizon, while technological development typically has a longer time-span, particularly before the investment made in the development of new technologies begins to be repaid and generate income. Gupta, Raj and Wilemon (1985) comment that R&D will tend to a long-term orientation, while marketing tends to involve short-term adjustments as a reaction to competitors. These two visions have to be adjusted to each other in order to develop useful new products. Brownlie (1987) suggests that a good solution for integration of technology and strategy has yet to be found. He points out that the time horizon for the development of a technology is much longer than the usual planning horizon. Furthermore, Kanter (1988) postulates that the combination of two different time horizons within an organisation is problematic, if not impossible.

A major consequence of the neglect of the technology component is that a lack of synergy can result between technology, technological direction and corporate plans; so much so that the development of technology results from almost a 'hobbyist' approach. Obviously, there is sympathy with this view because many new products have arisen through the work of creative individuals (Quinn 1985). However, the failure to take account of technology in strategic plans mean that a critical resource is not fully utilised.

Table 3.1   Various ways of looking at strategy

Choices for the product/market strategy	Strategic technological choices to be made
Distribution channel	Leader or follower/imitator
Product range	Process or product innovation
Price	Level of percentage of R&D
Region	Directed/undirected R&D
Client	Fundamental/applied R&D
Costleader or focus	Which core technologies
	Focus/diversified
	Synergy in the market
	Cooperation or solo
	How and what know-how to acquire
	Which know-how to sell
	Market- or technology domination
	How to do the idea-screening
	Attention to 'pull' or 'push'

A technology strategy entails decisions, including whether to strive to be a technological leader or follower, as well as decisions about the direction and focus of R&D, the priorities of R&D projects, and how (and which) technological knowledge has to be acquired and maintained. Technology strategy needs to be in tandem with corporate goals so that the technological direction of the company is likely to realise its commercial objectives. Table 3.1 contains some examples of product/market strategy decisions and their implications for strategic technological choices.

TOWARDS A TECHNOLOGY STRATEGY

The role of technology in corporate strategy has been neglected, and emphasis placed on financial and marketing concerns. Wilson (1986) concludes that the ultimate success of a firm is due to a combination of technological, economic and commercial success. But he maintains that the technological direction of a firm should not be guided by the vision and ambitions of R&D, but rather has to be defined at the firm level. Burgelman and Maidique (1988) support this.

Porter (1988) indicates that literature about the management of technology especially emphasises the internal conditions that might increase the probability of success of R&D programmes, and the relation between innovation and customer needs. However, he, on the one hand, misses the fundamental insight into how technological changes can also alter the structure of an industry and the 'rules' of competition and, on the other, the ways in which technology can form the basis for establishing a permanent competitive advantage. Technology strategy is a critical part of the company's overall competitive strategy and forms a powerful instrument for gaining a competitive advantage. This applies in particular when the pace of technological change is great and products are technologically complex.

One approach to the incorporation of technology in strategic planning is that of Japanese companies, which seem to acknowledge the role of technology in terms of 'technology push'. Investment in technology and the development of technology strategies that are linked with commercial goals are characteristic of Japanese business practice.

SUPPORT FOR TECHNOLOGY PUSH

In contemporary practice of strategic management, technology issues are often not taken into account explicitly, in particular by small and medium-sized firms, partly because an adequate framework for strategic technology management is lacking. This means that highly skilled technicians discuss the future of their firm in terms of products, markets, competitors and finance when they discuss strategic plans with their colleagues in the commercial and production departments. Much effort is put into market research and market positioning, whereas the availability of technology tends to be taken for granted or left to people outside the strategic management group. When it comes to strategic decision making, managers – even those with a background in engineering – usually confine themselves to the concepts and techniques as taught in traditional business schools, such as Porter's (1988) concepts of generic market strategies and techniques such as product portfolio analysis or SWOT (strengths, weaknesses, opportunities, threats) analysis. By doing so, crucial technology issues – for example, deciding on the type of process or machinery, what to make or buy, and so on – are not included in strategic decision making, but are instead overlooked or left to operational middle-line managers.

It is apparent that firms that rely heavily on highly developed technology should not focus only on 'today's market'. 'Technology push', as well as 'market pull' (the current market demand, often based on existing knowledge), is very important for business success. The Research Institute, Battelle, according to Quinn (1985), states that it takes an average of almost 20 years to put a technological idea into commercial practice. It is unlikely that a customer plans that far ahead. The development of new technologies, components and products is often started long before customer demand exists, so that the firm is able to meet the potential, future demand of customers. The firm cannot look ahead or predict with certainty the customer demand 20 years hence, but what it can do is build on its strength – its (core) technologies – and be ready to respond to changing technological needs.

The next section discusses a framework for a technology strategy. This framework can be helpful in the analysis and decision making on behalf of a technology strategy. It is placed in the context of strategic management. The chapter concludes by demonstrating how the framework was put into practice by a number of Dutch firms.

A FRAMEWORK FOR A TECHNOLOGY STRATEGY

This framework describes a method with regard to technological strategic planning. It is derived from existing theory, in particular Stacey and Ashton (1990) and insights gained from research and consultancy (Nagel 1992). This method aims to assist in the analysis and decision making of a technology strategy.

Table 3.2   The framework for a technology strategy

1. Assessment of current technological strengths and weaknesses
2. Assessment of externally available technologies
3. Generation of strategic technological alternatives
4. Decision making
   a. new R&D projects to be developed
   b. priorities for existing projects and technologies
   c. acquisition of technology
   d. exploitation of redundant technology
5. Action planning and preparation of implementation
6. Implementation
7. Review and evaluation of technology strategy implementation

The differences between a product/market strategy and a technology strategy are indicated in Table 3.1. This recognises that these strategies are mutually dependent, so that the choice for a product range, for example, is closely related to the available technology. Other areas of strategy, such as production strategies, could be regarded in a similar way as in Table 3.1.

In Table 3.2, a framework for a technology strategy is presented as a seven-step procedure. The various steps of the procedure are discussed below.

STEP I: ASSESSMENT OF CURRENT TECHNOLOGICAL STRENGTHS AND WEAKNESSES

Assessment of current technological strengths and weaknesses analyses the technological potential of the company, in particular its core technologies. Hamel and Prahalad (1989) propose to carry out this assessment by interviews with key figures in the company, and they suggest that the assessment address the questions: What are the current level of skills and knowledge? What has to be developed (in the future) by the company itself?

These questions are dealt with by focusing on:

- the goals for technology
- the selection of technologies
- the level of needed investments
- the appropriate level of know-how
- what needs to be developed by the firm itself
- what needs to be acquired

One aspect of such an assessment exercise concerns the determination of the objectives and position of the R&D function within the company. Sethi, Movsesian and Hickey (1985) mention decision parameters, such as:

- research versus development-intensive
- degree of linkage between the R&D function and other company functions
- the product life cycles (short life cycles require a stronger marketing approach than longer life cycles)
- the level of R&D investment
- distance from the state-of-the-art of technology
- past experience

STEP 2: ASSESSMENT OF EXTERNALLY AVAILABLE TECHNOLOGIES

The assessment of externally available technologies involves scanning and screening of the technological environment. This assessment should focus on what technologies the company can acquire, what is available to the competition and what the customer wants. From this, the company has a basis on which to direct its present and future core technologies. A collection of many proven techniques is known as *technology forecasting*, which concerns forecasting the influence and speed of a possibly profound development. Among the methods used for technology forecasting are scenarios, Delphi-time series and morphological analyses (Wills et al. 1972). Scenarios, for example, have to identify alternatives to a given change and consider the alternatives for a specific development. After the environmental screening the results have to be interpreted strategically, for example by means of a SWOT analysis, in order to develop a technology business plan.

STEP 3: GENERATION OF STRATEGIC TECHNOLOGICAL ALTERNATIVES

The purpose of this phase is to decide on the technological strategy for the company. Cooper (1985) has identified five distinct strategies:

1. The balanced and focus strategy: a coalescing of both a technological and a market orientation. This strategy serves as a focus strategy directed towards potentially attractive markets.
2. The conservative, low budget strategy. A smart 'me too' (follower) strategy with synergy between the existing technology and marketing orientation.
3. The technologically driven strategy, directed towards a high technological advancement, but with a weak market orientation.

4. The technologically deficient or market strategy, which is characterised by a weak technological orientation and a constant search for new markets, new needs and superior products.
5. The high budget or 'shotgun' strategy, which is characterised by a high level of R&D expenditure and a direction towards new markets.

These are only some possible strategies. In reality additional decisions have to be made, for example about collaboration with other companies, whether the accent lies on product or process innovation, and so on. Nonetheless, it is important to produce ideas creatively for the future direction of the firm and to take account of the following themes:

■ Searching for a new market for an existing product, for which the relevant process and product technologies are available.
■ Developing a new product for a known market, based on available technologies (obtained via other projects/products or available in other business units).
■ Searching for new or complementary technologies for an existing product line in an existing market (product adjustments, process improvements), which may lead to a product that fulfils its function for the customer in a more satisfying way, or that is cheaper or easier to produce.

In order to make the alternatives for a technology strategy visible, technology portfolios have been developed by several authors, including Stacey and Ashton (1990), who confine themselves to two dimensions (Figure 3.1):

■ The value of the application of the technology on the market: the attractiveness of the technology on a specific market.
■ The position of the company in relation to the considered technology compared to competition: the relative technological competitive position.

For both dimensions, those elements which – for this specific technology, on that specific market – are presumed to be the most determinant (key factors for success) are identified first. Every element is given a weighting score, and for every element a score for the company is determined. Examples of elements to measure the attractiveness of a new technology are: stage of maturity, degree of renewal, application possibilities, acceptance by customers, influence on cost reductions, effect on quality improvements, invested and to be invested capital, risks, possible substitutes, number of competitors and environmental effects. Examples of elements that are of importance in estimating the technological competitive position of the company include: lead on the competition, industrial infrastructure, dependence on suppliers and customers, costs structure, financial opportunities, invested capital in R&D,

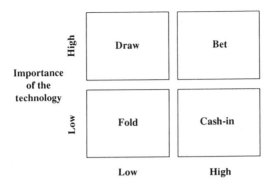

Figure 3.1   An example of a technology portfolio matrix. The four quadrants are described as follows:

- Bet: the company is in a technologically excellent position in a business segment where that technology is important; objectives should be to sustain and increase competitive advantage. This is the business where one must commit oneself to the newest equipment.
- Draw: the company is in a borderline position. One needs to make two decisions: either bet against the competition and invest to attain a leadership position, or develop a plan to disengage from, or even abandon, that technology and invest in more lucrative areas.
- Cash-in: the company is in a technologically strong position, but the technology where it excels is not really important in market-place terms. This situation occurs most often in a rapidly changing industry, such as electronics or engineered plastics, where existing technology is continually being supplanted by new techniques. Technologies underlying ageing product families (frequently a company's original product lines) tend to lie in this quadrant too.
- Fold: the company is technologically weak in an unimportant field. If heavy investment has taken place, this money may have to be considered to be sunk costs. If not, then a financial redeployment strategy is essential (and the sooner the better).

patents, capacity and position on the market. With the aid of this portfolio, the strengths of a company can be estimated for its most important technologies. The analysis can be extended by looking at the developments chronologically, representing the position with respect to the strongest competitor, estimating alternatives, and so on.

STEP 4: DECISION MAKING

Choice of Technology Strategy

Taking account of the above, the technological direction for the future of the company has to be determined. All functional areas (marketing, finance,

R&D and production) should make a contribution. Four major themes need to be addressed, as discussed in the following subsections.

New R&D Projects to be Developed

White (1988) notes that tools available for management to judge or guide technological innovations are rudimentary. He proposes the use of management criteria (filters) by which new technologies, innovations or innovative ideas can be selected. The criteria he uses relate to the technology, the context of the innovation(s), the business context and the subsequent market dynamics. For each of these four areas, there are pertinent issues to consider. The technology filters are:

1. What constraints of the prior technology are lifted?
2. What are the constraints of the new technology?
3. Is the new technology really better than the old one, given the pros and cons?

The main benefit arising from a questioning process is that it forms a basis for a discussion about new ideas and the judgement of these ideas.

Priorities for Existing Projects and Technologies

Current projects are open to appraisal based on their results (Foster 1988):

- technological opportunity/promise
- commercial opportunity/promise

These two points need to be supplemented by consideration of the following:

- Does the project fit with the chosen core technology?
- To what extent does it contribute to the knowledge and skills with regard to other projects?

Acquisition of Technology

Technologies and/or knowledge/skills can be acquired by:

- internal development, i.e. R&D projects within the company
- external acquisition
- externally via other business units (resources, capacity)
- completely externally:
  - buying or licensing of technologies

- acquisition of appropriate people/companies/means
- using external R&D and knowledge centres, contracting-out
■ strategic cooperation: joint ventures, co-makership, R&D partnership or innovation networks (Biemans 1989)

The choice of the method of acquisition depends mainly on the availability of suitable partners, time-scale, cost, proprietary nature of the development and strategic objectives.

Exploitation of Redundant Technology

Ford and Ryan (1988) posit that a company should strive for a maximal return on investments in a given technology, by exploiting this technology as much as possible. The technology can be exploited by incorporation in existing and new products, as well as by being sold as a product under license to other companies. Reasons for a company wishing to exploit its technological knowledge include:

■ The highest return on investment in R&D is being pursued; the company is not only making money by selling products realised by the technology, but also by selling the idea behind the product.
■ The company cannot, or does not wish to, apply the technology. Given this situation, a company that wants to get the highest return from its technologies will have to verify carefully the market value of the technology.

STEP 5: ACTION PLANNING AND PREPARATION OF IMPLEMENTATION

The implementation of technology strategy is most effective if carried out in phases. It seems to be prudent to do the following:

■ concentrate attention on the core technologies
■ first gain experience in a pilot implementation
■ ensure top-level commitment
■ specify action plans for each function

STEPS 6 AND 7: IMPLEMENTATION AND EVALUATION

The phased planning approach is the basis for the actual implementation of the technology strategy. Finally, at predetermined times, but at least once a year, the results need to be evaluated. The evaluation can be used to modify the technology strategy and plan.

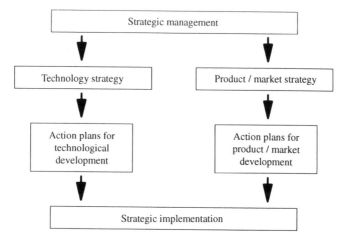

Figure 3.2   Linking technology strategy to product/market strategy

TECHNOLOGY STRATEGY WITHIN THE CONTEXT OF STRATEGIC MANAGEMENT

Technology is an important aspect of strategic decisions and should be treated in a complementary manner to the market strategy. They interact and interlace (Figure 3.2).

To avoid communication problems, it is essential that in formulating both the technology and market strategies, a continuous exchange of information between technical and commercial functions occurs, so that a balanced strategy can be produced. The technology strategy has to be given top-level commitment, and senior management need to:

- Create the innovative environment, which is needed for the process of new product generation.
- Direct specialists towards the intended goals.
- Provide the infrastructure needed for the process of new product generation (Quinn 1985; Wrapp 1967).

ACHIEVING A TECHNOLOGY STRATEGY IN PRACTICE

The framework for technology management was tested in a number of companies in the Netherlands (Nagel 1992). Eight firms, ranging in size from 2 to

350 personnel, participated in the action research. They were involved in the field of developing, producing and selling medical equipment. Companies were selected by an assessment of their present position and behaviour in technology management via interviews with managers and by studying documents, such as strategic plans. Workshops were then held with senior executives to identify their approaches to technology management. The workshops resulted in an 'action plan', the progress of which was evaluated in a subsequent workshop. Five of the larger firms adopted the ideas developed in the action plans and changed their strategic plans accordingly. One factor that facilitated acceptance of the action plans was that the staff were receptive to thinking and working strategically. Three small companies did not adopt the action plans, but the participants thought that their awareness of technology management had increased overall. One of these companies was facing bankruptcy, another was very small and the third used little technology, so the technology framework was deemed to be inappropriate. Two examples of workshop companies are given in the following subsections.

COMPANY A

In one R&D-intensive and high-tech firm, formal approaches of strategy formulation were used, and one of the central techniques was the product portfolio analysis. However, the company wanted to develop new products and required a procedure for facilitating this.

Taking steps 1 and 3 of the model (analysis and idea generation), during the workshops the management team was divided into three groups with representatives from market, technology and product to develop an action plan. Each group had to make an analysis and to come up with new products. During plenary sessions at the end of the workshop, the results were discussed and a plan to guide the strategic direction was devised for new product ideas.

After a few months, it was evident that a number of the new ideas produced were poor, but – more importantly – the groups were beginning to gain a deeper understanding of strategic thinking and to connect their technology plans with their corporate goals. As a matter of course, elements of a technology strategy are now incorporated in the company's strategic plans.

COMPANY B

In another R&D-intensive high-tech firm (150 personnel) a workshop was organised to:

- Raise the awareness of technology as an important factor in dealing with strategy.
- Identify the firm's core technologies.
- Devise a procedure for selecting a new product idea.

Four groups were formed, with representatives from different functions, and each group was led by a company director. In advance of the workshop, the following questions were put forward for discussion:

- What are the core technologies, both now and in the near future?
- What are the relevant strategic choices in production?
- What are the relevant technology choices for the firm?
- What are the relevant choices for R&D?

The greatest problem the company had was identifying its core technologies, and these were typically regarded in terms of existing products and components. Hence, technologies were described in terms of techniques (how to do it), rather than technologies (what to do, knowledge). Breaking down barriers between production, R&D and commercial functions so that they communicated with each other on these matters in a language that all understood was another problem.

At the end of the workshop a procedure for a technology strategy was accepted, similar to the framework developed by Nagel (1992). The chief executive claimed that, 'strategy will be different from now on and it will be better'. One major outcome was recognition that new products should be developed only if there was evidence that these products also satisfied the needs of the clients in the firm's distribution channels.

CONCLUSION

This chapter is an attempt to combine insights from literature and field experiments in a pragmatic way. It began by pointing out the relevance of technology corporate strategy issues and then proceeded with a framework for devising a technology strategy. The intention is to produce a balanced strategy that takes account of both technology and market needs. Achieving this balanced strategy is complex, and varies from context to context. Nevertheless, it is important that technology issues are taken account of in the strategic planning process.

Frameworks and techniques are merely vehicles to serve this process, and one approach to a technology strategy is presented here. In none of the cases was

the framework accepted as such. What matters is that the companies started –
for the first time – to think strategically about technology.

REFERENCES

Biemans, W.G. (1989). Developing innovations within networks, with an application to
the Dutch medical equipment industry, PhD Dissertation, Eindhoven University of
Technology, The Netherlands.
Brownlie, D.T. (1987). The strategic management of technology: A new wave of
market-led pragmatism or a return to product orientation, *European Journal of
Marketing*, **21**(9), 45–65.
Burgelman, R.A. and Maidique, M.A. (eds) (1988). *Strategic Management of Technol-
ogy and Innovation*, Richard Irwin, Homewood, IL.
Capon, N. and Glazer, R. (1987). Marketing and technology: A strategic coalignment,
Journal of Marketing, **54**, 1–14.
Cooper, R.G. (1985). Overall corporate strategies for new product programs, *Indus-
trial Marketing Management*, **14**, 179–193.
Foster, R.N. (1988). Linking R&D to strategy, in Burgelman, R.A. and Maidique,
M.A. (eds), *Strategic Management of Technology and Innovation*, Richard Irwin,
Homewood, IL, pp. 161–172.
Ford, D. and Ryan, C. (1988). Taking technology to market, in Burgelman, R.A. and
Maidique, M.A. (eds), *Strategic Management of Technology and Innovation*,
Richard Irwin, Homewood, IL, pp. 189–200.
Frambach, R.T., Nijssen, E.J. and de Freytas, W.H.J. (1989). Technologie, strategisch
management en marketing, Research Memorandum, Katholieke Universiteit
Brabant, Tilburg.
Gupta, A.K., Raj, S.P. and Wilemon, D. (1985). R&D and marketing dialogue in high-
tech firms, *Industrial Marketing Management*, **14**, 289.
Hamel, G. and Prahalad, C.K. (1989). Strategic intent, *Harvard Business Review*, May/
June, 63–66.
Kanter, R.M. (1988). The middle manager as innovator, in Burgelman, R.A. and
Maidique, M.A. (eds), *Strategic Management of Technology and Innovation*,
Richard Irwin, Homewood, IL, pp. 374–388.
Nagel, A.P. (1992). Verhogen van het strategisch produkt innovatie vermogen, PhD
dissertation, Eindhoven University of Technology, The Netherlands (in Dutch).
Porter, M.E. (1988). The technological dimension of competitive strategy, in Burgel-
man, R.A. and Maidique, M.A. (eds), *Strategic Management of Technology and
Innovation*, Richard Irwin, Homewood, IL.
Quinn, J.B. (1985). Managing innovation, controlled chaos, *Harvard Business Re-
view*, **53**, 73–84. (Also in Mintzberg, H. and Quinn, J.B. (1991). *The Strategy
Process, Concepts, Contexts, Cases*, 2nd edn, Prentice Hall, Englewood Cliffs, NJ,
pp. 746–758.)
Sethi, N.K., Movsesian, B. and Hickey, K.D. (1985). Can technology be managed
strategically? *Long Range Planning*, **18**(4), 89–99.
Stacey, G.S. and Ashton, W.B. (1990). A structured approach to corporate technology
strategy, *International Journal of Technology Management*, **5**(4), 389–407.
White, J.R. (1988). Management criteria for effective innovation, in Burgelman, R.A.
and Maidique, M.A. (eds), *Strategic Management of Technology and Innovation*,
Richard Irwin, Homewood, IL, pp. 103–113.

Wills, G., in association with Wilson, W., Manning, N. and Hildebrandt, R. (1972). *Technological Forecasting: The Art and its Implications*, Penguin, Harmondsworth.

Wilson, I. (1986). The strategic management of technology: corporate fad or strategic necessity? *Long Range Planning*, **19**(2), 21–22.

Wrapp, H.E. (1967). Good managers don't make policy decisions, in Mintzberg, H. and Quinn, J.B. (eds), *The Strategy Process, Concepts, Contexts, Cases*, 2nd edn, Prentice Hall, Englewood Cliffs, NJ, pp. 32–38.

MANAGING THE DESIGN–MARKETING INTERFACE

INTRODUCTION

Margaret Bruce

One of the critical interfaces in the product development process is that between design and marketing. Identifying market trends, assessing the competition and finding out end-user needs are the primary tasks of marketing. Converting the market information into a form that can be effectively utilised by designers and engineers to facilitate the creation and development of products that meet market demands and end-user needs is a key aspect of the design–marketing interface. Chapter 4, by Davies-Cooper and Jones, addresses this issue. The authors argue that a major cause of product failure is poor communication between design and marketing and a lack of understanding about their respective roles, ways of working and relative strengths. They have developed and implemented a diagnostic tool to help companies to assess the main problems that exist between the marketing and design functions in the product development process.

More and more companies are outsourcing design expertise. However, the overriding emphasis of the current literature is concerned with in-house approaches to managing product development. Chapter 5, by Bruce and Morris, compares three different approaches to design management: in-house, outsourcing and a mixture of in-house and outsourcing. The main points of difference focus on issues of control, particularly the desire to combine openness with a fear of leakage of proprietary information; accessibility, that is to appropriate design skills, as and when required; and familiarity, which refers to the designer's understanding of the client's market needs, production processes, etc., to create an optimum design solution. Some discussion is made about the nature of the design–client relationship and the benefits and disbenefits of shorter- or longer-term relationships.

Evaluation of new product concepts is often left to designers and marketers. Typically, consumers are asked, if at all, for their reactions to products *after* they have been launched onto the market. Loosschilder and Schoormans, in Chapter 6, outline their research into consumers' perceptions and interpretations of product concepts. The authors have applied a means–end chain model for consumer evaluation of product concepts. This takes account of consumers' perceptions of different concepts, the consequences of using the product and the individual's value set. The model is used to assess various concepts of telephone handsets.

CHAPTER FOUR

THE INTERFACES BETWEEN DESIGN AND OTHER KEY FUNCTIONS IN PRODUCT DEVELOPMENT

Rachel Davies-Cooper and Tim Jones

Design is an integral part of new product development, which, until recently, has been given little attention by researchers. This chapter discusses the key functions involved in new product development, such as marketing, design and technology, and focuses on their interfaces with design. The authors have developed a diagnostic tool for evaluating these interfaces and describe its application in six firms. The chapter closes with an overview of common areas of weakness in product development, then identifies the foundations of best practice.

INTRODUCTION

In the competitive market-place that organisations find themselves in today, there is an increasing sense of urgency in the need to develop new products, to reduce the development time and to be innovative. Not only is new product development (NPD) a fundamental factor in stimulating and supporting manufacturing growth, but it is also becoming a key issue for economic survival in many industrialised nations. The subject has been examined from the perspective of various management disciplines, and numerous studies have

Product Development: Meeting the Challenge of the Design–Marketing Interface.
Edited by M. Bruce and W.G. Biemans.   © 1995 John Wiley & Sons Ltd.

indicated factors that affect – positively or negatively – the success of the NPD process.

In contrast, 'design', an integral element of NPD, has been given relatively little attention by researchers. Rothwell, Gardiner and Pick (1990), in their study on design and innovation, concluded that there was a tendency for British goods to try to compete on price rather than on superior design and technical quality, making Britain doubly vulnerable to high price and high quality imports from mature manufacturing centres *and* to low price competition from newly industrialising countries. Therefore, design and innovation are now essential to the survival and success of all types of organisations.

This chapter discusses the key functions that affect NPD and considers their interfaces with design during the NPD process.

SUCCESS/FAILURE FACTORS IN NEW PRODUCT DEVELOPMENT

The NPD literature reveals a number of factors that contribute to success and failure in NPD (see also Hart, Chapter 1 and Johne, Chapter 2, this volume). In considering these, it is important to note that criteria for success and failure differ, for example from successful product launch to capturing a new market and to an increase in profits from new products. However, most studies find that the factors discussed in the following subsections are significant contributors to success.

STRATEGY

Most research suggests that a clear strategy is an essential contributor to success. In the first instance, corporate strategy must be well defined and based on sound data, which must be accurately translated into market, design and technology strategies.

STRUCTURE, CULTURE AND CLIMATE

Organisation for NPD is a field that is currently being given much attention from all areas of management and manufacturing. For instance, success is usually found using matrix structures, linking mechanisms or small business units. Also, there is a move away from the traditional 'over the wall' sequential approach towards periods of overlapping and cooperation between departments, or the use of dedicated teams (Francis and Winstanley 1988; Takeuchi and Nonaka 1986).

In addition, it is important to have committed personnel on projects and for them to be encouraged and stimulated by product champions or entrepreneurs (Cooper and Kleinschmidt 1987). Indeed, leaders of innovation, creative scientists, agents of change, teams and personnel with multifunctional perspectives have all been cited as contributing to success (Hopkins 1981).

The culture must also be one in which teams and product champions can operate; innovation requires a dynamic environment where initiative and risk taking are encouraged and where ideas can develop across disciplines (Barczak and Wilemon 1989). The support of senior management for programmes, but without too much interference (Johne and Snelson 1988) on projects, is essential (Topalian 1989).

NPD PLANNING AND PROCESS

NPD strategies and plans, both at programme and project level, have been identified as essential to success, either in the form of charters (Crawford 1980), business plans (Day 1975) or project manuals (Thomsen 1990).

EXTERNAL FACTORS

There are a number of factors that are often out of the control of an organisation, which can affect the success or otherwise of a new product, and should be noted:

- The economic climate: influencing the ability of the consumer to buy, obviously has an impact on the commercial success of a new product, and the investment available for the potentially risky NPD programmes.
- The market: the size of the market, the competitors and the changes in the market-place are all known to have an impact on new product success. Also, the relationships between the company and its suppliers, distributors and users have been identified as influential in NPD (Biemans 1991).
- Environmental issues: environmental legislation and market forces in this area are of increasing importance in the acceptance or uptake of a product in the market (see Frambach, Chapter 12, this volume), as well as determinants of the cost in design, material and manufacture.

The NPD process, therefore, must be planned and managed effectively. This cannot be achieved without the organisational structure to create the right teams, within an appropriate and supportive climate, with active communication and management commitment. Much of this depends on the people involved, their skills, their 'actual' and 'perceived' role and the value placed on their function both by themselves and by others in the organisation.

KEY FUNCTIONS IN NEW PRODUCT DEVELOPMENT

In addition to the organisation, culture, climate and NPD planning, the literature indicates that there are broadly three key function areas involved in successful NPD: marketing, design and technology.

MARKETING

Reliable and up to date market research has been identified as critical to NPD success (Hopkins 1981; Maidique and Zirger 1984; Townsend 1976, Utterback et al. 1976). It is essential that the market has been read early, that there is a well-defined market need, and, indeed, that the company understands the market-place and is aware of both its present and its likely future competitors in that market-place.

Marketing is concerned with most stages of the NPD process, from product planning, screening and testing through to launch. Attention to the promotion, for instance, is critical to the effective launch of a product into the market (Rothwell 1972; see also Biemans and Setz, Chapter 10, this volume).

DESIGN

Different design disciplines exist, including engineering, industrial and other specialisms (e.g. graphic design, interior design), and design activities that are diffused throughout the organisation have been described by Gorb and Dumas (1987) as 'silent design'.

In manufacturing, in particular of consumer products, industrial design is becoming an increasingly important factor in differentiating products from their competitors by giving them a coherent identity or higher levels of perceived value. Potter et al. (1991) identified the use of industrial design as a valuable commercial investment.

Engineering design has an essential role in the development of products in manufacturing industry, generating the solutions to technical problems, that use the available technology in the most effective manner, and integrating the product development with the requirements of efficient production (Rothwell and Gardiner 1984).

There are other design disciplines whose skills are required, depending on the business. For instance, although we have primarily discussed consumer products and manufacturing industry, new products form part of any business, whether it is in the manufacturing, service, retail, financial or public sector. If, for instance, a company is involved with the insurance industry, any new product will require promotional material, forms, certificates and so on, which must all be designed, and the aim of the product must be communicated clearly to customer or consumer. Therefore, a graphic designer will be involved. Similarly for a hotel chain, interior designers would be essential to make the best use of available space and develop the appropriate atmosphere for restaurants, reception areas and coffee shops.

Whatever the 'new product', whether it be purely technical as in a turbine blade, purely aesthetic as with textiles and fabrics, or, as is more common, a combination of both technical and aesthetic design, some design discipline will be involved.

TECHNOLOGY

The term 'technology' links together many of the functions and activities that occur in NPD. The most identifiable area where technology has a significant presence is R&D, where, throughout the development of innovations, new processes and materials, technology is the dominant feature and essentially drives the research. Technical innovators and creative scientists have been identified as necessary since the early 1970s (Roberts 1977; Rothwell 1972), and strong management of technology was found to be important to NPD success by Cooper and Kleinschmidt in 1987.

Manufacturing is the fundamental application of new technology. Whether adopting new techniques developed within the company or externally, the processes and materials selected and used in manufacturing are all technologically based. In choosing which particular process, machines and materials are appropriate for a product, production engineers are inherently influencing aspects of the design of the product, in terms of both its manufacture and its assembly. Hopkins (1981) found failure associated with technical problems such as 'trying to convert full scale production from laboratory or pilot development work and manufacturing problems when using novel materials or components bought from outside suppliers'.

FINANCE

There are, of course, a number of other functions within an organisation that have a significant bearing on that organisation's success, but when addressing NPD specifically, there is one function in particular that has considerable influence on the success or otherwise of the process: finance. Projects need to be appropriately and adequately supported, yet checks on costs, profit margins and return on investment must be part of the process (Hopkins 1981). Many organisations now use phase reviews to keep a check on the progress of the projects, the budget and the authorisation to spend.

THE INTERFACES

It is clear that in terms of the NPD process, while having a good corporate strategy, the appropriate process in place and the right external environment are important, unless the organisational climate is supportive and the key functions operate effectively success may not be achieved. Much management research has focused on the interface between marketing and manufacturing; both industry and academia have placed emphasis on the building up of awareness of the importance of being market orientated, of understanding the customer, improving the use of technology and using tools and techniques for more effective manufacture. In the past few years quality has become an issue that has been used to focus all functions and to develop cross-functional relationships.

However, despite the importance of design to the end product, until recently little attention has been given to the role of design and considerably less to the interfaces between design and other functions in the NPD process. How it is perceived (Hart and Service 1988), what its role is in the organisation, who is responsible for it (Gorb and Dumas 1987; Topalian 1989) and how it is managed and interfaced during the NPD process (Bruce and Roy 1991) are all areas that have, to date, received little examination.

As the separate functions begin to work together, a need develops to improve the cross-functional processes, and research indicates that the success or failure of the project can be influenced significantly by the interfaces between these functions (Rosenthal 1990): It is therefore necessary to examine the dynamics of each of the interfaces, specifically those within the design function and those between design and the other key function areas.

THE INTERFACES WITHIN DESIGN

Within the design function in manufacturing industry there are three separate design disciplines: ergonomics, engineering and industrial design. Although the relative importance of each can vary from product to product, most products have inputs from all three (Barlow 1988; Walsh et al. 1992). When purchasing a product, the customer does not differentiate between the different types of design, and so, to produce a coherent design, there has to be an integration of the different disciplines from the start. This can be difficult, particularly as there is often perceived to be a cultural gap between design engineers and industrial designers. Many engineers are confident that they can deal with all aspects of the design, and feel that they represent the most important discipline. Some consider that they understand aesthetics and can undertake the industrial design themselves, while others consider industrial design to be merely the 'tarting up' of the product (Moody 1980). However, even though some industrial designers are only used for styling, many engineers do recognise their importance; to work together successfully, the disciplines have to respect each other's skills (Black 1973).

THE MARKETING–DESIGN INTERFACE

Throughout the development programme, it is claimed that there ought to be a continuous interaction between marketing and design (Hopkins 1981). Not only do designers need to know about the product, the competition, the target market and the price, but, as well as information on the characteristics of the consumer, they also need to be regularly updated on any changes in their requirements (Dace 1989). This range of information needs to be presented clearly and, at all times, must be appropriate to the needs of the designers (Slade 1989). In order to achieve this successfully, it is often recommended that marketing should fully understand the design process and that there should also be regular communication between marketing, production and manufacturing to ensure that all products are appropriate to the company's existing or planned manufacturing capability (Rothwell and Whiston 1990).

As one of the primary means of communicating the product information from marketing to the rest of the development team, the initial brief and the subsequent specification have been identified as critical documents. Usually written by marketing, the brief ought to be clear and concise, because a vague and ambiguous brief can be the source of major problems in the project (Slade 1990). Furthermore, early discussion of the brief allows design to comment on it and feedback their understanding before acceptance (Rosenthal 1990). This ensures that all parties understand and agree with the briefing document and that design do not have to clarify omissions later on. Although involving all of the NPD functions means that the specification often takes longer to prepare, it is also important that this document should be communicated clearly before any detailed design work is undertaken (Slade 1990).

THE RESEARCH–DESIGN INTERFACE

As with the marketing interface, it is recommended that there should also be regular contact between design and R&D (Walsh et al. 1992). In order to operate effectively, designers need to be aware of both the current research taking place within the company and relevant developments in new materials and processes occurring outside, particularly during the early stages of a project. They need to be able to consult with R&D, who themselves also need to communicate with market research and marketing over new products which may be developed in the future (Hopkins 1981). Finally, to further ensure maximum transfer of the required information, design and R&D both need to be brought together with production and manufacturing in the team, right from the earliest stages (Rothwell and Gardiner 1984).

THE MANUFACTURING–DESIGN INTERFACE

Studies have found that it is beneficial to involve production and manufacturing from the start and that there needs to be a continuous interaction between them and design (Francis and Winstanley 1988). There should be regular consultation between design, production and manufacturing to discuss any problems that arise, the outcomes of which have to be fed back to the design team to ensure that the final product is entirely appropriate to the manufacturing capabilities of the company (Rosenthal and Tatikonda 1992). Achieving this level of contact between the functions through the use of multifunctional teams increases the efficiency of the overall development programme significantly. As a means of further improving the design to manufacture transfer, CAD is cited as a useful tool available to manufacturers (de Meyer 1992).

THE STUDY

It is clear, therefore, that the interaction between design and other functions is significant in creating effective NPD programmes. A study undertaken by the authors is based on the hypothesis that the interfaces between design and other functions in the NPD process are critical to its success, and that companies need to identify interface problems more precisely, enabling solutions to be found and, subsequently, an improved NPD process to be implemented.

The overall objective of the work described below was to develop diagnostic tools that would enable companies to identify problems in the NPD process, and, in particular, in the interfaces between functions. The remainder of this chapter describes the development of these tools and the findings that resulted when the tools were tested in a number of companies.

THE METHOD

The study involved two stages:

1. The development and testing of a diagnostic questionnaire.
2. The refinement and further development of a diagnostic tool.

Stage One

Initial research involved an extensive literature review followed by in-depth interviews with design, marketing and technical personnel involved with NPD in 12 UK companies. The companies were chosen to represent a broad cross-section of manufacturing industry, in terms of both sector and size. This was to overcome the problem of developing a sector-specific tool. The companies ranged from large, high-tech companies through medium-sized consumer products and textile companies to smaller furniture manufacturers.

Using statements from these interviews, a diagnostic questionnaire was then developed to identify differences in functional perceptions. The questionnaire used attitude statements and a 'Likert'-type scale to measure the attitudes of each function towards each other and the NPD process. It was divided into separate sections, addressing in turn NPD, design, the design–marketing, design–research and design–manufacture interfaces, and the use of consultants.

The diagnostic tool was then tested in the 12 participating companies and was found to be successful in diagnosing areas of disagreement between functions within the companies. In the main, the findings replicated those from the initial interviews and, in several instances, a number of new problems that were previously unknown were also identified.

Stage Two: Revision of Diagnostic Questionnaire

Using feedback from this pilot study, a number of changes were made to improve the questionnaire and produce a revised version. The majority of the statements used in the initial questionnaire were again included, mostly unchanged. Some, however, were rephrased, while a number of additional statements from the original interviews were added to clarify issues. The format was revised to improve ease of completion and analysis. The tool subsequently comprised a section on NPD divided into strategy, creativity, the use of teams and project management, separate sections covering each function and an additional section on specifications.

Using an original database where a number of UK manufacturers were mapped into 10 separate product sectors, 16 companies were selected and approached. Of these 16, 6 expressed interest in participating and, during September 1993, each was visited and given up to 40 questionnaires to distribute to personnel involved in NPD. These were given to senior management, project managers, design engineers, industrial designers, ergonomists and personnel from marketing, R&D, production and manufacturing, as well as to staff from other functions involved in the development process, such as quality, finance and purchasing.

A summary table of the responses obtained for every statement was compiled for each company. This incorporated a frequency count of the responses, the percentages of agreement and disagreement for each statement, and both the overall and the functional mean responses. From these it was possible not only to identify points where disagreement occurred but also to determine between which functions these differences of opinion existed.

FINDINGS

The following short summaries represent the main findings presented to each of the companies participating in this second stage of the study, and indicate the issues that the companies were advised to address.

Company A: A Large International Manufacturer of Domestic Appliances

The analysis for company A identified a number of important areas:

■ Individual roles and responsibilities were not made clear to all, and projects were felt to be neither well chosen nor well funded. Projects were not considered to be well managed; there were no clear project goals nor was there good communication between personnel. Furthermore, NPD was not felt to occur in a creative environment, nor were personnel well motivated. Multidisciplinary teams were not considered to be used and key functions identified more with their separate departments than with the team as a whole.

■ The contribution of design was not recognised, and design felt burdened with routine work.

■ Marketing did not understand the design process and was therefore unable to provide design with the necessary information at the appropriate times. There was no clear idea of how market research was undertaken and coordinated with other marketing areas.

■ Design was not aware of what R&D is undertaken by the company, the use of new technologies was not encouraged and it was felt that a good technical library was not available.

■ Neither production nor manufacturing was considered to be involved early enough, while design felt constrained by production and were not made to understand the implications of their design decisions.

Company B: A Large Manufacturer of Consumer Products

For company B, the conclusions were more specific to the functions and their interfaces:

■ Design staff in particular were not happy with their role and position within the company. They did not feel that their responsibilities were clear and were scared of making mistakes. They thought that resources were wasted and that the reasons for terminating projects were not communicated to them. They tended to identify more with their department than with the team, and considered that their contribution was not recognised. In addition, other functions felt that design did not respond quickly to the needs of the market and had an insufficient input into NPD.

■ Although design was felt to undertake its role within the company effectively, marketing neither respected design, nor were in turn respected by design and were not felt to understand either the design process or the needs of design. Designers did not feel that enough market research was undertaken and considered that it typically addressed only the present and not future demands. In addition, managers felt that marketing was not innovative.

■ Although R&D was well integrated with design, a good technical library was not considered to be present within the company, nor was information on new materials and processes made available to design. Moreover, the use of such new technologies was not encouraged.

■ The relationship between design and production was generally effective. However, design felt that production constrained design and a close inter-action between the functions in the early stages of projects was considered to be lacking.

Company C: A Medium-Sized Manufacturer of Building Products

In company C the conclusions pointed to some serious problems within NPD:

■ Individual roles and responsibilities were not made clear, and projects were felt to be neither well chosen nor well funded. NPD was not considered to be well managed, nor were targets well defined. In addition, communication between functions was felt to be poor.

■ Design was not felt to be good at identifying new products and was not considered able to do anything challenging. Designers were felt to have a resistance to change and to take the low risk alternative whenever possible.

■ Marketing was not felt to communicate effectively with other functions and considered itself more as a department than as members of a team. Again, marketing staff neither respected design nor were respected by design, and did not understand the design process or the needs of design. Market research and sales were not well coordinated with market research, not understanding their role in NPD, and sales was not involved early enough in the process. In addition, the briefs and specifications prepared by mar-keting were felt to be late, too short, vague and often ambiguous.

■ The design–production interface appeared to be generally effective, with a good relationship existing between the two functions. However, there was uncertainty over whether design dealt with manufacturing problems and if design wholly understood the production implications of their decisions.

■ R&D felt that people were scared of making mistakes and that failure was not tolerated. There was little communication between design and R&D, with little awareness of what research was being undertaken within the company. Again, a good technical library was not considered to exist within the company, nor was the use of new materials or processes encouraged.

Company D: A Medium-Sized Manufacturer of Electrical Equipment

The study of company D revealed fewer identifiable problems:

■ Although projects were perceived to be well managed, individual roles and responsibilities were not made clear to all, and some felt that communication between functions was poor and that resources were not well utilised. Ideas received support, yet some felt that people were scared of making mistakes and that failure was not tolerated. There was perceived to be a lack of innovation in NPD and therefore in the company's products.

■ Marketing did not understand the needs of design and, it was felt, should learn more about the design process. Not enough market research was undertaken.

Company E: A Small Manufacturer of Measurement Systems

In company E the conclusions indicated that:

■ Although clearly an innovative company, NPD was not considered to be well managed and project goals were not felt to be well defined. In addition, some felt that resources were not well allocated and were sometimes wasted on unrealistic projects. Production staff did not believe that their role and responsibilities were clear and did not feel part of the team, considering themselves instead to identify more with their department. This feeling was emphasised by their belief that communication between NPD personnel was not very good.

■ Production staff also did not feel that design understood the implications of their design decisions and considered them to take the established, low risk option.

■ Marketing staff were not considered to understand the design process or the needs of design, and, consequently, design felt that marketing did not provide them with enough information. Market research and sales were not considered to be well coordinated, and marketing did not feel themselves to be a key part of the NPD process. Specifications were felt to be brief, vague and often late.

Company F: A Medium-Sized Manufacturer of Medical Products

In Company F the study found that:

■ Although NPD was felt to be generally well organised, there was no overall belief that projects were well chosen or well funded. In addition, marketing and quality considered that there was a lot of bureaucracy.

■ Multidisciplinary teams were clearly felt to be beneficial to NPD; however, neither marketing nor production felt strongly integrated into the NPD team.

■ The relationship between design and production was generally effective. However, quality felt that production constrained design, and production felt that designers did not understand the implication of their designs.

■ Neither production nor marketing was felt to be involved early enough in the development process.

Table 4.1   Common areas of weakness in NPD across six UK companies

New product development:
- Unclear roles and responsibilities
- Badly chosen projects with no clear project goals
- Inadequate funding and resourcing of projects
- Poor communications
- Not using multidisciplinary teams
- Little toleration of failure
- Lack of encouragement of innovation

Design:
- Over-burdened with routine work
- Slow response to the needs of the market
- Unable to do anything challenging
- Resistance to change

Marketing and design:
- Marketing not understanding the design process
- Lack of clear information supplied to design
- Little mutual respect between functions
- Lack of market research and no coordination with sales

Specifications:
- Late arrival
- Too brief, vague and ambiguous

Research and design:
- Little contact between R&D and design
- No awareness of current research being undertaken within the company
- Little encouragement to use new technology, materials or processes
- Lack of a good technical library

Manufacturing and design:
- Design not understanding production implications
- Production constraining design
- Production and manufacturing not being involved early enough in the project
- Not using the same components for prototypes as intended for production

DISCUSSION

The tool clearly demonstrated a significant diagnostic capability and was able to identify functional perspectives and provide more specific findings for each company.

In addition, the use of the diagnostic tool revealed overall areas of weakness across the companies in their NPD processes and the interfaces between design and the other key functions. These are summarised in Table 4.1.

EPILOGUE

The 'product' is central to successful business. The product's form, function, manufacture, price, promotion, distribution and customer perception are all determined during the NPD programme. Typically, each function considers itself to be the primary contributor to success, and designers, in particular, believe that their skills determine a product's success or failure. Although this is not wholly true, they are key in the interface with marketing, production and other main contributors to a project.

The authors' research to date suggests that individual corporate problems at functional interfaces can be identified, and it has also found four foundations of best practice in organising for NPD:

- Understanding: this means each function understanding not only its own role and responsibility but also that of others in the team.
- Awareness: each function and team member must be aware of, and respond to, the needs of the others during the process.
- Communication: good communication in terms of frequency and content must occur between functions, both at the beginning of a product development programme, in order to develop an accurate product concept description or design brief, and throughout the process in terms of the findings of market testing and product testing through to launch.
- Commitment: a culture of commitment to the project must be evident from the onset. That commitment must be based on respect and understanding of the value of all functions contributing to the design and development process.

REFERENCES

Barczak, G. and Wilemon, D. (1989). Leadership differences in new product development teams, *Journal of Product Innovation Management*, **6**(4), 259–267.

Barlow, W. (1988). The importance of design, in Gorb, P. (ed.), *Design Talks*, The Design Council, London, pp. 85–103.

Biemans, W.G. (1991). User and third-party involvement in developing medical equipment innovations, *TechnoVation*, **11**(3), 163–182.

Black, M. (1973). Engineering and industrial design, *Chartered Mechanical Engineer*, January, 51–57.

Bruce, M. and Roy, R. (1991). Integrating marketing and design for commercial benefit, *Marketing Intelligence and Planning*, **9**(5), 29–39.

Cooper, R.G. and Kleinschmidt, E.J. (1987). New products: What separates winners from losers? *Journal of Product Innovation Management*, **4**(3), 169–184.

Crawford, C.M. (1980). Defining the charter for product innovation, *Sloan Management Review*, 3–12.

Dace, R. (1989). Japanese new product development, *Quarterly Review of Marketing*, **14**(2), 4–13.

Day, G.S. (1975). A strategic perspective on product planning, *Journal of Contemporary Business*, **4**, 1–34.

de Meyer, A. (1992). The development/manufacturing interface: Empirical analysis of the 1990 European manufacturing survey, in Sussman, G. (ed.), *Integrating Design and Manufacturing for Competitive Advantage*, Oxford University Press, Oxford.

Francis, A. and Winstanley, D. (1988). Managing new product development: Some alternative ways to organise the work of technical specialists, *Journal of Marketing Management*, **4**(2), 249–260.

Gorb, P. and Dumas, A. (1987). Silent design, *Design Studies*, **8**(3), 150–156.

Hart, S.J. and Service, L.M. (1988). The effects of managerial attitudes to design on company performance, *Journal of Marketing Management*, **4**(2), 217–229.

Hopkins, D.S. (1981). New product winners and losers, *Research Management*, **24**(3), 12–17.

Johne, F.A. and Snelson, P.A. (1988). Success factors in product innovation: A selective review of the literature, *Journal of Product Innovation Management*, **5**(2), 114–128.

Maidique, M.A. and Zirger, B.J. (1984). A study of success and failure in product innovation: The case of the US electronics industry, *IEEE Transactions on Engineering Management*, **31**(4), 192–203.

Moody, S. (1980). The role of industrial design in technological innovation, *Design Studies*, **1**(6), 329–339.

Potter, S., Roy, R., Capon, C.H., Bruce, M., Walsh, V and Lewis, J. (1991). The benefits and costs of investments in design: Using professional design expertise in product, engineering and graphics projects, report DIG-03, Design Innovation Group, Open University and UMIST, Milton Keynes/Manchester.

Roberts, E.B. (1977). Generating effective corporate innovations, *Technology Review*, **79**, 27–33.

Rosenthal, S. (1990). *Building a Workplace Culture to Support New Product Introduction*, Boston University Manufacturing Round Table, Boston, MA.

Rosenthal, S. and Tatikonda, M. (1992). Competitive advantage through design tools and practices, in Sussman, G. (ed.), *Integrating Design and Manufacturing for Competitive Advantage*, Oxford University Press, Oxford.

Rothwell, R. (1972). Factors for success in industrial innovations: Project SAPPHO – A comparative study of success and failure in industrial innovations, Science Policy Research Unit, University of Sussex, Brighton.

Rothwell, R. and Gardiner, P. (1984). Design and competition in engineering, *Long Range Planning*, **17**(3), 78–91.

Rothwell, R. and Whiston, T.G. (1990). Design, innovation and corporate integration, *R&D Management*, **20**(3), 193–201.

Rothwell, R., Gardiner, P. and Pick, K. (1990). *Design and the Economy*, The Design Council, London.

Slade, M. (1989). The Walkman factor, *Engineering*, **229**, 37.

Slade, M. (1990). Understanding the brief, *Engineering*, **230**, 21.

Takeuchi, H. and Nonaka, I. (1986). The new product development game, *Harvard Business Review*, **64**(1), 137–146.

Thomsen, T.H. (1990). Product development and an effective interface with design and marketing in product strategies for the 90s, *The Financial Times*, 15–16 October, 2.1–2.4.

Topalian, A. (1989). Organisational features that nurture design success in business enterprises, in proceedings of the second international conference on engineering management, Toronto.

Townsend, J.F. (1976). Innovation in coal machinery, The Anderton Shearer loader –
The role of the NCB and supply industry in its development, SPRL occasional
paper series, No. 3, Brighton, Sussex.

Utterback, J.M., Allen, T.J., Holleman, J.H. and Sirbu, M.H. (1976). The process of
innovation in five industries in Europe and Japan, *IEEE Transactions in Engineering Management*, **23**(9).

Walsh, V., Roy, R., Bruce, M. and Potter, S. (1992). *Winning by Design*, Basil Blackwell, Oxford.

CHAPTER FIVE

APPROACHES TO DESIGN MANAGEMENT IN THE PRODUCT DEVELOPMENT PROCESS

Margaret Bruce and Barny Morris

Outsourcing of design expertise is an increasingly common practice for UK companies. Approaches to managing external design expertise are wide ranging and rather *ad hoc*. In this chapter, a taxonomy of different approaches to design management is presented, and issues raised by different approaches to design management are discussed. The nature of the relationship between design suppliers and buyers can vary, from a long-term, close relationship to an arms-length and distanced relationship. The nature of this relationship is considered and a model is outlined that assists in the management of the design–client relationship.

INTRODUCTION

Effective products have to be designed, developed and marketed, and the interfaces between design, marketing and development are critical in the product development process (Cooper and Kleinschmidt 1987; see also Davies-Cooper and Jones, Chapter 4, this volume). The central role that design plays in the product development process is recognised; however, attention has been placed on the management of design as an activity inside the firm. A noticeable trend towards the outsourcing of design expertise is evident

Product Development: Meeting the Challenge of the Design–Marketing Interface.
Edited by M. Bruce and W.G. Biemans.   © 1995 John Wiley & Sons Ltd.

(Westamocott 1992), which has implications for the management of product development. At a strategic level, companies may be losing a core competence in design and a basis of proprietary knowledge, which, once lost, may not be easy to regain. At a tactical level, skills in the acquisition and management of external design expertise have to be found. The nature of the relationship with the external design supplier has to be decided, particularly whether a long-term, close relationship between client and design professional, or an arms-length and more distanced relationship is preferred (Bruce and Docherty 1993).

This chapter addresses some of the key issues raised by the outsourcing of design expertise. A taxonomy of the different ways of organising the design function is outlined, covering solely in-house, solely outsourcing and a mixture of the two. Different approaches to the relationship between design buyers and design suppliers are discussed, and critical management issues raised by the outsourcing of design expertise are highlighted. A model is outlined to help design managers to 'get the most out of' their design relationships.

OUTSOURCING OF DESIGN EXPERTISE

The trend towards outsourcing [is likely to have] a major impact on the structure, organisation and traditional working relationships between industry and design firms.

(Westamocott 1992)

Over the past ten years, changes have occurred in the organisation of the design function. Design activities are being displaced from the firm and are being outsourced. In 1983, 65% of design capability in the UK was estimated to be located within the firm (Chris Hayes Associates and Keller Dorsey 1983); by 1991 this had been reduced to 55% (Potter et al. 1991). Related to this movement of design out of the firm, and within the same time-frame, the design consultancy profession has burgeoned to become one of the fastest growing service sectors in the UK (McAlhone 1987). Another effect of this change is the emergence of design management as a distinct management function. The tasks, responsibilities and skills required by design managers cover:

1. the selection and commissioning of design expertise
2. preparation of design briefs
3. evaluation of design work
4. project management skills

A major survey of UK companies found that those companies that possess effective design management capabilities have a sustained competitive advantage (Potter et al. 1991).

TAXONOMY OF APPROACHES TO DESIGN MANAGEMENT

Three main types of approaches to the perception of design expertise exist (Bruce and Morris 1994b), and these are examined in detail in this chapter. The types are:

1. in-house design function
2. solely external expertise
3. a mixture of in-house and external design expertise

Each of these has benefits and disadvantages.

- In-house: design skills lie within the firm and can be located in a design department, or be dispersed through R&D, production or marketing. As well as full-time design staff, other personnel such as the technical director may be counted as an additional design resource. In-house designers may be expected to generate income by serving as consultants to other companies.
- External: design competencies lie outside the firm and design professionals are selected and commissioned to carry out the design activities required by the firm. Design managers, or those with responsibility for design, source, commission, liaise and evaluate the external design skills.
- Mixture: design capability comprises a mixture of in-house and external design skills. The external design professional is brought in to supply additional resources to ensure that the project is completed on time, to input fresh ideas, or to provide a specific expertise.

RELATIVE MERITS

The merits of an in-house capability are attributed to the view that in-house designers are:

> intimately aware of company practices . . . and are always on hand to give advice or deal with problems that may arise through the stages of product development . . . also [they are] more closely integrated into the overall design team.
> (Bruce and Morris 1994b)

Against this is the concern that in-house designers may become complacent, produce 'me-too' ideas and fail to provide innovative solutions.

The positive contribution of external design professionals is that they are regarded as injecting fresh inputs and insights. On the down side, they can make mistakes because they have insufficient knowledge of the firm's practices or are not sensitive to the organisation's market needs. One source of tension is that between wishing to be open and provide the external designer(s) with knowledge to complete the design task and the risk of losing proprietary knowledge.

Utilising both in-house and external design expertise appears to overcome the problems and builds on the positive aspects of each situation. However, the integration of the in-house and external professionals has to be managed carefully to ensure that they are truly working together. The tension between fear of giving away commercially sensitive information and the need to build up an open and trusting relationship is particularly acute.

Whatever the approach adopted, the interface between the design resource and other functions in the product development process has to be managed, and the nature of this interface considered, planned and integrated within the firm.

IMPLICATIONS FOR DESIGN MANAGEMENT AND THE PRODUCT DEVELOPMENT PROCESS

Attention has been paid to identifying 'best practices' for the management of product development (see Hart, Chapter 1, this volume). A critical success factor for new product development is that of effective management of the different functions involved in this process. Souder (1988) argues that a positive outcome is likely to arise from '. . . openness, good cross-functional cooperation and communication, and mutual respect and trust'. In terms of the organisational structure, Bentley (1990) suggests that:

> flat, or decentralised, systems of control . . . [coupled with] . . . integrative mechanisms, good communication systems and individuals who can take broad perspectives, solve problems and cope with risks . . . are the best performers.

These 'rules of best practice' refer to a situation where the design capability resides inside the firm. But how do they relate to a situation of outsourcing? Mutual respect and trust, which eventually lead to openness and cooperation, take time to build and may not be required when an external designer is engaged to work on a 'one-off' project. Can 'shared values and mutual goal commitments' be achieved with an external design function? Using an external design professional often leads to a formalised *modus operandi* to try to ensure that proprietary information is not 'leaked' and to tighten up control of the process. This in itself may undermine the feeling of openness and may constrain the free flow of ideas across the boundaries of the client and design firms involved in product development.

A strong theme in the product development literature is that of multidisciplinary teams that work together from inception to completion of the process (Craig and Hart 1992). When using an external design consultant, to what extent is their design expertise openly involved in the team? Can the external design professional truly be regarded and treated as a full team member? At what stages in the process can the external designer be actively involved in the process? Which function in the team is to have responsibility for liaison with the external design professional?

METHODOLOGY

The research design was chosen to explore approaches to design management practice and to provide insight into design issues associated with the outsourcing of design expertise. The research design was divided into a three-stage process. To begin with, a 'judgemental' or convenience sample (Morris 1993) of eight UK manufacturers was created based on three criteria:

1. The sample had companies that utilised one of the three models of design expertise, i.e. in-house, out-house or a mixture.
2. The sample covered a range of company sizes and geographical areas.
3. The sample used industrial design expertise in the development of its products.

The Design Council (North West) and the Design Council (London) were approached to help with company selection and to gain access at chief executive or director level within the companies.

DATA COLLECTION

Data was collected using a semi-structured questionnaire administered by personal interview with those responsible for design and product development, for example, directors of marketing, design or R&D. The interviews were tape recorded. In addition, secondary company information was gathered either at source or by follow-up telephone conversations. This included such items as background of the company, nature of product lines and company structure. The interview began with questions covering a broad range of company issues and information, including management experience, policy on in-house/out-house design usage, company development process activities and procedures, product planning and design management practices.

DATA ANALYSIS

Tape recordings and interview notes were transcribed, and combined with the secondary sources of information to create interview reports. The interview material was analysed by categorising the data and looking for 'patterns' that corresponded from one company to another. Where there was data deficiency, follow-up telephone interviews with the original interviewee were undertaken. The initial draft of the interview report was returned to the interviewee to cross-check for accuracy. The final stage of the analysis involved revisiting the data, where the researcher constantly 'zigzagged' between conceptualisation and the data (Bonoma 1985) to produce meaningful conclusions about what may or may not be happening.

COMPANY SUMMARIES

Of the eight companies interviewed, three summaries are presented below. For a fuller account of the eight companies, see Morris (1993). Company A represents the 'in-house' model, company B is indicative of the 'out-house' model and company C illustrates the 'mixture' model.

COMPANY A: IN-HOUSE

Company A designs and manufactures mostly 'white goods' for the consumer market using an in-house design department. The industrial design manager describes the design department's role as 'appearance designing', with the result that the 'nuts and bolts' of products for each group company are similar, if not the same, while the products have been styled differently. Product development projects are achieved in a team atmosphere at company A, the team consisting of a project engineer, product coordinator, and marketing and design personnel. Marketing has a dominant role in the team, particularly in the initial stages of product development, by generating effective marketing research from which ideas for products are created. While the design department would like to have more authority and involvement in this initial stage of product development, more often than not, design is brought in by marketing at the latter stages of product development. Thus, design in company A is used as a reactive resource in the product development process, rather than as a proactive resource.

A large proportion of new product development is undertaken by R&D, who create the 'bare bones' of the product. Around this 'skeleton' the designers wrap an outer skin based on a tightly defined specification created by marketing. Different appearances are evaluated in a presentation to marketing, where the 'designs' are compared in terms of the 'bottom line cost versus appearance' compromise. Good rapport with marketing is critical, because this leads to generation of appropriate solutions by design first time round.

The marketing department at company A is perceived to be in a more influential position than design. Marketing at company A is very strong; they hold the 'purse strings' and perceive design as subservient. However, the design manager is trying to change this situation by raising the status of design within the company. Tension between marketing and design at company A is rare, however. When there are differences it is mainly due to the different departments' 'time horizons', as the designers work to a two- to four-year time horizon compared to marketing's time horizon of 12 months. This leads to two problems:

1. 'Prostitution' of a product occurs; this is the modification of a product to meet different market needs after product launch, usually triggered by marketing. This causes technical problems that could have been avoided had they been addressed earlier in the product development process.
2. 'Marketing change the goal posts', where the specification changes during the development stages of a product (unlike 'prostitution', which refers to changes after product launch). This lengthens the development time of the product, and causes design to generate inappropriate work.

The design manager at company A believes that in order to reduce the lengthy development times of products, design needs more resources to become proactive in product development. An alternative solution would be to involve design at earlier stages in the process. Company A is described as bureaucratic. Despite this, the in-house design team has a free rein within the company, particularly if sidestepping bureaucracy is seen to save time, and so they are described as a 'breed unto themselves'.

Relationships with Consultants

The design manager was adamant that in-house designers have a level of familiarity with the company that puts any external designer at a disadvantage.

When external design consultants have been used, they have slowed down the design process. For these reasons, the use of external designers is not considered a 'serious option'. The design manager admits that in-house design departments can become 'stagnant', leading to lower work rates and less creativity when compared to external designers, but sees the advantages as:

- cost (because they are a fixed overhead)
- familiarity of production practices, marketing and corporate culture
- stability
- appropriateness of work (because of familiarity)
- control of the resource (to produce appropriate and creative work)
- proprietary nature of the work guaranteed

COMPANY B: OUTSOURCE

Company B is a multinational company manufacturing a large range of heavy duty tools and equipment for the construction industry.

Company B uses a multifunctional product development process, consisting of manufacturing, marketing, a design engineer and an external product design consultant. Product development uses customer input at various stages in the process, particularly to help with the specification of the product, to test the product at the prototype stage, and in general to give feedback on the project to ensure that it is 'on the right track'. Identifying 'gaps' in the market is undertaken by the team via competitive benchmarking, which involves analysing competitor product attributes (vibration, price, weight, etc.), and competitors' products are reverse engineered, whereby they are stripped down and analysed.

Relationship with the External Design Consultancy

Company B believes that consultants should be 'indoctrinated into the ethos of the company'. Design consultants have to know what the company can and cannot do, and 'become almost an employee of the company'. They provide specialist knowledge that the company does not possess internally. The company tends to use the same design consultancy to maintain continuity, and believes that long-term relationships are important: 'once you've built up that relationship in terms of trust and respect, it would be folly to change'.

When they initially chose their current design consultancy, they were looking for a consultant who was prepared to 'come to the party'. Company B believe that the external design consultant must take on some responsibility, and 'put his/her own stake in'. The marketing manager was not looking for a standard consultancy relationship; that is, someone who would listen to the problem, go away and solve it and come back with the solution. The marketing manager had the objective of maintaining a product design facility in Europe for company B. Thus, he wanted 'someone who was a part of the team' on a longer term basis.

COMPANY C: MIXTURE

Company C is a subsidiary of a large textile producing plc which manufacturers garden and car products for large car/DIY retailers. With no resources to fund an in-house design department, the company uses external design expertise for developing most of its products, together with input from internal R&D.

In terms of marketing strategy, where company C is 'going' is dictated by its product range, which is in turn driven by its customer base. In particular, the larger customers play a significant role in the direction of marketing strategy. Design is seen as providing 'a vital role in product development, but it is not the overriding factor; making money is'.

The Relationship

Marketing initially relied on the design firm's reputation as a means of gauging competency. Now, after a number of successful projects, track record is more important. Thus, 'there's a difference between initially looking at the consultancy, and the ongoing project or next project when you've worked with somebody'. Trust and respect are considered important factors in the relationship, and are built up by high levels of communication at the beginning of a relationship.

Company C believes that consultants are less expensive than full-time employed designers. If the costs of using the consultant are too high, or the project costs are high, the marketing manager will sit down and talk to the consultancy about how the costs can be reduced. He believes that costs can be reduced without having to 'shop around for cheaper design', and is a part of effective management of the client–consultant relationship.

Company C use a single design consultancy because of the benefits of the designer knowing 'our markets and our business, and knowing what we want. We consider them sort of as an employee. We are working with them, rather than them working for us'. In between design projects, the marketing manager believes in 'keeping in touch' with the consultancy, as it is important to see 'what the consultancy is up to and how their business is going'.

Relationship with Consultants

External and internal design expertise have been used at company C for at least the past 10 years, with external consultants accounting for approximately 20% of all design work undertaken. Products are designed completely in-house or completely outsourced, depending on the type of project.

External expertise is mainly used if there is a problem that cannot be resolved internally or because of excessive internal workloads, and in this respect consultants tend to be used as and when required. The design consultant has little input in formulating the product specification; this is an internal under-taking between R&D and marketing only. Consultants are criticised because 'they tend to be full of bright ideas, but when it actually comes to the crunch they don't actually deliver: their ideas just aren't practical'.

While external designers are needed for their design skills, the project engineer perceived that in-house designers have more advantages, such as:

- Accessibility: with an in-house department, problems are sorted out immediately.
- Familiarity: in-house designers know the history of the product because of the amount of upgrading and modification work that is required.
- Commitment: in-house staff seem more committed to meeting deadlines.
- Briefing: this is a problem with out-house consultants: 'we will say we want so and so, and when we get it back it's nothing like what we asked for. Consultants don't know what you really want or what the product really does, they don't listen to you properly'.

Company C has 'been through more external design consultants than hot dinners', with only 30% of their relationships with consultants deemed successful, indicating that they still have a lot to learn regarding design management. While one or two good designers have had repeat business from the company, these are the exceptions to the rule.

UTILISATION OF DESIGN EXPERTISE

All of the three companies regarded design as a central resource that adds value to the product, builds a brand proposition, keeps the product ahead and abreast of the competition and reduces manufacturing costs. The use of design in product development was triggered initially by a 'need to change' (e.g. the customer requirements changed). The customer requirements drove the product base, thus the need to be 'close to the customer' at all times during the product development process was stressed. The translation of customer and company requirements into design requirements that allow the company to plan design input (long- and short-term) is a critical aspect of product development. In this sense, the design resource interacts with marketing for its strategic direction.

MANAGEMENT IMPLICATIONS

The management process for in-house and outside designers differs in two important respects. Firstly, management of the external designer raises potential communication and control difficulties. Table 5.1 shows the purposes and implications of different approaches to design management for in-house, outsourcing and a mixture of these types. Secondly, the relationship between design buyer and supplier has to be managed, both on a short-term basis at the project level and on a long-term basis at the relationship level.

Table 5.1   Comparison of approaches to location of design

	In-house	Outsource	Mixture
Purposes	Accessible	Solve short-term problems	Flexibility
	Integrated within company practices and product development team	Relieve workloads	
		Access new ideas	
	Cost efficient	Access specialist expertise	
		Easier to abort unsuccessful projects	
		Cost efficient	
Management characteristics	Encouraging creativity	Evaluation of work more intense during the design process	Creation of design team complex
	Less anxiety over control factors	Level of contact higher in the initial relationship stage	
		Choosing the designer is critical	
		Communication factors uppermost	
		Fear of leakage of proprietary information	

Source: Bruce and Morris (1994b); reproduced by permission of Elsevier Science

Concern about potential communication and control difficulties was dealt with in various ways:

1. Close evaluation of external designer's work.
2. Intense level of contact (enforced familiarisation) in the initial stages of the relationship.
3. Selection of the external designer entailed an analytical procedure.
4. The brief was treated as a 'formal' document, rather than one that evolved as the design work progressed, as was more likely to be the situation for in-house design.

COMPATIBILITY

A key issue influencing the client–design relationship is that of compatibility between the client and the design parties. Dimensions of compatibility relate to the characteristics of the individuals involved in the relationship, the type of expertise required and offered by the client and design professional and the respective company cultures and *modus operandi* (see Figure 5.1).

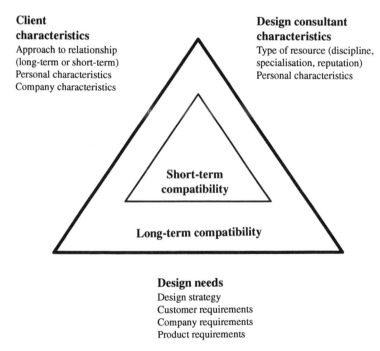

Client characteristics
Approach to relationship (long-term or short-term)
Personal characteristics
Company characteristics

Design consultant characteristics
Type of resource (discipline, specialisation, reputation)
Personal characteristics

Short-term compatibility

Long-term compatibility

Design needs
Design strategy
Customer requirements
Company requirements
Product requirements

Figure 5.1   Compatibility model of client–design relationship (Bruce and Morris 1994a; reproduced by permission)

Buying-in design from the same design supplier suggests that the relationship is compatible between the partners involved. Long-term relationships were typical for the companies participating in the research, because such relationships were perceived as having benefits, such as stability, understanding the client's needs and markets, and loyalty and trust, which can help the client to relax and give consultants more creative freedom (Bruce and Docherty 1993).

IN-HOUSE OR EXTERNAL DESIGN RESOURCE

Choosing between an in-house or external design resource involved consideration of accessibility, familiarity and control factors (Bruce and Morris 1994b), and these factors were viewed in different ways by the companies in the sample:

- Accessibility: while company A suggested that external designers were not sufficiently accessible because they were located externally, company C experienced no difficulties with meeting or contacting external design professionals. The complexity of the product, the amount of design work required and the need to meet deadlines influence the choice of using in-house or external designers.
- Familiarity: in-house designers were more familiar with past products, manufacturing processes, materials and market requirements. However, familiarity was viewed as a 'factor of communication' remedied by good project and relationship management, rather than an inherent disadvantage of external designer consultants. Long-term relationships between client and design firms ensure that familiarity is developed over time, and facilitate the building up of trust, respect and understanding, which are important in producing effective design solutions.
- Control: company A believes that out-house designers are difficult to control, in particular with respect to their creativity, whereas company B suggests lack of control of external consultants is due to weak project management skills by the client company. Regular contact to ensure that the external designer is 'along the right lines' is important.

MODEL OF RELATIONSHIP MANAGEMENT

Design management at a strategic level entails making a decision about the location of design expertise, particularly whether this should lie inside or outside the firm. The trend towards outsourcing is partly driven by cost

Table 5.2   'Pros' and 'cons' of short-term versus long-term relationships

Short-term advantages	Long-term advantages
1. Comparison purposes Having a relationship with more than one consultant enabled the client to compare quality and efficiency factors between consultants 2. Cost Relationships were open to market forces 3. Access to different expertise Gave the client more choice in the type of expertise required 4. Time Consultants were used to relieve short-term in-house design workloads 5. Compatibility By maintaining a short-term relationship with a consultant, if the relationship is 'difficult' it gives the client the freedom to choose a more compatible designer partner	1. Familiarity This improved the effectiveness of the design input from project to project 2. Stability Once a project had been completed successfully with a consultant, management anxiety and uncertainty about the relationship and product development in general reduced 3. Continuity Retaining the same consultant ensured that the brand proposition within and, if required, across product ranges remained the same. It also made the initial stages of each new project much easier because the 'process' of using the same consultant remained consistent

Source: Bruce and Morris (1994b); reproduced by permission of Elsevier Science

considerations and a belief that this may be cheaper than having design in-house. Keeping design in-house is partly driven by control factors, as well as by fear of leaking proprietary information and loss of expertise. The client's previous experience and the individual design manager's personal preferences have a role to play in the decision about the location of design expertise, so a wide range of design management practices exist.

At a tactical level, design management, where outsourcing occurs, entails the procurement, commissioning and project management of the design resource. Compatibility is an aspect influencing the selection of design company. A major facet of the management process is that of fostering close and long-term relationships, or arms-length and short-term relationships. Long-term relationships may have certain perceived benefits in attaining security, trust and understanding (Bruce and Docherty 1993). A comparison of the relative merits of long- and short-term relationships is shown in Table 5.2.

By investing in an in-house design capability, accessibility, familiarity and control are perceived to be more likely to be ensured. The design process differs, particularly in terms of procurement, briefing and management of the

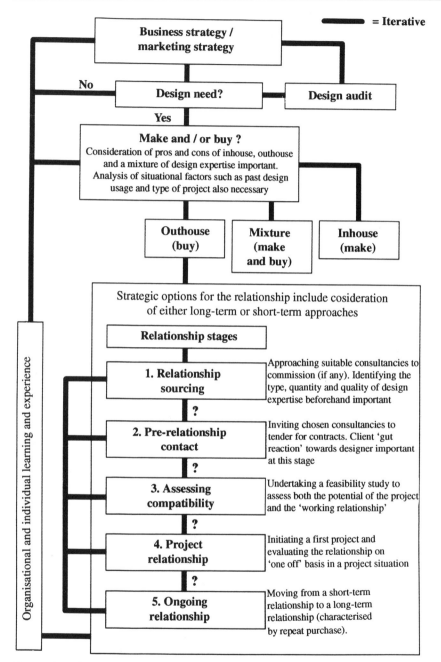

Figure 5.2   Diagnostic tool, depicting the choice decisions for the types of expertise required and the approach taken towards the relationship between client and designer (Bruce and Morris 1994a; reproduced by permission)

relationship. Complacency and lack of creative solutions is a major cost of relying solely on in-house design expertise. The stages in the client–design relationship are outlined in Figure 5.2.

The model formalises the types of decisions required at different stages in this relationship. Each client relationship entails a set of stages, from initial contact, to appraisal of client–design compatibility, to the project and its completion. Once a project has ended, then ongoing contact is required between parties to ensure that the client–design relationship is continued, if there is a potential to establish a longer term relationship. Moving from a one-off project to an ongoing relationship takes time and commitment in building up a personal relationship. Compatibility between client and design firms also entails a resonance of operating procedures and the design company's ability to understand the client's business, in order to devise effective design solutions. Good design, a positive personal relationship and company compatibility all have to dovetail to facilitate a longer term relationship.

CONCLUSIONS

The trend towards outsourcing has been identified in the product development process, and the product development literature for management practice has been discussed. Three different approaches to the management of design expertise have been identified – in-house, out-house and mixture – coupled with two main approaches towards client–design relationships – short-term and long-term.

The main issues affecting outsourcing of design expertise centre on accessibility, familiarity and control. Where the company wishes to ensure that all of these issues are 'secure', it will tend to have an in-house facility. Outsourcing can lead to fresh insights and effective design solutions at a reduced cost, but only if it is well managed and the client company is confident of attaining an effective outcome. The choice of approach to the location of design expertise, whether in-house or out-house, is undertaken on rather an *ad hoc* basis and depends on the client's previous experience and individuals' personal preferences. This leads to a wide range of design management practices.

It is important to stress that for companies relying on external design expertise, the long-term benefits of familiarity (resulting in more effective design) associated with long-term successful relationships outweigh the cost savings of regularly switching design suppliers (associated with efficient design and short-term relationships). The personalities involved play an important role in the long-term development of the relationship. The core question to be asked is: which type of expertise gives the most effective (quality) design for the same cost? Effective design depends upon the management of the relationship between client and designer in both the long- and short-term situations, and an acknowledgement at the highest management levels of the strategic significance for the company's product development process of the external design resource (see also Jevnaker, Chapter 9, this volume).

The model sets out the stages in the client–design relationship, whether long or short term, and serves to formalise the types of decisions required at different stages. There is a need for design managers to acquire, preserve and use experience of relationship management for the future.

ACKNOWLEDGEMENTS

The authors wish to acknowledge the support of the Economic and Social Research Council (ESRC) and the British Design Council.

REFERENCES

Bentley, K. (1990). A discussion of the link between one organisation's style and structure and its connections with its market, *Journal of Product Innovation Management*, **7**, 19–34.

Bonoma, T. (1985). Case research in marketing: Opportunities, problems and process, *Journal of Marketing Research*, **XII**, 199–208.

Bruce, M. and Docherty, C. (1993). It's all in a relationship: A comparative study of client–design consultant relationships, *Design Studies*, **14**(4), 402–422.

Bruce, M. and Morris, B. (1994a). *Strategic Management of UK Design Consultants: Policy and Practice*, Manchester School of Management, UMIST, Manchester.

Bruce, M. and Morris, B. (1994b). Managing external design professionals in the product development process, *TechnoVation*, **14**(9), 585–599.

Chris Hayes Associates and Keller Dorsey (1983). *The Industrial Design Requirements of Industry*, a report for the Design Council.

Cooper, R.G. and Kleinschmidt, E.J. (1987). What makes a new product a winner? Success factors at the project level, *R&D Management*, **17**(3), 175.

Craig, A. and Hart, S. (1992). Where to now in new product development research? *European Journal of Marketing*, **26**(11), 2–49.

McAlhone, B. (1987). British design consultancy: An anatomy of a billion pound business, Design Council, London.

Morris, B. (1993). The management of design consultants in the product development process, MSc dissertation, Manchester School of Management, UMIST.

Potter, S., Roy, R., Capon, C.H., Bruce, M., Walsh, V and Lewis, J. (1991). The benefits and costs of investments in design: Using professional design expertise in product, engineering and graphics projects, report DIG-03, Design Innovation Group, Open University and UMIST, Milton Keynes/Manchester.

Souder, W.E. (1988). Managing relations between R&D and marketing in new product development projects, *Journal of Product Innovation Management*, **5**(1), 6–19.

Westamocott, T. (1992). Decentralised design market: Where the trends are leading us, *Design Management Journal*, **3**(2), 40–43.

CHAPTER SIX

A MEANS–END CHAIN APPROACH TO CONCEPT TESTING

Gerard H. Loosschilder and
Jan P.L. Schoormans

Concept testing is one area where the field of product development may benefit from the application of consumer research. This chapter proposes a means–end chain model for the design of concept testing. The means–end chain model suggests that the form characteristics of a product influence consumers' overall evaluations through the functional and psycho-social consequences that are inferred from the product's form. The results of an empirical study are presented to illustrate the importance of the amount and nature of the information presented in a concept. The chapter ends with a discussion of the implications for the practice of concept testing, and suggestions for further research.

INTRODUCTION

Consumer research is regarded as an important discipline in product development. Essentially, the purpose of consumer research is to gather information about the potential market for the product, with the intention of improving the success rate of the new product and identifying problems with it and its marketing strategy (Mahajan and Wind 1992).

Frequently, consumer research is applied in product development for concept testing (Moore 1982). In a concept test, product ideas are presented to a

Product Development: Meeting the Challenge of the Design–Marketing Interface.
Edited by M. Bruce and W.G. Biemans.   © 1995 John Wiley & Sons Ltd.

sample of consumers and evaluations about these preliminary ideas are collected. The product ideas are presented in the form of a concept. This concept can refer to the new product's form, size or all kinds of other product characteristics, such as overall appearance, colour, and so on. Different modes can be used to present the idea, ranging from a verbal description, to a pictorial representation to a three-dimensional model, such as a dummy or mock-up. The consumer evaluations are usually assessed in terms of appreciations and preferences about the product idea. These evaluations are used to optimise product ideas or to screen and select from different product ideas, ultimately ending up with the product idea with the highest probability of market success.

A product idea can be represented by a concept in many different ways. The amount and nature of the information presented in a concept will influence the respondent's evaluation of the concept. For this reason, it is recommended by different authors (for example, Green and Srinivasan 1978) that a concept should resemble the new product as closely as possible. Only in such a case can valid results be obtained. In our opinion it is necessary for the essence of the product to be conveyed in the concept, so that the consumer has an understanding and appreciation of the product from the concept. Here, an important decision to make in the practice of concept testing is which information to include in the concept. Unfortunately, guidelines to underscore this decision, other than that a concept should resemble the idea, or the future product, as closely as possible, are rarely found in the literature.

The lack of direct guidelines is due to the absence of a theory of concept testing. The aim of this chapter is to provide a theory about how concepts should be considered. This theory would be very helpful in determining aspects such as:

- What information should a concept show?
- What kinds of questions should be asked in a test?

Furthermore, a theory can give insights into the appropriateness and accuracy of concept testing *per se*.

THE EFFECT OF INFORMATION IN CONCEPTS ON EVALUATIONS

A major concern in concept testing is the meaning that consumers extract from products. They use different layers of product meaning to assess the

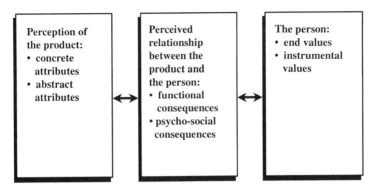

Figure 6.1   The means–end chain model

product's utility and hence their preference. Finn (1985) expressed this as follows:

> For valid predictions, the stimulus presented at the time of the concept test must convey to the subjects the same meaning that they would extract from a marketplace exposure to the (new) product at the time of launch. So when considering concept testing, it is first necessary to understand the layers of meaning that consumers extract from products in the marketplace.

Gutman (1982) describes in his *means–end chain* model how consumers structure a product's meaning. In this model, different layers are recognised:

1. the perception of a product
2. the perceived relationship between a product and the person (the consequences of using the product)
3. the person (human values)

Figure 6.1 shows the means–end chain model.

PRODUCT PERCEPTION

Characteristics are aspects of a product itself; when these characteristics are perceived and denominated by consumers, they are referred to as attributes. The way in which the product is perceived is defined in terms of two kinds of attributes: *concrete* and *abstract* product attributes. Concrete attributes are the perceived objective, physical, tangible product characteristics, such as the four doors of a car. Concrete attributes are perceived in similar ways by all consumers. Abstract attributes are the perceived, subjective and intangible characteristics of a product, such as quality. Substantial differences can exist between consumers with respect to the recognition and perception of these kinds of characteristics.

RELATIONSHIP BETWEEN PERSON AND PRODUCT

Product consequences also affect the person's perceptions of a product. Two types of product consequences have been identified: functional consequences and psycho-social consequences. Functional consequences are the direct utilitarian outcomes of the product for the consumer, such as the transport possibilities of a car. They are more or less objective. Psycho-social consequences are the psychological and social effects of using and owning a product, such as the perception of status that accrues with owning an expensive car. These consequences are often symbolic, and are to some extent emotional in nature and more subjective than functional consequences.

HUMAN VALUES

Each person has a set of values, which Rokeach (1973) defines as 'instrumental' and 'end' values. He assumes that these values are the fundamental states that a person is striving for, such as 'happiness' and 'health'. Although values guide human behaviour, in general they have less direct influence on the evaluation of specific concepts and so will not be elaborated here.

RELATIONSHIPS BETWEEN THE ELEMENTS OF THE MODEL

An important assumption of the means–end chain model is that these three layers of product meaning are interconnected. Furthermore, elements of the model that are more product-orientated are instrumental in influencing (in terms of recognition and perception) aspects that are related to the person. The recognition of concrete attributes is instrumental for the recognition of abstract attributes. Both concrete and abstract attributes affect the perception of consequences and values. For example, the anti-lock braking system of a car (concrete attribute) affects the consumer's perception of the car's safety (abstract attribute). Recognition of concrete, as well as perception of abstract, product attributes leads to an inference of functional and/or psycho-social consequences. For example, a car with an anti-lock braking system will be safer (functional consequence) and will give the driver a feeling of safety (psychological consequence). The form of a car gives consumers the impression that it has a low 'CW-value' (functional consequence) and indicates status (psycho-social consequence).

The means–end chain model can be used to describe the relationship between the perception and recognition of product characteristics and consumer product evaluation. However, in research to date concepts have been described or visualised in terms of objective, tangible characteristics such as form. For example, the concepts shown in Page and Rosenbaum's 1987 and 1992 research display almost exclusively the objective attributes of different products (food processor, spin drier and steam iron). Concepts reflecting abstract product characteristics are common. This is also the case for concepts that indicate possible consequences of the product for the consumer, for instance, 'this product has a high quality' or 'it comes in handy when cooking'.

There may be several reasons why abstract characteristics and consequences are not taken into account. Firstly, it is almost impossible to match concrete and abstract characteristics. For example, from the perception that a bicycle rides smoothly, it is difficult to infer which product characteristics cause 'smoothness'. Secondly, only concrete characteristics are directly actionable by the designer. For instance, a designer can only make a car appear 'sporty' by controlling those characteristics, including form, that will cause the abstract attribute 'sportiness'. The designer cannot control 'sportiness' directly. Only the more concrete design characteristics are open to the designer to influence the perception of abstract characteristics, and the perception of functional and psycho-social consequences.

Nonetheless, not only the use of objective characteristics in concept evaluation needs to be addressed because, depending upon the product, consumers are more likely to be interested in the product's abstract characteristics and its functional and psycho-social consequences. As Snelders, Schoormans and de Bont (1993) state, 'the product's meaning is not apparent from the perceived product characteristics themselves, but from what these do for the consumer.' This idea is endorsed by a number of authors (e.g. Ratchford 1975) and is related to the idea of benefit segmentation (Haley 1968). Therefore, in order to grasp the meaning of a product, the concept should not only indicate concrete characteristics but should also propose probable abstract characteristics, and consequences of the product for the consumer.

The relation between concrete and abstract product characteristics is rather complex. Snelders and Stokmans (1994) show that the presentation of concrete characteristics leads to differences in the perception of abstract characteristics between consumers. Furthermore, Maheswaran and Sternthal (1990) indicate that only specific groups of consumers are able to infer product consequences from concrete characteristics. These studies indicate that concepts in which only objective product characteristics are included have different meanings for different consumers. This may apply to the product's form. The way in which form influences the meaning that consumers attribute to a product is discussed in the following section.

THE ROLE OF PRODUCT FORM IN CONCEPT TESTING

The fundamental question is: do consumers infer abstract attributes and product consequences from the product's form and material characteristics? To examine this question the relation between the concrete product characteristic form, on the one hand, and abstract product characteristics and product consequences, on the other, has to be confronted.

Muller (1990) proposes that the product characteristic form has three levels: an elementary level, a structural level and a metaphorical level. At the *elementary* level, form is the configuration and organisation of the product's parts and components in three-dimensional space, such as the form and position of the parts of the product. Each part of the product can be described in terms of its geometric properties, such as primitive shape (sphere, cylinder, cube, torus), curved surfaces or polygonals. Other form characteristics at the elementary level are size and dimensionality of the product.

The configuration of the parts and components of the product's overall shape is referred to as the *structural* level. At the structural level, the form confers the product's membership of a product category, such as telephone, car, etc. This configuration and organisation of parts and components in the product's overall shape is called the prototypicality of the form, which is stated as a degree. The degree of prototypicality of a product is proposed to have an effect on the consumer's recognition of the product as an example of a given product category, such as 'telephone', 'coffee maker' etc. The more the shape of the product resembles the prototypical design for the given product category, the higher the probability of the product being recognised as a member of the product category. For instance, the recognition of a compact car as a member of the category 'compact car' will be heavily influenced by the organisation of the main parts, e.g. the main body, the number of doors and the size of the product.

Both the elementary and the structural level of form indicate abstract characteristics and consequences. Muller (1990) has himself also recognised this reference of form, in what he refers to as the *metaphorical* level. At this level, the form reveals the product's functionality in its purchase and usage situation.

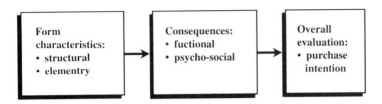

Figure 6.2 Theoretical model in the concept test

In terms of the means–end chain model, the elementary and the structural levels of form constitute concrete product characteristics. Therefore, variations of the elementary level of form can be expected to affect the perception of abstract characteristics and product consequences. Variations of the structural level will affect abstract product characteristics by changing the perception of the character of the product; e.g. 'this car is not a luxury car but a compact car'. Variations of the elementary and the structural level of form will create distinctive, appealing or functional products. From the elementary level of form, consumers can learn which functions are part of that product; for example, a large, four-door car is designed for family households and is more functional for them than a small, two-door car. A Jaguar or Porsche confers more status than an Austin or Nissan.

The means–end chain model can be used as a theoretical framework to study the meaning that consumers attach to concepts. More specifically in this chapter, the differences in structural and elementary levels of form are expected to influence consumers' evaluation of the product concept, by their reference to abstract characteristics and to functional and social/psychological consequences. An experiment is described that was conducted to investigate this hypothesis (Figure 6.2).

THE INFLUENCE OF FORM CHARACTERISTICS ON CONCEPT EVALUATION

To investigate whether product evaluations are guided by inferences that consumers make about the product's consequences on the basis of elementary and structural form characteristics, six concepts of telephone sets were evaluated by consumers. These concepts differed systematically in their structural and elementary form characteristics.

Two research propositions were formulated, as follows:

- Proposition 1: overall product evaluation will be affected by elementary and structural form characteristics.
- Proposition 2: the influence of form characteristics on overall evaluation is mediated by the perception of certain abstract attributes and/or functional and psycho-social consequences.

SAMPLE

The concepts were presented to 41 subject (27 males, 14 females; average age 21.5 years), all of whom were students at the School of Industrial Design Engineering of the Delft University of Technology. The respondents were recruited by means of posters in the public areas of the school.

PROCEDURE

The experiment was conducted in the laboratory of the School of Industrial Design Engineering. Six concepts of telephone sets were shown to the respondents, one by one. The respondents filled in a questionnaire designed to measure the overall evaluation of the product concept and perceived product consequences for each specific concept.

METHOD

Operationalisation of Elementary and Structural Characteristics of Form

The effect of the elementary and structural characteristics of form was assessed by measuring the evaluations of a number of concepts that differed systematically on these two characteristics of form. In other words, the operationalisation of differences in structural and elementary form characteristics was achieved by creating a number of concepts that differed systematically on these form characteristics.

The geometric properties of the product are an important part of the elementary form level. In this respect, two classes of telephones are found:

1. Spherical telephones, characterised by rounded corners and rounded edges.
2. Flat telephones, characterised by flat corners and flat edges.

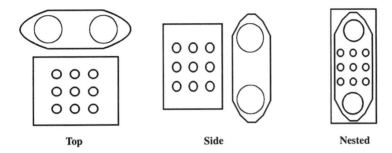

| Top | Side | Nested |

Figure 6.3   Structural form characteristics of telephone set design

In the telephone set concepts used in the experiment, differences in the elementary level of form were induced by creating three spherical and three flat telephones.

Structural form characteristics refer to the configuration of the parts and components of the product in an overall shape. According to Muller (1990), the overall shape of the telephone consists of the receiver, the dialling mechanism and the main body. Three almost prototypical configurations of the telephone can be made on the basis of altering the configuration of these three parts (Figure 6.3):

1. The receiver is positioned on top of the dialling mechanism (Top).
2. The receiver is positioned alongside the dialling mechanism (Side).
3. The receiver is nested in the main body, in front of the dialling mechanism (Nested).

Concepts of telephones were designed to differ on these three configurations. The differences in elementary and structural level were combined, which led to six (very abstract) product ideas that differed systematically in terms of structural and elementary form characteristics (see Table 6.1). Telephone set A in Table 6.1 has a spherical shape and the receiver is positioned on top of the dialling mechanism.

The concept ideas of telephone sets forms were generated by a team of designers on the basis of specifications defined by the experimental research

Table 6.1   The six concepts with their form characteristics

		Structural form characteristics		
		Top	Side	Nested
Elementary form	Spherical	A	B	C
characteristics	Flat	D	E	F

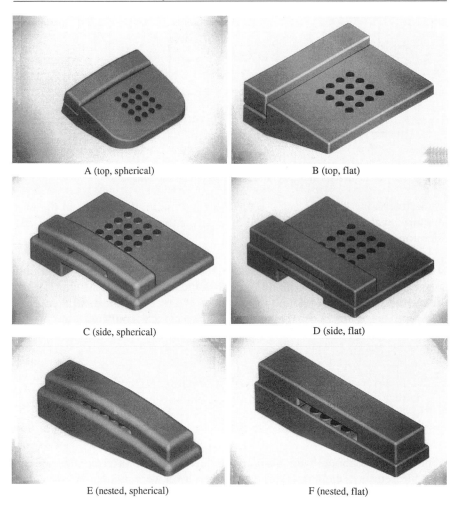

A (top, spherical)   B (top, flat)

C (side, spherical)   D (side, flat)

E (nested, spherical)   F (nested, flat)

Figure 6.4   Six concepts of telephone set design

design. These form ideas were transformed into concepts by means of Pro/Engineer, a computer-aided design (CAD) program. These concepts were created by CAD to guarantee a comparable degree of elaboration for all of the concepts. The program ran on a Digital DEC 3100 workstation, with a 19-inch colour graphics display. The concepts were photographed from the colour graphics display (Figure 6.4).

Operationalisation of the Perceived Product Consequences

Perceived consequences of the use of the product were taken from a study by Snelders and Stokmans (1994). They asked consumers to indicate the potential consequences of using a telephone. Only the consequences that were regarded as being the more important ones were included in the experiment. The evaluation of these consequences was measured on the basis of five-point scales, with the following anchors: beautiful versus ugly; attractive versus unattractive; distinctive versus usual; stark versus non-stark; modern versus old fashioned; functional versus unfunctional; practical versus impractical; pleasant versus unpleasant; and handy versus unhandy.

Operationalisation of the Overall Evaluation

The overall evaluation of the concepts was measured by a 5-point purchase intention scale, ranging from 1 (no intention to buy at all) to 5 (almost sure about buying).

RESULTS

Preliminary Analyses

The first step in the analysis was to factor analyse (principal components analysis) the scores on the nine items that were used to assess product consequences. In this analysis the overall evaluation of the six concepts was used. The principal components analysis resulted in a two-factor solution (eigenvalue criterion: eigenvalue larger than 1). The first factor explained 44.2% of the variance in the data. Three items that referred to the perceived aesthetic quality of product use load high (>0.60) on this factor (beautiful versus ugly, attractive versus unattractive and pleasant versus unpleasant). The second factor in the factor analysis explained another 19.3% of the variance in the data. The items that load high on this factor were all items that indicated the perceived functional consequences of product use (functional versus unfunctional, handy versus unhandy, practical versus impractical).

Separate factor analyses gave more or less the same solution for each concept. These results indicate that the perceived consequences of using the telephones separate into two dimensions: a psycho-social dimension (which consists solely of aesthetic consequences) and a functional dimension. This division of the consequences into two separate dimensions corresponds with the division of product consequences according to the means–end chain model.

Subsequently, the high loading items of every factor were added to form two scales (Cronbach's alpha 0.79 and 0.90). These scales were formed to simplify further analyses. We refer to these two scales as 'functionality' and 'aesthetic quality'.

Testing the Research Propositions

Our two research propositions are redefined in the form of one single theoretical model. Such a model can be tested by using LISREL (Jöreskog and Sörbom 1986), a statistical technique that can be used to test whether collected data match a theoretical model. The theoretical model that we used to test our research propositions is now described in operational terms.

The elementary and structural form characteristics of the telephone sets were operationalised by systematically varying the form of the six concepts. This provided the opportunity to calculate the influence of the difference between the two elementary form characteristics and between the three different structural form characteristics. Four independent comparisons were made:

1. The comparison of the effect of flat versus spherical shape.
2. The comparison of Top against Side and Nested.
3. The comparison of Side against Top and Nested.
4. The comparison of Nested against Top and Side.

In a number of statistical techniques, comparisons between two nominal data items can be made by using dummy variables. Dummy variables have a binomial character. In this experiment, a dummy variable (shape) assessed the influence of the difference between the flat (value 0) and spherical (value 1) shapes. The structural characteristics of form were translated into two dummy variables. The dummy variable Side reflected the effect of Side (value 1) against the joint effect of Nested and Top (value 0). The dummy variable Top was used to measure the effect of Top (value 1) against the joint effect of Nested and Side (value 0).

After the transformation to dummy variables, the theoretical model was translated into the empirical model shown in Figure 6.5, and this model was tested. Figure 6.5 also specifies the results of the LISREL analysis. The data fit the model (chi-square = 4.78, $df = 3$, $p = 0.13$). In other words: the relations in the empirical model do not differ significantly from the relations found in the collected data. The set of relations specified in the empirical model explains about 41% of the variance in the evaluations. This means that a significant degree of the variation in purchase intention can be attributed to the joint effect of form characteristics and perceived consequences. This result indicates that our data fit with the model that we have proposed, which means that (i) our research propositions can be accepted, and (ii) the model that underlies our research propositions – the means–end chain model – has proved to be more or less accurate in this context.

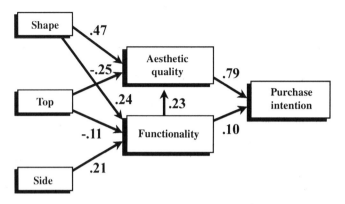

Figure 6.5   Estimated model on the basis of the LISREL analysis

All of the arrows in Figure 6.5 indicate significant effects of the variable at the tail of the arrow on the variable at the point of the arrow (t-value ≥ 1.69). The weights found can be compared with beta-weights, which are calculated in regression analysis. Some very interesting effects can be observed. The effect of shape on aesthetic quality is straightforward (ß = 0.47). This positive beta-weight indicates that the telephones with a spherical shape are believed to have a higher degree of aesthetic quality than those with a flat shape. Furthermore, effects of Side and of Top (structural form characteristics) on functionality and on aesthetic quality are found. A telephone with the receiver alongside the dialling mechanism is regarded as most functional (ß = 0.21), followed by the sets with the receiver nested in the body. The telephones with the receiver on top of the dialling mechanism are regarded as least functional (ß = –0.11) and least aesthetically qualified (ß = –0.25).

The significant effect of shape on functionality (ß = 0.24) is quite surprising. This effect indicates that a spherical shape is considered as more functional than a flat shape.

The positive effects of functionality (ß = 0.10) and aesthetic quality (ß = 0.79) on purchase intention are straightforward. The relative dominance of the effect of aesthetic quality on purchase intention over functionality may be due to the small variation in actual functionality between the telephone sets. The telephone sets all consist of a receiver and a dialling mechanism, and none has additional features. One of the unexpected results was the indirect effect of functionality on purchase intention via aesthetic quality (ß = 0.23). Respondents attributed aesthetic quality to the degree that a telephone set was regarded as more or less functional. Thus, a more functional telephone was considered to have more aesthetic quality.

DISCUSSION AND CONCLUSIONS

The first research proposition, that 'overall product evaluation will be affected by elementary and structural form characteristics', could not be rejected. Hence, form characteristics influence purchase intentions. This conclusion is expected, since the form of products is likely to have a profound effect on consumers' purchase intentions. Nonetheless, this result is important for the practice of concept testing because it highlights the relevance of showing a product's form in concept testing. One implication of this is that the use of verbal descriptions of products, as is typical of conjoint measurement studies (Wittink and Cattin 1989), can lead to less valid results. Recent developments show that form can be included in conjoint analysis studies by means of computer graphics (Loosschilder et al. 1994).

The second proposition, that 'the influence of form characteristics on overall evaluation is mediated by the perception of certain abstract attributes and/or functional and psycho-social consequences' is tentatively accepted. This result indicates that the means–end chain model seems, to a certain degree, valuable for the practice of concept testing. These results show that in a concept test situation, the overall product evaluation is not guided directly by concrete characteristics, but rather indirectly via the product's consequences inferred by the respondents. Although not tested by this study, this is likely to hold true for abstract attributes. This again indicates that respondents in a concept test do not judge a product directly on its characteristics, but base their overall evaluation on the meaning that the product can have for them. The study has implications for concept testing. Firstly, more attention needs to be paid to the perceived abstract attributes and the perceived product's consequences. This will give more insight into the reasons that respondents use when they judge a concept. In practice, this can be achieved by asking respondents which abstract attributes and consequences they perceive when shown a concept. Another possibility is to let respondents judge the degree to which certain important consequences are found in a concept. This last procedure can be used when it is already known what the most important product consequences are for the consumer.

Studies like the one described here have been accused of leading to a 'me-too' design, simply because uncommon and innovative forms are likely to be rejected. To countermand such an accusation, it is important to consider the results of concept testing very carefully. For instance, it is known that certain consumer groups are more innovative (or conservative) than others. De Bont, Schoormans and Wessel (1992) showed that deviant design was preferred more by younger people and men than by older people and women. Also, from innovation adoption and diffusion theories it is known that there are 'innovators' and 'laggards'. Taking a random sample of consumers for a concept test may lead to rejection of an innovative form simply because innovators are a minority in the market, and hence, in the sample. As a consequence, a sample of innovative consumers can be devised. It must be noted, however, that the individual degree of innovativeness may differ between product categories. For example, one can be very innovative in one's preference of car styling, but a laggard with respect to furniture design.

Secondly, the data set can be analysed at the level of the individual respondents, rather than aggregating this data. Since 'innovators' will probably be a minority in the sample, their evaluations will be dominated by the evaluations of more 'conservative' respondents, which will lead to 'regression to the mean'. It may be advisable to analyse data on the individual level first, and then to look for more specific, group-wise evaluation patterns, for instance by means of clustering techniques.

The value of concept testing can be enhanced by a strong theoretical foundation. The means–end model can be of value in learning to understand how product preferences come about in concept testing. However, much more research is needed before the means–end chain model can be regarded as *the* theory about the way in which consumers perceive the information in concepts. Furthermore, we believe that for concept testing, a theoretical foundation should be developed with respect to the use of the different modes in which product ideas are formulated, with respect to the value of the attribute form, also in relation to other product characteristics, and with respect to the selection criteria for respondents.

REFERENCES

de Bont, C.J.P.M., Schoormans, J.P.L. and Wessel, M. (1992). Consumer personality and the acceptance of product design, *Design Studies*, **13**, 200–208.

Finn, A. (1985). A theory of the consumer evaluation process for new product concepts, in Sheth, J.N. (ed.), *Research in Consumer Behaviour*, JAI Press, Greenwich, CT, pp. 35–65.

Green, P.E. and Srinivasan, V. (1978). Conjoint analysis in consumer research: Issues and outlook, *Journal of Consumer Research*, **5**, 103–123.

Gutman, J. (1982). A means–end model based on consumer categorization processes, *Journal of Marketing*, **46**, 60–72.

Haley, R.I. (1968). Benefit segmentation: A decision-oriented research tool, *Journal of Marketing*, **32**, 30–35.

Jöreskog, K.G. and Sörbom, D. (1986). *LISREL – Analysis of Linear Structural Relationships by the Method of Maximum Likelihood*, Scientific Software Inc., Mooresville, IN.

Loosschilder, G.H., Rosbergen, E., Vriens, M. and Wittink, D.R. (1994). Computer-generated pictorial stimuli for consumer input to durable product styling decisions, research memorandum 564, Institute of Economic Research, University of Groningen, Groningen, The Netherlands.

Mahajan, V. and Wind, J. (1992). New product models, practice, shortcomings, and desired improvements, *Journal of Product Innovation Management*, **9**, 128–139.

Maheswaran, D. and Sternthal, B. (1990). The effects of knowledge motivation and the type of message on ad processing and product judgements, *Journal of Consumer Research*, **17**, 66–73.

Moore, W.L. (1982). Concept testing, *Journal of Business Research*, **10**, 279–294.

Muller, W. (1990). *Vormgeven, Ordening en Betekenisgeving*, Lemma, Utrecht (in Dutch).

Page, A.L. and Rosenbaum, H.F. (1987). Redesigning product lines with conjoint analysis: How Sunbeam does it, *Journal of Product Innovation Management*, **4**, 120–137.

Page, A.L. and Rosenbaum, H.F. (1992). Developing an effective concept testing program for consumer durables, *Journal of Product Innovation Management*, **9**, 267–277.

Ratchford, B. (1975). The new economic theory of economic behaviour: An interpretive essay, *Journal of Consumer Research*, **2**, 65–75.

Rokeach, M. (1973). *The Nature of Human Values*, Free Press, New York.

Snelders, H.M.J.J. and Stokmans, M.W.J. (1994). Product perception and preference in consumer decision making, in Greenacre, M., Blasius, J. and Kristof, W. (eds), *Correspondence Analysis in the Social Sciences: Recent Developments and Applications*, Academic Press, New York.

Snelders, H.M.J.J., Schoormans, J.P.L. and de Bont, C.J.M. (1993). Consumer–product interaction and the validity of conjoint measurement: The relevance of the feel/think dimension, in Van Raaij, F. and Bamossy G. (eds), *European Advances in Consumer Research*, Vol. 1, ACR, Provo, Utah, pp. 142–147.

Wittink, D.R. and Cattin, P. (1989). Commercial use of conjoint analysis: An update, *Journal of Marketing*, **53**, 91–96.

NETWORKS AND RELATIONSHIPS

INTRODUCTION

Wim G. Biemans

Collaboration is one of the key words characterising product development in the 1990s, with successful firms emphasising the development of relationships and networks in their product development strategies. The three chapters in this section describe several aspects concerning relationships and networks, involving both internal and external partners.

In Chapter 7, Biemans discusses a number of changes in the market-place (e.g. increasing product complexity and decreasing product life cycles) that cause firms to emphasise collaboration, both with external partners and internally. Firstly, companies develop strategic alliances with other organisations, such as key suppliers, competitors and major customers, which lead to complex structures of organisations connected by interactive relationships, called external networks. The purpose of the networks is to exchange ideas and knowledge and to share the risks and costs of product development. Secondly, companies build high-performance cross-functional teams within their organisations, and these teams constitute the core of the internal networks. These teams may facilitate idea generation and 'time to market'. Biemans reviews the relevant literature and argues that the concepts of external and internal networks are closely related and need to be integrated. To this end, he presents a simple framework that may assist academic researchers in formulating new research projects.

Companies collaborate with all kinds of organisations during product development. Many authors have discussed the numerous benefits of collaborative product development and the factors leading to success. In Chapter 8, Bruce, Leverick and Littler present the major findings from the literature and combine it with the results of their empirical study of collaborative product development by UK information and communication technology companies.

They point out that, despite the various benefits of collaborative product development, there are potential disadvantages and the level of success of collaborative product development is difficult to establish. In addition, they identify and categorise the major factors that, according to the respondents in their investigation, are more likely to contribute to the success of collaborative product development.

Design is an important area where firms increasingly collaborate with outside organisations. In Chapter 9, Jevnaker focuses on long-term relationships between external design consultants and their clients. In the context of such long-term relationships, it is inevitable that some of the design knowledge and approach will be transferred from the design consultant to the client firm. Jevnaker demonstrates the issue of organisations 'absorbing' new design skills and blending them with existing competencies and capabilities by using a comprehensive case of a Norwegian manufacturer in the furniture industry. The concept of 'inaugurative learning' is identified as a missing link in explaining the adoption of new competencies in product design.

CHAPTER SEVEN

INTERNAL AND EXTERNAL NETWORKS IN PRODUCT DEVELOPMENT: A CASE FOR INTEGRATION

Wim G. Biemans

Changing market conditions make product development an expensive and risky endeavour, and strongly influence the way it is being managed. In response to these changes, firms follow two broad strategies. They (i) develop strategic alliances with various external organisations and (ii) build high-performance cross-functional teams within their organisation. The management literature has typically treated these two strategies as separate issues. This chapter presents a survey of the literature and argues that successful firms develop ways of integrating internal and external networks. It closes with a simple framework to study such integration.

INTRODUCTION

For some years now, the management of product development has been the subject of increasing attention from both academics and practitioners (see, for instance, the survey by Hart, Chapter 1, this volume). The seminal studies of the New York-based management and technology consulting firm of Booz, Allen and Hamilton (1968, 1982) contributed significantly to the state-of-the-art knowledge about the management of product development, as well as to a general awareness in firms that their future existence depends strongly on

Product Development: Meeting the Challenge of the Design–Marketing Interface.
Edited by M. Bruce and W.G. Biemans.   © 1995 John Wiley & Sons Ltd.

their capability to generate a continuous stream of new products. This has led companies like 3M to set explicit targets for the percentage of sales generated by products that are less than five years old.

The Booz, Allen and Hamilton studies have inspired a large number of empirical investigations into the management of new product development, undertaken to determine the underlying causes of success and failure. Especially well known in this context are the extensive NewProd projects among several hundred Canadian firms (summarised in Cooper 1993) and the SAPPHO studies. Other researchers focused on various specific issues, ranging from the role of marketing (Biemans 1992; Workman 1993) and implementing a market orientation (Harmsen 1994) to the importance of human resources (Gupta and Singhal 1993) and specific practices of Japanese firms (Czinkota and Kotabe 1990; Kennard 1991).

During the past ten years, changing market conditions have resulted in two major areas of interest to both academics and practitioners:

1. Developing and managing strategic alliances with other organisations.
2. Creating a high-performance cross-functional team with representatives of all departments involved in the development of new products.

This chapter briefly summarises these issues and argues that internal and external networks should be integrated. The limited empirical material available is used to construct a framework for further empirical study.

CHANGING MARKET CONDITIONS

Drastically changing market conditions have fuelled a growing practical interest in the management of product development. An increasing number of firms find themselves facing changing circumstances that strongly impact on the way they are doing business. The most relevant changes concern the competitive structure, complexity of products and production processes, length of product life cycles, and demands made by customers.

INCREASING COMPETITION

The integration of the European market, deregulation of industries, tumbling trade barriers in various parts of the world (e.g. Europe and NAFTA) and democratisation processes (e.g. the former Soviet Union and China) increase both the number of players and the intensity of competition. For instance, growing deregulation coupled with significant technological advances is causing sweeping changes in the competitive structure of the global telecommunications industry, where once secure national monopolies are now being eliminated.

INCREASING COMPLEXITY OF PRODUCTS AND PRODUCTION PROCESSES

New products are becoming increasingly complex, and their development necessitates the combination of different areas of knowledge. In addition, the development of new products may necessitate the production of complex production processes and tools, as well as the acquisition of new technologies. For instance, the 'Information Superhighway' and the accompanying flood of multimedia products and services require the integration of consumer electronics and digital cable and telephone networks, as well as the development of computerised compression techniques to further reduce redundant information in digital signals.

DRAMATICALLY SHORTENED PRODUCT LIFE CYCLES

Technological developments have accelerated to a level where product life cycles have shortened considerably, with product life cycles of advanced consumer electronics often being measured in months rather than years (as is the case with the current generations of notebook computers). As Ed McCracken, chief executive of Silicon Graphics, recently stated in an interview (Prokesch 1993):

> There has never been a commodity market with the rate of technological change that exists in the computer industry. The performance, or computing power relative to price, is now increasing tenfold every 3½ years. . . . Our feeling is that this rapid, chaotic rate of change will continue forever and will continue to accelerate. . . . Long term product planning is dangerous in our industry and many others . . . No one can plan the future. Three years is long-term. Even two years may be. Five years is laughable.

However, this trend does not just affect high-tech products: for instance, life cycles of such mundane products as washing powders have decreased from 30 years to 5 or 6. This implies that a manufacturer can no longer count on a steady demand over many years for a newly developed product, and the time available for a manufacturer to recoup its product development expenditures has been significantly reduced (Von Braun 1990). Time becomes a critical factor in obtaining competitive advantage. Japanese firms in particular have proven to be adept at cutting product development times in half, and their methods and techniques are currently being applied by an increasing number of western firms.

HIGHER DEMANDS BY CUSTOMERS

Customers make increasingly sophisticated demands upon suppliers and their products. For instance, rejection levels are being formulated in parts-per-million (ppm), while some strive for zero defects:

> L.L. Bean Inc., the American retailer of outdoor gear, during one stretch in the spring of 1991, mailed 50,000 packages and claims to have correctly filled every order. Its fill rate hasn't dropped below 99.9% in 1991, even during the Christmas season, when the company mailed as many as 134,000 packages a day. Manchester Stamping Corp., an American auto parts supplier, tells a similar story. It now sneers at a record many companies would envy: in 1989, it delivered 540,000 parts to Honda of America Manufacturing Inc.'s assembly plant – of which only seven were bad. But President Wayne T. Hamilton isn't content. His new goal is perfection.
>
> (Port et al. 1992)

In addition, firms demand that their suppliers are certified. While some firms develop their own norms, others use international standards, such as the ISO 9000 series. Motorola, the 1988 winner of the Malcolm Baldridge National Quality Award, demands from all of its suppliers that they also apply for this award. Suppliers that do not comply are removed from the approved vendor list. Motorola monitors its selected suppliers closely. Motorola teams tour suppliers' plants every two years, while commodity managers rate suppliers monthly on an index that combines cost and quality, in both cases comparing the suppliers with their competitors (Magnet 1994).

These general trends are closely intertwined and together demonstrate the need for continuously developing new products, thus putting pressure on the management of product development and emphasising the need to reduce time to market. As a result new product development has become an expensive and high-risk activity.

Firms react to these changing market conditions in a variety of ways, as witnessed by the profusion of new terminology: among others, co-makership, co-design relationship, co-destiny relationship, partnership, value-adding partnership, network, strategic alliance, hybrid organisation, virtual organisation, concurrent engineering, parallel product development, fast track product development, multidisciplinary team and cross-functional team.

However, closer inspection of these related concepts shows that they can be divided into two groups, representing two clearly different strategic responses undertaken by firms: external and internal collaboration.

COLLABORATION WITH OTHER ORGANISATIONS: DEVELOPING EXTERNAL NETWORKS

Over the years the development of new products has been studied from a number of perspectives, reflecting the changes in the market-place. Four overlapping phases can be distinguished.

EVOLVING PERSPECTIVES OF PRODUCT DEVELOPMENT

The Manufacturer as the Only Party Involved

Traditionally, the management of product development processes has typically been considered from the manufacturer's perspective. The process of new product development is usually divided into a series of subsequent stages, and the various empirical studies aimed at formulating specific recommendations for the manufacturer to improve its management of the new product development process and increase both the chances and extent of success. The manufacturer is considered to be the only party involved, controlling the process and influencing the environment. The overwhelming majority of studies of new product development belong to this category, including the renowned studies by Booz, Allen and Hamilton (1968, 1982).

The User as Initiator

In the mid-1970s Von Hippel published the results of two empirical investigations demonstrating that, in some industries, it is the user rather than the manufacturer who initiates the development of a new product. Based on his studies of the scientific instruments and the semiconductor and electronic subassembly industries, Von Hippel (1978) formulated the *customer-active paradigm* (CAP) as the counterpart of the *manufacturer-active paradigm* (MAP). MAP describes the more traditional situation discussed above, where the manufacturer employs traditional methods of market research to investigate user demands and uses the information thus gained to guide new product development. In other words, the user is involved only passively. With CAP, on the other hand, it is the user who has an idea for a new product and who initiates the development of new products. Sometimes, the user may even go beyond this and, for example, develop a crude prototype and test it in practice. Subsequently, a manufacturer is approached to further develop (if necessary), manufacture and market the product.

Manufacturer–User Interaction

Von Hippel's findings inspired a large number of similar studies by researchers, who demonstrated user involvement in product development processes in areas as diverse as industrial machinery (Foxall and Tierney 1984), medical instruments (Biemans 1991; Shaw 1986), applications software (Voss 1985), machine tools (Parkinson 1982) and consumer products (Ciccantelli and Magidson 1993). However, in so doing, these researchers did not *a priori* limit the user's involvement to the idea generation stage, and the focus gradually shifted from characterising the product development process as being either manufacturer-active or customer-active to determining the role of users during the whole process of product development. Von Hippel's concept of CAP evolved into a broad range of manufacturer–user interaction, where many researchers used the interaction model of the Industrial Marketing and Purchasing (IMP) group as a starting point (Håkansson 1982). Recently, Flores (1993) offered a sociological/ psychological approach to this subject.

Collaboration within Networks

The Swedish branch of the international IMP group subsequently started to elaborate on the concept of manufacturer–user interaction by emphasising that the involvement of external parties need not be limited to users. Indeed, the growing complexity of products and increasing competition led firms to collaborate with all kinds of external organisations (e.g. key suppliers, major customers, competitors, universities, research institutes, government agencies) in an effort to reduce costs and manage risks, for instance by sharing development costs, gaining entry to each other's markets or exchanging technologies. Bruce, Leverick and Littler (Chapter 8, this volume), in their discussion of the complexities of collaborative product development, provide more information about the reasons for collaboration, the expected benefits, the potential disadvantages and the relevance of contextual factors.

Another major reason for increased collaboration with external organisations is the increasing tendency of firms to focus on their core activities and subcontract everything else. Indeed, management guru Tom Peters (1994) even points to examples of companies outsourcing core activities, such as the newly founded Australian telecommunications company, Optus Communications, which decided to subcontract most of its information-systems activities.

With respect to product development, this tendency causes companies to buy in expertise for specific parts of the process. For instance, firms may employ organisations to develop exciting ideas for new products, conduct extensive market scanning studies, or perform technical tests on prototypes. Bruce and Morris (Chapter 5, this volume) show that companies increasingly outsource design expertise and discuss the major issues involved in managing external design.

Thus, in the second half of the 1980s, academics started to view product development as an interplay between a number of actors and therefore as taking place within networks (Biemans 1992; Håkansson 1987). In order to distinguish these forms of external collaboration from the teamwork taking place within the company (discussed in the next section), these often complex structures of interactive relationships will be referred to as *external networks*.

THE RISE OF STRATEGIC ALLIANCES

The development of the interaction and network concepts was accompanied by an observed increase in the relevance and use of strategic alliances. Both academics and practitioners point to the same changing market conditions to explain the rise of strategic alliances:

> The significant change in the business environment due to economic conditions, high costs, the globalization of business and increasing political control has changed the focus of alliance strategies to the point where they are now becoming the rule rather than the exception.
>
> (James 1985)

> It's too complicated and too expensive for any size company to go it alone all the time. Today, going alone means missing opportunities. Tomorrow, it means going out of business.
>
> (Lipnack and Stamps 1993)

Nevertheless, one should realise that whereas the network concept is typically closely related to the issue of product development, strategic alliances refer to a broad range of management activities. For instance, the well-publicised alliance between Ford and Mazda is basically built on swapping products and gaining access to each other's markets. Bucklin and Sengupta (1993) focused on co-marketing alliances, i.e. contractual relationships undertaken by firms whose respective products are complements in the market-place. These co-marketing alliances 'involve coordination among the partners in one or more aspect of marketing and may extend into research, product development, and even production' (Bucklin and Sengupta 1993). Particularly in industries that are changing rapidly (e.g. the telecommunications industry) or just coming into existence (e.g. multimedia), the development of strategic alliances is critical in ensuring long-term viability. According to a *Biotechnology '91* survey, the larger biotechnology firms, numbering 300 or more employees, participate in nine strategic alliances on average.

Some academics have tried to explain strategic alliances and formulate conceptual tools to study them. For instance, a group of Dutch academics developed a general framework for studying strategic alliances, and demonstrated that the development of new products is just one of the many possible objectives in forming a strategic alliance (Huyzer et al. 1990). This framework was subsequently employed to analyse the use of strategic alliances by a number of firms in the Netherlands (Huyzer et al. 1991). Others explained the functioning of strategic alliances by linking them to the concept of embedded knowledge (Badaracco 1991), or focused on specific kinds of alliances, such as the ones between large and small firms (Botkin and Matthews 1992) and alliances formed by entrepreneurial companies (Larson 1991). Many researchers focused on the process of managing strategic alliances (Bronder and Pritzl 1992; Devlin and Bleackley 1988; Lorange and Roos 1991, 1992; Lynch 1993; Niederkofler 1991; Slowinski, Farris and Jones 1993; Sonnenberg 1992). Typically, they describe the management of strategic alliances according to a limited number of growth stages, such as strategy decision, configuration of the alliance, partner selection and management of the ongoing partnership. A number of researchers explicitly focused on the issue of dependence and stressed the importance of learning (Hamel 1991; Hamel, Doz and Prahalad 1989; Lei 1993; Lei and Slocum 1992; Reich and Mankin 1986), while others also mention the disadvantages of strategic alliances (Leverick and Littler 1993) or warn against the use of universal solutions and emphasise the need for taking contextual factors into account (Bruce, Leverick and Littler, Chapter 8, this volume).

COLLABORATION WITHIN THE ORGANISATION: DEVELOPING INTERNAL NETWORKS

In addition to the focus on collaboration with external partners (whether the resulting structures are called networks or strategic alliances), the product development literature shows a preoccupation with internal organisational issues, such as the allocation of resources, involvement of top management and the relationship between marketing and technology. In this section we focus on cooperation issues, and briefly discuss the marketing–R&D interface and cross-functional teams.

Table 7.1 Marketing and R&D's perceptions of each other

Marketing people about technical people	Technical people about marketing people
Have no sense of time	Want everything now
Don't care about costs	Are aggressive and too demanding
Have no idea of the real world	Are unrealistic
Hide in the laboratory	Are quick to make promises they cannot keep
Can't communicate clearly	Are involved only in advertising, promotion
Should be kept away from customers	and public relations
Require customers to adapt themselves	Are focusing on customers that don't know
Lack a feeling for service and a customer-	what they want
orientated attitude	Make bad predictions
Do not pay attention to competitors and	Can't make up their minds
competitive advantage	Change the design specifications frequently
Are always looking for standardisation	Are too impatient
Are inflexible	Are more interested in playing golf
Are very conservative	Are always in a hurry
Have a very narrow view of the world	Don't trust technical people
Always underestimate costs	Set unrealistic goals for profit margins
Have no sense of humour	Can't possibly understand technology
Are off in another world	Aren't interested in the scientists' or
Are passive	engineers' problems
Don't understand customers	Are too quick in introducing a new product
Can't stick to schedules	Want to ship products before they are ready
Are interested only in technology	
Are slow	
Never finish developing a product	

THE MARKETING–R&D INTERFACE

Considerable research efforts have been dedicated to the relationship between the two major departments involved in product development: marketing and R&D. Researchers formulated frameworks to study the relationship
between marketing and R&D (Gupta, Raj and Wilemon 1986), investigated
the barriers between the two departments (Gupta, Raj and Wilemon 1985;
Souder 1981) and discussed the problem from R&D's perspective (Gupta and
Wilemon 1990). Many of the problems in the relationship between marketing
and R&D can be traced to the different backgrounds and nature of marketers
and developers, which foster a lack of interest in each other's work and
thinking in stereotypes. Table 7.1 summarises how marketing people and
technical people perceive each other (based on Himmelfarb 1992; Van der
Hart 1993). The results of such prejudiced attitudes and opinions can be
disastrous:

> Because of such misconceptions, technical people are often intentionally kept
> away from the customers. This keeps them further isolated and out of touch with

the real world. As a result, their ideas for new products are even less likely to match real needs of the marketplace. . . . As a result of such misconceptions, marketing people are often intentionally kept in the dark about developing technologies that might yield exciting new products. They are less likely to be able to respond to the needs of a changing marketplace because they have no idea of what might be possible. Further, they are likely to be blind-sided by a competitor who may be more capable of converting new technologies into saleable products.

(Himmelfarb 1992)

However, differences in cultures and attitudes do not only exist between marketers and developers. See, for instance Chapter 4, this volume, in which Davies-Cooper and Jones analyse the interface between design and marketing. In describing the challenges in developing a conducive workplace culture, Rosenthal (1992) demonstrates that even representatives from closely related specialties, such as design engineers, manufacturing engineers, industrial designers and human factors specialists (i.e. ergonomists), have very different cultural backgrounds.

The importance of striving at good relationships between marketers and developers is demonstrated by the empirical work of researchers who have related the cooperation between marketing and R&D to product success and concluded that 'collaborative efforts between marketing and R&D during the actual designing of new products appear to be a key factor in explaining the success levels of new products' (Hise et al. 1990). Nevertheless, it should be emphasised that successful product development is realised through the combination of diverse inputs from people with different backgrounds. The objective of eliminating all differences of viewpoints and perspectives is not only unattainable, but also undesirable. The combination of conflicting points of view increases the organisation's creativity!

CROSS-FUNCTIONAL TEAMS

As a result of the changing market conditions, especially the increased costs of product development and shortening product life cycles, the product development literature has started to emphasise the need for speed (Gold 1987; Mabert, Muth and Schmenner 1992; McDonough and Barczak 1991; Smith and Reinertsen 1991; Starr 1992; Vesey 1992). (Although Crawford (1992) endorses this new strategy, he points to the hidden costs of accelerated product development.) An increasing number of firms employ the management techniques developed by Japanese companies to reduce the time to market by up to 50%.

Probably the most frequently mentioned piece of advice to realise high product quality and drastically reduce product development times is the practice of concurrent engineering (also known as parallel product development, overlapping stages and the rugby approach), combined with the use of cross-functional teams (see also Hart, Chapter 1, this volume). After all, marketing and R&D are not the only departments involved in the development of new products; engineering and production are obviously involved as well, while purchasing is also frequently mentioned as an additional member of the product development team, because of its network of relationships with suppliers (Burt and Soukup 1985; Williams and Smith 1990). The practice of using cross-functional teams was pioneered by Toyota Motor Company and is now standard practice in an increasing number of firms. The benefits of using cross-functional teams are (Parker 1994):

- decreased product development times
- improved organisational ability to solve complex problems
- increased customer focus
- increased creative potential
- increased learning by team members
- single point of contact

However, management by cross-functional teams is not always easy to achieve in practice, as is implied by the following mission statement, formulated by a director of the R&D operations of a food company: 'I have a DREAM: Development by Research, Engineering And Marketing' (cited in Moenaert et al. 1994). Several authors have described the challenges in the development and management of cross-functional project teams, the tasks and qualifications of the project leader and the relationship between the project organisation and the regular functional departments (Himmelfarb 1992; House and Price 1991; Howard and Guile 1992; Thamhain 1990).

Nevertheless, for many firms the results of using cross-functional teams have proved to be nothing short of spectacular. Chrysler used the team approach to reduce by 40% the time it takes to develop a new car or truck (Power et al. 1993). Honeywell's Building Controls Division used cross-functional teams to cut product development time by 50%, reduce product costs by 5–10%, and make products 97.6% defect free (Parker 1994). Hewlett-Packard credits horizontal teaming with the following results (Lipnack and Stamps 1993):

- manufacturing cost reduced by 45%
- development cycle reduced by 35%
- field failure rates reduced by 60%
- scrap and rework reduced by 75%

In the area of product development, the cross-functional teams are the main point of focus. However, in making the product development project a success, the team members (i) frequently draw upon the expertise of additional individuals within the firm, and (ii) depend on the functioning of various internal departments. By analogy to the external networks, these internal structures of individuals and departments involved in product development can be considered to constitute *internal networks*.

THE NEED FOR INTEGRATION

An increasing number of firms seem to be integrating external and internal networks in order to successfully develop and launch new products.

PRACTICES OF WORLD-CLASS FIRMS

The relationship between the concepts of external and internal collaboration has been touched upon by both academics and practitioners. Biemans (1991) studied how Dutch manufacturers of medical equipment collaborate with other organisations during the development of new products. As a result of his investigation, he distinguished between external and internal networks and concluded that 'the functioning of each of the internal networks directly influences the efficiency and efficacy of the external network'. Dan Ciampa, chief executive of the Rath & Strong consulting firm, put it as follows: 'unless an organization knows how to foster collaborative relationships internally, it won't be good at making such relationships outside' (Magnet 1994). The close relationship between internal and external networks led Lipnack and Stamps (1993) to introduce the concept of 'Teamnets', which bring together two powerful organisational ideas:

- Teams: small groups of people working with focus, motivation and skill to achieve shared goals.
- Networks: disparate groups of people and groups 'linking' to work together based on a common purpose.

In practice, the integration of internal and external networks can be found in leading firms in various industries. For instance, companies as diverse as Toyota, Honda, Mazda, Ford, Harley-Davidson, Black & Decker, Motorola, Bose, Xerox and Kodak are developing effective new ways to work together with key suppliers in optimising product design and development (Asmus and Griffin 1993; Håkansson and Eriksson 1993). A good example is provided by

Kodak, which introduced its Early Production Supplier Involvement (EPSI) programme, designed to involve suppliers more closely in the design and manufacturing of a product (Aleo 1992). EPSI helps to define a product's functional needs, including assembly requirements, especially in light of the supplier's manufacturing process. By including suppliers – on a non-disclosure basis – on its project teams from early product development through to product introduction, Kodak combines the expertise of the manufacturer and its supplier. Among the benefits of the programme are:

- Selection of proper material and processes that lead to manufacturable products.
- Class A certification recognises the items that consistently meet requirements, especially functional and quality requirements.
- Shortened lead times, which allow Kodak to arrive in the market-place ahead of the competition.
- Lowest overall cost for Kodak products, which enables them to meet customer needs at competitive prices.
- Improved communication, which gives suppliers the ability to meet Kodak's expectations in areas of cost, delivery and quality.
- An established production supplier base that allows Kodak to develop long-term relationships and commitments with suppliers.

Another example is Douglas Aircraft which, in the beginning of the 1990s, projected the cost to build the first copy of its next-generation, wide-body, long-haul vehicle at $5 billion. These kinds of investment call for innovative organisational solutions. Douglas Aircraft struck the following deal with its suppliers. Each manufacturer of the MD-12's major parts, such as the wing, tail, avionics and computer systems, will not be a supplier in the traditional adversarial sense. Instead, the manufacturers become risk-sharing partners: they invest their components and get paid when the airlines buy the planes. This increases the intensity of the supplier partnerships, and adds organisational problems and opportunities to the numerous technical ones (Lipnack and Stamps 1993).

Through improvements such as these, companies have managed to reduce their development times by as much as 40% and reduce the cost of purchased materials by between 15% and 35%.

Similarly, firms involve key customers in their product development efforts and include them in their product development teams. In developing the new 300-seat 777, Boeing's most ambitious project of the past 25 years, Boeing involved customers by making them members of its design/build teams. As Philip Condit (1994), president of the Boeing Company, put it:

advanced technology did not drive the design process. On the contrary, we defined this airplane by 'aggressively listening' to customers. We brought together a number of airlines, representing the major regions of the world, to create the aircraft they would most prefer. And that was two years before we began the design process.

United Airlines, which has thirty-four 777s on order and will be the 777 'launch airline', had a permanent representative at 777 headquarters (Nelson 1994). Although initially there was resistance to the idea of bringing the customer in, the experiences were quite positive: 'Once the customer was involved in the meetings, people stopped acting like they were surrogates for the customer, trying to understand how they thought the customer might react' (Condit 1994).

Kodak's Black and White Film organisation (also known as 'Team Zebra') also regularly included customers on its product and service development teams, where they were involved in the design from the beginning.

In their report on an extensive study of practical measures to improve product development processes, Howard and Guile (1992) state that 'membership in [cross-functional] teams may be quite flexible and may even include suppliers, customers, consultants and members of technical advisory groups as needed'.

These world-class practices notwithstanding, most firms persist in treating external and internal cooperation as two separate issues. But more and more firms realize that the present competitive conditions require them to integrate both areas in order to generate the required continuous stream of successful new products and reap the full benefits of their investments in product development.

A CONTINUUM OF COLLABORATION OPTIONS

As regards collaboration with external parties, the discussion in this chapter suggests that firms can choose between two basic alternatives: develop new products internally or use external expertise to complement internal development capabilities.

Develop New Products Internally

The practice of performing all product development activities internally used to be widespread, and some companies (such as IBM and the Dutch Philips Electronics) used to be famous for it. However, the present-day complexity, speed, costs and competitiveness of product development make this strategy difficult to uphold.

Complement Internal Development Capabilities with External Expertise

This strategy of external collaboration may involve (i) outsourcing selected product development activities to specialised organisations (e.g. market research, prototype testing or design) and (ii) hiring experts to complement comparable capabilities available within the organisation (e.g. having the design department join forces with an external design consultant; see also Bruce and Morris, Chapter 5, this volume).

Naturally, firms will use external collaboration in varying degrees, depending on the specific circumstances, so both alternatives can be considered to be points on a collaboration continuum. The first alternative, developing products internally (i.e. no external collaboration), would lie at one extreme of the continuum. The logical counterpart would involve a situation of 'only external collaboration', with a whole range of combinations of internal and external collaboration in between. Using external collaboration only is incorporated in the concept of the 'virtual corporation'.

Constructing a Virtual Corporation

The cover story of the February 1993 issue of *Business Week International* describes the virtual corporation as follows (see also Davidow and Malone 1992):

> The virtual corporation is a temporary network of independent companies – suppliers, customers, even erstwhile rivals – linked by information technology to share skills, costs, and access to one another's markets. . . . this new, evolving, corporate model will be fluid and flexible – a group of collaborators that quickly unite to exploit a specific opportunity. Once the opportunity is met, the venture will, more often than not, disband.
>
> (Byrne et al. 1993)

Peters (1994) discusses the same idea when he talks about the corporation as Rolodex. Truett and Barrett (1991) focus on the role of electronic networks, and suggest that Corporate Virtual Workspaces (CVWs) will be highly productive replacements for current work environments, which all but eliminate the need for the physical corporation: 'having no need for physical facilities other than the system hosting the CVW, the cyberspace corporation will exist entirely in cyberspace.'

Needless to say, all of the various forms of external collaboration still need to be integrated with the collaboration inside the organisation. Although some leading firms seem to be doing this quite successfully, the theoretical knowledge about this kind of integration is limited. The next section presents a simple framework for studying the integration of internal and external networks.

INTEGRATION OF INTERNAL AND EXTERNAL NETWORKS

Figure 7.1 shows a simple framework that illustrates how the literature of both external and internal collaboration can be used to investigate a number of major research questions. The figure distinguishes between four groups of issues. The first three categories correspond to the familiar stages of scientific research: description, explanation and prediction. The research questions from the descriptive stage aim at analysing the current situation within firms. The questions from the explanatory stage can be derived from the results of the descriptive stage and used to formulate research models and hypotheses. Finally, the research questions from the predictive stage are based on the results of the explanatory stage, and aim at formulating normative advice for management practice. The fourth and final category of questions concerns issues related to theory building. The questions build on the results from the previous stages by tying conceptual constructs into a coherent whole. The results of the theory-building stage can be used as input for subsequent empirical investigations. The lists of questions in the following subsections are not exhaustive, but are meant to provide some indication of the major issues to be raised at the various research stages.

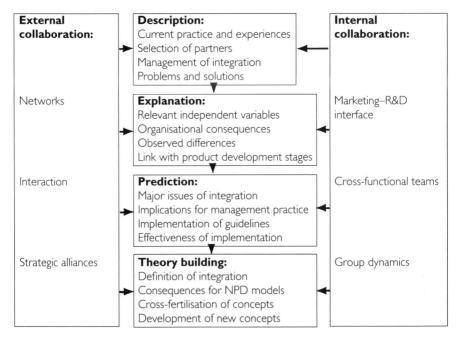

Figure 7.1   A simple framework for investigating the integration of internal and external networks

DESCRIPTION

The following research questions are directed at describing how firms integrate internal and external networks and identifying the major issues involved:

- To what extent do firms actually attempt to integrate internal and external networks?
- Which type of organisations (e.g. suppliers, customers, universities) are involved in the product development team?
- How many organisations of each type are typically involved in the product development team?
- How do firms select the organisations, departments and individuals to be involved in the product development team?
- How do firms deal with conflicting interests (e.g. when they want to involve two major competing suppliers)?
- What kind of integration mechanisms do firms use?
- What do firms consider to be the major issues concerning the integration of internal and external networks?
- What are the major problems experienced by firms when integrating internal and external networks?
- Which solutions to these problems have been tried and what were the results?
- What are the general experiences of firms in integrating internal and external networks?

EXPLANATION

These research questions aim at explaining the integration of internal and external networks, as well as their consequences. Although these questions will be based on the results of the preceding descriptive phase, in general they will include questions like:

- What variables do managers perceive as determining a firm's efforts at integrating internal and external networks?
- Are there any significant differences concerning the integration of internal and external networks determined by industry, organisational size, type of product and so on?
- During which stages of the product development process can external parties be involved, and what determines their contributions?
- What are the organisational consequences of integration of internal and external networks for the cross-functional team? For example, what are suitable organisational structures, and what is effective management of the interaction (both from a human resources and an information systems perspective)?

■ To what extent are there differences in observed organisational behaviour, and what determines these differences?

PREDICTION

These research questions are meant to provide management with normative advice and implementable managerial guidelines for effectively establishing and managing the integration of internal and external networks:

■ What are the major issues to be addressed by the integration (e.g. involvement in short-term projects versus long-term strategy)?
■ What are the major implications for management practice in integrating internal and external networks?
■ What are the major issues involved in implementing the managerial guidelines (e.g. major bottlenecks and suggested solutions)?
■ What variables determine the effectiveness of implementation efforts?

THEORY BUILDING

These final questions go beyond individual observations and contribute to existing theory about collaboration during product development:

■ How do you define the concept of 'integration'? Should a distinction be made between levels of involvement, such as being consulted on an *ad hoc* basis versus actual membership of the product development team?
■ What are the characteristics of a flexible model of the product development process that allows for the integration of internal and external networks? For instance, what are the basic building blocks? How do you accommodate for the large number of different possibilities? How can such a model be depicted graphically?
■ Which existing theoretical concepts provide opportunities for cross-fertilisation of ideas?
■ Which existing theoretical concepts can be used or easily modified to describe and analyse the integration of internal and external networks?
■ What are the major issues or areas for which new theoretical concepts need to be developed?

A number of these research questions have already been (partly) addressed in other chapters in this book. For instance, at the end of her survey of product development research, Hart (see Chapter 1) proposes a multiple convergent process model which was specifically designed to accommodate for the involvement of various internal functions and external organisations in product development. Similarly, in discussing the outsourcing and management of external design, Bruce and Morris (see Chapter 5) raise various issues involving the contribution, selection and management of external design consultants. The research questions outlined above combine a great number of related issues into a coherent whole, and are meant to inspire researchers in formulating new research projects that address the integration of internal and external networks.

CONCLUSION

Collaboration is a frequently recurring theme in the current product development literature, as is evidenced by the attention paid to issues such as joint product development, customer involvement in product development, developing products within networks, strategic alliances, cross-functional teams, marketing–R&D interface, virtual corporations, and so on. In discussing these themes, academics typically treat the issues concerning external collaboration (e.g. product development within networks and strategic alliances) as separate from the ones concerning internal collaboration (e.g. the marketing–R&D interface and cross-functional teams).

However, on taking a closer look at the concepts of internal and external collaboration it becomes obvious that these concepts are closely related. For instance, the efficiency and effectiveness of collaboration with other organisations (such as suppliers, competitors and customers) is influenced by the quality of the collaboration between the various functions within the organisation that are involved in product development. Therefore, it is not really surprising that successful firms seem to integrate the concepts of internal and external networks into a coherent whole to improve their development of new products, for example by making key suppliers and major customers members of the product development team and involving them from day one.

To bridge this gap between academic research and management practice, academics not only need to follow up on these developments, but to try to lead the way. This requires the translation of contributions from various fields of scientific research (network theory, management of strategic alliances, management of cross-functional teams, and possibly even group dynamics, motivation theory and leadership) to the area of product development, and integrating them into a coherent whole.

This chapter provides a survey of the most relevant literature concerning internal and external networks, and brings them together by formulating a number of major research questions in a simple framework. These research questions can be used by academics as a starting point for new research efforts aimed at improving the understanding of these phenomena, with the dual aim of contributing to theory and providing management with detailed guidelines to improve their development of new products.

REFERENCES

Aleo, J.P., Jr (1992). Redefining the manufacturer–supplier relationship, *Journal of Business Strategy*, **13**(5), 10–14.

Asmus, D. and Griffin, J. (1993). Harnessing the power of your suppliers, *The McKinsey Quarterly*, No. 3, 63–78.

Badaracco, J.L., Jr (1991). *The Knowledge Link – How Firms Compete Through Strategic Alliances*, Harvard Business School Press, Boston, MA.

Biemans, W.G. (1991). User and third-party involvement in developing medical equipment innovations, *TechnoVation*, **11**(3), 163–182.

Biemans, W.G. (1992). *Managing Innovations within Networks*, Routledge, London.

Booz, Allen and Hamilton (1968). *Management of New Products*, Booz, Allen and Hamilton Inc., New York.

Booz, Allen and Hamilton (1982). *New Products Management for the 1980s*, Booz, Allen and Hamilton Inc., New York.

Botkin, J.W. and Matthews, J.B. (1992). *Winning Combinations – The Coming Wave of Entrepreneurial Partnerships between Large and Small Companies*, John Wiley & Sons, New York.

Bronder, C. and Pritzl, R. (1992). Developing strategic alliances: A conceptual framework for successful co-operation, *European Management Journal*, **10**(4), 412–421.

Bucklin, L.P. and Sengupta, S. (1993). Organizing successful co-marketing alliances, *Journal of Marketing*, **57**, 32–46.

Burt, D.N. and Soukup, W.R. (1985). Purchasing's role in new product development, *Harvard Business Review*, September/October, 90–97.

Byrne, J.A., Brandt, R. and Port, O. (1993). The virtual corporation – The company of the future will be the ultimate in adaptability, *Business Week International*, 8 February, 36–40.

Ciccantelli, S. and Magidson, J. (1993). Consumer-idealized design: Involving consumers in the product development process, *Journal of Product Innovation Management*, **10**, 341–347.

Condit, P.M. (1994). Focusing on the customer: How Boeing does it, *Research and Technology Management*, January/February, 33–37.

Cooper, R.G. (1993). *Winning at New Products*, 2nd edn, Addison-Wesley, Reading, MA.

Crawford, C.M. (1992). The hidden costs of accelerated product development, *Journal of Product Innovation Management*, **9**, 188–199.

Czinkota, M. and Kotabe, M. (1990). Product development the Japanese way, *Journal of Business Strategy*, November/December, 31–36.

Davidow, W.H. and Malone, M.S. (1992). *The Virtual Corporation – Structuring and Revitalizing the Corporation for the 21st Century*, HarperCollins, New York.

Devlin, G. and Bleackley, M. (1988). Strategic alliances – Guidelines for success, *Long Range Planning*, **21**(5), 18–23.

Flores, F. (1993). Innovation by listening carefully to customers, *Long Range Planning*, **26**(3), 95–102.

Foxall, G.R. and Tierney, J.D. (1984). From CAP1 to CAP2: User-initiated innovation from the user's point of view, *Management Decision*, **22**(5), 3–15.

Gold, B. (1987). Approaches to accelerating product and process development, *Journal of Product Innovation Management*, **4**, 81–88.

Gupta, A.K. and Singhal, A. (1993). Managing human resources for innovation and creativity, *Research Technology Management*, May/June, 41–48.

Gupta, A.K. and Wilemon, D. (1990). Improving R&D/marketing relations: R&D's perspective, *R&D Management*, **20**(4), 277–290.

Gupta, A.K., Raj, S.P. and Wilemon, D. (1985). The R&D–marketing interface in high-technology firms, *Journal of Product Innovation Management*, **2**, 12–24.

Gupta, A.K., Raj, S.P. and Wilemon, D. (1986). A model for studying the R&D–marketing interface in the product innovation process, *Journal of Marketing*, **50**, 7–17.

Håkansson, H. (ed.) (1982). *International Marketing and Purchasing of Industrial Goods: An Interaction Approach*, John Wiley & Sons, Chichester.

Håkansson, H. (ed.) (1987). *Industrial Technological Development: A Network Approach*, Croom Helm, London.

Håkansson, H. and Eriksson, A.K. (1993). Getting innovations out of supplier networks, *Journal of Business-to-Business Marketing*, **1**(3), 3–34.

Hamel, G. (1991). Competition for competence and interpartner learning within international strategic alliances, *Strategic Management Journal*, **12**, 83–103.

Hamel, G., Doz, Y.L. and Prahalad, C.K. (1989). Collaborate with your competitors – and win, *Harvard Business Review*, **67**(1), 133–139.

Harmsen, H. (1994). Product development practice in medium-sized food processing companies: Increasing the level of market orientation, *Proceedings of the EIASM Conference on New Approaches to Development and Engineering*, May, Gothenburg, Sweden, 286–300.

Himmelfarb, P.A. (1992). *Survival of the Fittest – New Product Development During the 90s*, Prentice Hall, Englewood Cliffs, NJ.

Hise, R.T., O'Neal, L., Parasuraman, A. and McNeal, J.U. (1990). Marketing/R&D interaction in new product development: Implications for new product success rates, *Journal of Product Innovation Management*, **7**, 142–155.

House, C.H. and Price, R.L. (1991). The return map: Tracking product teams, *Harvard Business Review*, January/February, 92–100.

Howard, W.G., Jr. and Guile, B.R. (eds) (1992). *Profiting from Innovation – The Report of the Three-Year Study from the National Academy of Engineering*, Free Press, New York.

Huyzer, S.E., Luimes, W., Spitholt, M.G.M., Slagter, A.H. van Wijk, van der Leest, D.J. and Croese, D. (1990). *Strategische Samenwerking*, Coopers & Lybrand Dijker Van Dien, Amsterdam, Samsom BedrijfsInformatie, Alphen aan den Rijn.

Huyzer, S.E., Moëd, J., Spitholt, M.G.M., Luimes, W., Kroodsma H. and Douma, M.U. (1991). *Strategische Samenwerking; De Praktijk in Nederland*, Coopers & Lybrand Dijker Van Dien, Amsterdam, Universiteit Twente, Faculteit der Technische Bedrijfskunde, Enschede, Samsom BedrijfsInformatie, Alphen aan den Rijn.

James, B.G. (1985). Alliance: The new strategic focus, *Long Range Planning*, **18**(3), 76–81.

Kennard, R.B. (1991). From experience: Japanese product development process, *Journal of Product Innovation Management*, **8**(3), 184–189.

Larson, A. (1991). Partner networks: Leveraging external ties to improve entrepreneurial performance, *Journal of Business Venturing*, **6**, 173–188.

Lei, D. (1993). Offensive and defensive uses of alliances, *Long Range Planning*, **26**(4), 32–41.

Lei, D. and Slocum, J.W., Jr. (1992). Global strategy, competence building and strategic alliances, *California Management Review*, Fall, 81–97.

Leverick, F. and Littler, D. (1993). *Risks and Rewards of Collaboration: A Survey of Product Development Collaboration in UK Companies*, Manchester School of Management, UMIST, Manchester.

Lipnack, J. and Stamps, J. (1993). *The TeamNet Factor – Bringing the Power of Boundary Crossing Into the Heart of Your Business*, Oliver Wight Publications, Essex Junction, VT.

Lorange, P. and Roos, J. (1991). Why some strategic alliances succeed and others fail, *Journal of Business Strategy*, January/February, 25–30.

Lorange, P. and Roos, J. (1992). *Strategic Alliances – Formation, Implementation and Evolution*, Blackwell, Cambridge, MA.

Lynch, R.P. (1993). *Business Alliances Guide – The Hidden Competitive Weapon*, John Wiley & Sons, New York.

Mabert, V.A., Muth, J.F. and Schmenner, R.W. (1992). Collapsing new product development times: Six case studies, *Journal of Product Innovation Management*, 9(3), 200–212.

Magnet, M. (1994). The new golden rule of business, *Fortune*, 21 February, 28–32.

McDonough, E.F., III and Barczak, G. (1991). Speeding up new product development: The effects of leadership style and source of technology, *Journal of Product Innovation Management*, 8, 203–211.

Moenaert, R.K., Souder, W.E., De Meyer, A. and Deschoolmeester, D. (1994). R&D–marketing integration mechanisms, communication flows, and innovation success, *Journal of Product Innovation Management*, 11, 31–45.

Nelson, E. (1994). Boeing gets airlines on board, *Business Marketing*, 79(5), 3.

Niederkofler, M. (1991). The evolution of strategic alliances: Opportunities for managerial influence, *Journal of Business Venturing*, 6, 237–257.

Parker, G.M. (1994). *Cross-Functional Teams*, Josey-Bass, San Francisco, CA.

Parkinson, S.T. (1982). The role of the user in successful new product development, *R&D Management*, 12(3), 123–131.

Peters, T. (1994). *The Tom Peters Seminar – Crazy Times Call for Crazy Organizations*, Vintage Books, New York.

Port, O., Carey, J., Kelley, K. and Anderson Forest, S. (1992). Quality – Small and midsize companies seize the challenge – Not a moment too soon, *Business Week International*, 7 December, 64–69.

Power, C., Kerwin, K., Grover, R., Alexander, K. and Hof, R.D. (1993). Flops – Too many new products fail. Here's why – and how to do better, *Business Week International*, 16 August, 34–39.

Prokesch, S.E. (1993). Mastering chaos at the high-tech frontier: An interview with Silicon Graphics's Ed McCracken, *Harvard Business Review*, November/December, 135–144.

Reich, R.B. and Mankin, E.D. (1986). Joint ventures with Japan give away our future, *Harvard Business Review*, March/April, 78–86.

Rosenthal, S.R. (1992). *Effective Product Design and Development – How to Cut Lead Time and Increase Customer Satisfaction*, Business One, Richard Irwin, Homewood, IL.

Shaw, B. (1986). The role of the interaction between the manufacturer and the user in the technological innovation process, PhD thesis, Science Policy Research Unit, University of Sussex, Brighton.

Slowinski, G., Farris, G.F. and Jones, D. (1993). Strategic partnering: Process instead of event, *Research Technology Management*, May/June, 22–25.

Smith, P.G. and Reinertsen, D.G. (1991). *Developing Products in Half the Time*, Van Nostrand Reinhold, New York.

Sonnenberg, F.K. (1992). Partnering: Entering the age of cooperation, *Journal of Business Strategy*, **13**(3), 49–52.

Souder, W.E. (1981). Disharmony between R&D and marketing, *Industrial Marketing Management*, **10**, 67–73.

Starr, M.K. (1992). Accelerating innovation, *Business Horizons*, July/August, 44–51.

Thamhain, H.J. (1990). Managing technologically innovative team efforts toward new product success, *Journal of Product Innovation Management*, **7**, 5–18.

Truett, S. and Barrett, T. (1991). In Bendikt, M. (ed.), *Cyberspace: First Steps*, MIT Press, Boston, MA.

Van der Hart, H.W.C. (1993). Techniek en marketing; Verschillen in opvatting en perceptie (1), *Tijdschrift voor Marketing*, February, 6–12.

Vesey, J.T. (1992). Time-to-market: Put speed in product development, *Industrial Marketing Management*, **21**, 151–158.

Von Braun, C-F. (1990). The Acceleration Trap, *Sloan Management Review*, **31**, 49–58.

Von Hippel, E. (1978). Successful industrial products from customer ideas, *Journal of Marketing*, **42**, 39–49.

Voss, C.A. (1985). The role of users in the development of applications software, *Journal of Product Innovation Management*, **2**(2), 113–121.

Williams, A.J. and Smith, W.C. (1990). Involving purchasing in product development, *Industrial Marketing Management*, **19**, 315–319.

Workman, J.P., Jr. (1993). Marketing's limited role in new product development in one computer systems firm, *Journal of Marketing Research*, **XXX**, 405–421.

CHAPTER EIGHT

A MANAGEMENT FRAMEWORK FOR COLLABORATIVE PRODUCT DEVELOPMENT

Margaret Bruce, Fiona Leverick and Dale Littler

It is apparent that more and more organisations are collaborating in the development of new products. The benefits of collaboration have been well documented and are linked to the complexity and costliness of product development and the need for inputs from wide and varied areas of expertise as well as shorter lead times for product development. This is particularly evident in information and communication technology (ICT) sectors, so much so that part of the 'received wisdom' of ICT companies is that collaboration is the preferred route for product development. But the risks and costs of collaborative product development have been less well articulated. It is argued that the alleged rewards of collaboration may not be achieved in practice. Management practice can facilitate the effective outcome of collaborative product development, and the critical management factors affecting the likelihood of 'successful' collaboration are presented here.

INTRODUCTION

The importance of new product development to business competitiveness has long been recognised. Yet product development is widely acknowledged as being risky: the rate of failure of new products is high and the costs of

---

Product Development: Meeting the Challenge of the Design–Marketing Interface.
Edited by M. Bruce and W.G. Biemans.   © 1995 John Wiley & Sons Ltd.

development can be prohibitive. Indeed, it has been suggested that new product development is becoming *more* complex, involving diverse technologies and rapidly mutating markets. Moreover, as product life cycles apparently shorten and the pace of technological change increases, there are pressures to reduce product development periods (Cooper and Kleinschmidt 1987; Millson, Raj and Wilemon 1992).

Collaborative product development has been promoted as a means of effectively managing some of these more problematic aspects of new product development. The supposed benefits of cooperation include spreading the costs and risks of product development, gaining access to technological expertise and acceleration of the product development process. As such, interest in collaboration as a strategy for product development appears to have increased markedly, especially in the new technology-based sectors of information and communications technology (ICT) and biotechnology, where collaborative ventures are widespread (Anonymous 1993). Indeed, in recent literature, there has been extensive and, at times, unquestioning promotion of the case for collaboration in new product development. Hamel, Doz and Prahalad (1989), for instance, state that:

> The case for collaboration is stronger than ever. It takes so much money to develop new products and to penetrate new markets that few companies can go it alone.

It is somewhat surprising, however, that the possible risks and costs of collaboration are often less prominently articulated, despite growing evidence that collaborations do not always meet the expectations of the collaborating partners. For example, in a study of over 895 collaborations, in only 45% of cases were both of the partners satisfied with the outcome (Harrigan 1986).

The focus of the research discussed in this chapter is on product development collaboration in ICT sectors, and it draws on a major UK study of the collaborative development of ICT products. After a review of the literature relating to collaborative product development, the relative costs and rewards of collaborative product development are discussed, and management practices and other factors contributing to the likelihood of a positive outcome are considered. A framework for effective collaboration management is suggested.

STIMULI TO COLLABORATIVE PRODUCT DEVELOPMENT

Collaboration may be stimulated by technological change, providing a means for organisations with an established technological base to secure access to other technologies or skills (Berg, Duncan and Friedman 1982; Hamel, Doz and Prahalad 1989), as has clearly been the case in the biotechnology industry (Burrill and Ernst & Young 1989). The allegedly increasing convergence of technologies is said to have led to greater collaboration in product development. Blonder and Pritzl (1992) argue that:

> the long-term benefit of strategic alliances is the access to complementary competencies and the exchange of information between partners. In the light of industries such as computer [sic] and telecommunication moving closer together, one company or business unit might not be able to exploit promising opportunities by itself.

Collaboration may also provide a means to market access, stimulated by the ostensibly increasing globalisation of industries and the rapid rate of product obsolescence in some industries. Through collaboration, new products may be marketed more quickly in several regions (Littler, Leverick and Wilson 1993), while collaboration may also be a means of overcoming various barriers to entry to foreign markets (Kent 1991).

Collaboration, it is alleged, may provide a means of sharing the costs and risks of product development (Gugler 1992; Lorange and Roos 1991; Rice 1991). It is debatable, however, whether such cost cutting is actually achieved in practice, with evidence from past research (Leverick and Littler 1993) suggesting that this may not always be the case.

Similarly, some authors further assert that collaboration can not only reduce the cost and risk of product development to a single organisation, but can also reduce the time taken in product development (Dodgson 1992; Guy and Georghiou 1991), the latter being particularly significant, given the increased emphasis on reducing 'time-to-market' (Millson, Raj and Wilemon 1992). Again, however, whether or not such time reductions are necessarily achieved in practice is certainly debatable (Leverick and Littler 1993). Furthermore, the empirical evidence to support the need for such rapid development *per se* is itself questionable. An organisation will not necessarily benefit from being the first to enter a market; indeed, the risks of such pioneer strategies in product development are well documented (Schaars 1986).

In addition to the more 'rational' cost and benefit analyses described, the belief that collaboration is an effective strategy for product development may in itself serve as a compelling driving force. We would suggest that in certain sectors, ICT included, such a belief in the merits of collaboration has apparently become part of the received wisdom of the sector, and an unquestioned part of product development strategy.

DISINCENTIVES TO COLLABORATE

However, the dogma of collaborative product development has been questioned. A small but growing number of studies indicate that collaboration can be costly and unsuccessful, and that the expectations of the collaborating parties are not always satisfied (Harrigan 1986; Killing 1982; Norburn and Schoenberg 1990). For instance, the costs associated with the time and effort necessary to manage the collaboration, including setting up the collaboration, monitoring its progress, and, where necessary, attempting to harmonise the different cultures and operating styles of the parties involved, can be considerable (Farr and Fischer 1992). The upfront work to establish time scales and operating procedures may be particularly demanding, as Lorange and Roos (1991) suggest: 'strategic alliances represent a demanding way of working for both parents' management teams, requiring top management's time and energy'.

Collaboration is also likely to lead to a reduction in the direct control held by one organisation over the product development in question (Ohmae 1989). As Collins and Doorley (1991) state, 'strategic partnership is appropriate only when you don't want control, you can't afford it, you don't need it, or you are not allowed it'.

Concerns about the leakage of information, experience and skills that are part of the 'core competencies' of an organisation and proprietary to its future operations (Hamel, Doz and Prahalad 1989) may hinder the formation of open organisational relationships, yet this is problematic in the light of studies suggesting that trust is an important lubricant of effective collaborations. It may be appropriate to draw boundaries, as it were, around certain company assets so that knowledge about other aspects of the business is not so freely disclosed (Gugler 1992; Hamel, Doz and Prahalad 1989), thereby protecting the key competencies that are the source of the firm's competitiveness. However, given the extent of communication at different levels of the organisation, this may not be effective in practice.

Furthermore, collaboration may also incur significant opportunity costs because undue effort and resources are directed towards developing a successful collaboration. Thus, it is the maintenance of this relationship *per se* which becomes the all-consuming objective, at the expense of other activities and the commercial contribution of the collaboration itself. It may be that a true calculus of alternative strategies to collaboration is not made because of the dominance of the view that collaboration is an essential ingredient of competitiveness.

FACTORS AFFECTING THE COLLABORATIVE PROCESS

Considerable attention has been directed towards the influences affecting the collaboration process, a subject made complex by the fact that what is regarded as a 'successful' outcome is by no means straightforward. As Dodgson (1993) states:

> It is notoriously difficult to define success in collaboration. The range of firms' circumstances and their expectations and experiences of collaboration are so variable as to make uniform definitions of success and failure unwise.

There are numerous ways of assessing the performance of a collaborative relationship aimed at developing a product, each of which could be used as a single measure or in conjunction with other measures. For example:

- Measurement by objectives and commercial outcomes: whether the particular collaborative project meets the objectives initially set for it, for instance in terms of time, profit and cost targets (although initial objectives may become less appropriate as a basis for measuring 'success' as circumstances change; see Hellan, Hovi and Nieminen (1992)) and whether its commercial outcomes are deemed to be 'successful' in terms of profit levels or other measures such as market share, although such measurement itself can be somewhat problematic (Crawford 1987; Leverick and Littler 1994).
- Strategic measures: whether, for example, the relationship opens up previously unavailable market opportunities, or lays the path for continuing and productive further relationships between the collaborating organisations.
- Measures of experience gained: the value of accumulating experience in collaboration management which may assist in improving the effectiveness of future collaborative projects (Hlavacek 1974; Littler, Leverick and Wilson 1993).

Research into the management factors contributing to 'successful' collaborative relationships, however these might be defined, has been extensive, tending to focus on collaboration inputs (such as the choice of a suitable partner, establishing clear collaboration objectives and drawing up procedures for accountability and control) and ongoing collaborative management factors (such as frequent monitoring of progress, building a climate of 'trust' and attempting to maintain equality of contribution and benefit) (Gyenes 1991; Lynch 1990; Lyons 1991).

It is against this background that the study of collaborative product development relationships in ICT sectors was conducted.

RESEARCH OBJECTIVES AND METHOD

The primary objective of the research reported here was to analyse various aspects of collaboration management aimed at the development of existing or new products. A mail questionnaire was administered to 300 UK companies involved in the information technology or telecommunications sectors. The companies were selected randomly from trade directories covering mobile communications, computer components, hardware or systems manufacturers and software suppliers (the *Computer Users Yearbook*, the *Software Users Yearbook* and the *Communications Users Yearbook*, all of 1992). A response rate of 36% was achieved. Details of the sample are shown in Table 8.1.

Table 8.1   Respondent sample details

Details	Respondents (%)
Nature of main business:	
Telecommunications equipment manufacturers	43
Computer hardware/systems manufacturers	23
Computer component manufacturers	15
Computer software producers	19
Number of employees:	
1–50	11.3
51–100	24.7
101–200	12.3
201–500	22.6
501–1000	10.3
1001 plus	20.6
Turnover (1992/93) (£ million):	
Under 5	19.6
5–9.99	13.4
10–19.99	19.6
20–49.99	17.5
50–99.99	12.4
100 plus	17.5
Pre-tax profit (loss) (1992/93) (£ million):	
Over 10	10.3
5–9.9	5.2
1–4.99	18.6
Up to 0.99	30.9
(Up to 0.99)	20.6
(1–4.99)	4.1
(5–9.99)	5.1
(Over 10)	5.1

These sample details are derived from the responses of 97 of the 106 respondents to the questionnaire, the remaining 9 respondents wishing to remain entirely anonymous.

Source: Bruce et al. (1995); reproduced by permission

Sixty-one per cent of the sample had been involved in a major collaborative product development project during the past two years, and all of the respondents had participated in collaborative product development to some extent. It is worth noting that this may reflect a degree of sample bias, in that respondents with a major involvement in collaborative product development would have been more likely to complete and return a questionnaire on the topic.

This chapter focuses on just one aspect of the study: the factors that improve the effectiveness of product development collaboration. This was approached from two angles in the questionnaire survey. Firstly, an analysis of the factors discriminating between examples of 'successful' and 'less successful' collaborations was undertaken. The issue of identifying 'successful' collaborations is one that has received some attention in the literature and was discussed earlier. In our analysis, examples of 'successful' and 'less successful' collaborations were self-nominated by respondents in order to avoid the difficulties of classification by the researchers. Further discussion of the way in which 'success' was defined by respondents is contained in Leverick and Littler (1993). Secondly, survey respondents were asked freely to indicate the factors that, from their own experience in collaboration management, contributed most to effective product development collaboration.

RESEARCH RESULTS

The impact of collaboration on the process of product development was considered. Respondents were asked:

> From your experience, how does collaboration affect the process of product development?

and to indicate their level of agreement with a set of statements about the effect of collaboration on the product development process. A five-point scale ranging from 'strongly agree' (1) to 'strongly disagree' (5) was used to assess each statement, and the average score for each statement was ascertained. The statements and scores are presented in Table 8.2; a lower average score denotes a higher level of agreement.

From Table 8.2, it is clear that many respondents regarded collaboration as making product development more costly, complex and difficult to control and manage. While these are subjective perceptions, nonetheless they question the widespread enthusiasm for collaboration, suggesting that this needs to be somewhat tempered.

Table 8.2   The effect of collaboration on the product development process: responses to the question, 'From your experience, how does collaboration affect the process of product development?'

Collaboration generally . . .	Agree/ strongly agree (%)	Disagree/ strongly disagree (%)	Average score
Makes product development more costly	51	22	2.66
Complicates product development	41	35	3.03
Makes it more difficult to control and manage the product development process	41	38	3.08
Makes product development more responsive to supplier needs	36	26	2.76
Makes product development more efficient	35	41	3.36
Emphasises accountability in product development	30	44	3.38
Allows product development to adapt better to uncertainty	27	43	3.30
Accelerates product development	25	58	3.46
Makes product development more responsive to customer needs	22	50	3.40
Allows product development to respond better to market opportunities	15	63	3.74
Enhances the competitive benefits arising through product development	12	65	3.72
Facilitates the incorporation of new technology in product development	7	70	3.77

Source: Bruce et al. (1995); reproduced by permission

These findings are supplemented by respondents' views on the major risks of collaborative product development. Collaboration was seen as involving such risks as leaking critical information to a partner, who may, at some stage, use this information to their own competitive advantage, and having to deal with a partner's changing commitment during the product development process. These and other risks are potential disbenefits which need to be weighed carefully against the potential benefits of collaborative product development.

However, the reservations expressed had not deterred the participants from embarking on collaborations for product development, and a proportion had considerable experience of collaborative ventures. Critical factors affecting the management of collaborations were identified in the survey and are discussed here.

Table 8.3 contains a list of 20 factors that, after a review of the literature, were considered by the researchers as possible influences on the outcome of product development collaborations. Respondents were asked to indicate the

Table 8.3 Discriminating factors between successful and less successful collaborations

Factor	Difference in mean score (less experience)	Difference in mean score (more experience)
The collaborating partners failed to contribute as expected	2.17	2.67
There was a lack of frequent consultation between the collaborating partners	1.67	1.64
Benefits between the collaborators were perceived as 'evenly' distributed	1.21	1.43
The relationship was perceived as being very important to the collaborators	1.17	1.14
There was a champion for the collaboration	1.07	1.27
There was little 'trust' between the collaborating partners	0.67	2.14
A long-term view of strategic benefits was taken	1.10	0.86
There was little consultation between marketing and technical personnel	1.17	1.05
There was clear project planning with defined 'task milestones'	1.14	0.76
Adequate staff resources were made available to the collaboration	0.89	1.19
Little attention was given to marketing issues	0.73	1.24
Sufficient budgetary resources were made available to the collaboration	0.66	0.90
Senior management was closely involved in the collaboration	0.50	0.95
Sufficient time resources were made available to the collaboration	0.71	1.10
Corporate systems and management style were flexible	0.43	1.33
Specific roles and responsibilities were not clearly allocated	0.82	0.23
The product development did not fit naturally with existing businesses	0.30	1.00
There was little previous experience of collaboration management	0.17	0.23
Purely financial measures of progress in the collaboration were avoided	0.37	0.24
The product or concept being developed was highly innovative	0.73	1.09

Source: Littler, Leverick and Bruce (1995); reproduced by permission of the editor from the *Journal of Product Innovation Management*, an international publication of the Product Development and Management Association and Elsevier Science, Inc.

extent to which each of the factors shown in Table 8.3 was present in a self-nominated example of a 'successful' collaboration and in an 'unsuccessful' collaboration using a scale of 1 (strongly disagree) to 5 (strongly agree). In order to achieve a measure of the importance of each factor in discriminating between 'successful' and 'unsuccessful' collaborations, the mean scores of each factor were calculated for both the 'successful' and 'unsuccessful' collaborations.

Further analysis was carried out by focusing on the responses of those organisations in the sample with proportionally more experience of collaborative product development in the past two years. The purpose of this exercise was to examine whether different factors became more or less significant in discriminating between successful and less successful collaborations as organisational experience in collaboration was accumulated. The difference between the mean scores for respondents with proportionally more and proportionally less experience of collaboration are both presented in Table 8.3. Experience in collaboration was proxied using the responses to one particular question in the questionnaire which required respondents to estimate the proportion of major new product developments that had been carried out collaboratively over the past two years. Responses were categorised as either 'under 25% of product development' (63% of respondents) or '25% of product development or over' (37% of respondents). It was this 37% of respondents which was classified as having 'more experience of collaborative product development'.

From Table 8.3, it is clear that a number of factors were particularly influential in contributing to effective collaboration. The most powerful discriminating factors between 'successful' and 'less successful' collaborations were:

- whether the collaborating parties contributed as expected
- whether there was frequent consultation between partners, particularly between marketing and technical staff
- whether benefits were perceived as evenly distributed
- whether the relationship was perceived as important by all parties involved
- whether there was a 'collaboration champion'
- whether there was a substantial degree of trust between collaborating parties
- whether there was clear project planning with defined task milestones

Clearly, it is possible to influence all of these factors to a greater or lesser degree. These findings are therefore of considerable importance to companies hoping to increase the probability of achieving a relatively successful collaboration.

When the responses of organisations with proportionally move experience of collaborative product development are considered, a number of factors increased considerably in their discriminatory power. Most notable were the presence of trust between collaborating parties, the attention paid to 'marketing issues', flexibility of management systems and style, and the fit of the project with existing businesses. These factors will be discussed in more detail when considering the second analysis of the factors affecting collaboration outcome: that of the responses freely specified by survey participants.

Respondents were asked to indicate the major factors that, in their experience, contributed most to the success of collaborative product development.

Table 8.4   Respondents' view of factors affecting
outcomes of collaborative product development

Factor	Respondents freely mentioning factor (%)
Choice of partner	**39**
Culture/mode of operation	13
Mutual understanding	12
Complementary expertise/strengths	12
Past collaboration experience	2
Establishing the ground rules	**67**
Clearly defined objectives agreed by all parties	41
Clearly defined responsibilities agreed by all parties	19
Realistic aims	10
Defined project milestones	11
Process factors	**45**
Frequent communication/consultation	20
Mutual trust/openness/honesty	17
Regular progress reviews	13
Ensuring collaborators deliver as promised	9
Flexibility	3
Ensuring equality	**42**
Mutual benefit	22
Equality in power/dependency	11
Equality of contribution	9
People factors	**54**
Commitment at all levels	11
Collaboration champion	21
Top management commitment	10
Personal relationships	10
Staffing levels	3
Environmental factors	**25**
Market need for product	17
Economic factors/recession	3

Source: Bruce et al. (1995); reproduced by permission

An open-ended question format was used, and the responses obtained were categorised by the researchers. These categorised responses were then grouped further to reveal that six types of response were particularly frequently mentioned (see Table 8.4):

- choice of partner
- establishing the ground rules
- ensuring equality
- process factors
- people factors
- environmental factors

It should be noted here that these groupings are somewhat arbitrary, and are significant only for the purposes of simplifying the presentation of results. However, they do reflect, to some degree, an existing emphasis in the literature on collaboration. As Table 8.4 shows, factors relating to establishing the 'ground rules' for collaborative product development, and agreement on clearly defined collaboration objectives, in particular, were the more frequently mentioned. However, confirming some of the results shown in Table 8.3, the importance of frequent consultation, perceived mutual benefit, the existence of a 'collaboration champion' and the presence of mutual trust and openness were also some of the most frequently mentioned factors. Each of the categories of factor shown in Table 8.4 is now discussed in more detail.

CHOICE OF PARTNER

Compatibility of culture, which embraces operating and management styles, is a critical aspect of 'choice of partner'. The experiences of survey respondents provide insight into this factor. One respondent stated that:

> A joint venture with a Japanese company failed in almost every sense and the resulting product lost a considerable amount of money. There were severe culture problems, a complete lack of understanding of each other and differing objectives, although this was not made open to each other at the time.

Up-front investment in attempting to develop an appreciation of each other and being willing to accommodate and adjust to another's point of view would appear worthwhile. Adaptability is required because it is not possible to ensure that perfect 'understanding' is obtained, and unanticipated changes, such as movement of personnel, can bring about altered conditions and circumstances. The nature of organisational differences is revealed by a brief examination of the experiences of one of the companies involved in the research, Comtel.

Case 1: Organisational Differences

Comtel and ATN collaborated for three years on the development of Product X. Company names have been changed for reasons of confidentiality. Comtel was proactive in establishing the relationship with ATN, because ATN was the only organisation that possessed the necessary expertise to develop Product X and it was not already working with Comtel's competitors. Product X was subject to considerable delays in production. Comtel places much of the blame for these delays on managers at ATN, who were not able to deliver what they promised:

ATN were not as honest as they might have been. They didn't understand what was involved and weren't prepared to admit the possibility of facing [delays in production] early enough.

Comtel felt that ATN held the balance of power in the relationship, because Comtel had no feasible alternative choice of partner and did not hold the necessary expertise and production capacity in-house. For this reason, the managing director of Comtel spent considerable time and effort trying to prevent the 'unthinkable' possibility of ATN withdrawing altogether.

From ATN's perspective, the balance of power appeared to lie firmly with Comtel. Such was the perceived strategic importance of the Comtel collaboration to ATN that, without it, there was some doubt that one ATN division would continue to be financed. As an ATN manager stated, 'we were desperate for the business'.

Overall, Comtel has found ATN a difficult organisation with which to do business. Comtel considers itself to be 'marketing led' and 'flexible'. ATN is seen by Comtel as 'engineering orientated', 'rigid and inflexible' and 'excessively formal'. Negotiating with ATN is described by Comtel as 'painful in the extreme', since ATN staff tended to adhere rigidly to formal procedures, involving lawyers in even minor negotiations. There is little doubt among managers at Comtel that the differences in culture and operating styles between the two organisations have considerably slowed progress in the collaboration. However, Comtel dealt with the situation simply by learning to live with these differences:

> In the end you have to accept. If [ATN] has to have everything in writing because they're scared stiff of getting the sack otherwise, you have to accept it.

Comtel has been able to effect such an acceptance primarily through the significant role played by its technical director, who describes himself as the collaboration 'mentor'. However, recent developments in the relationship indicate that even his patience has been exhausted, as Comtel has finally begun to work with additional partners.

ESTABLISHING THE GROUND RULES

Factors concerned with the process of initially setting up the collaborative development project – establishing the ground rules – were by far the most frequently mentioned in the survey as contributing to 'success'. Of these factors, the need for clearly defined objectives agreed by all parties was mentioned most frequently (41% of respondents). However, achieving what is desirable may differ from what is possible because circumstances can change; hence, a strict adherence to the initial objectives may not be feasible. There is clearly a need to agree procedures at the outset that can deal with possible changes.

PROCESS FACTORS

Another dimension is that of the process of managing the collaboration relationship, mentioned by 45% of the sample. This includes the need for frequent communication, mutual trust, regular progress reviews and ensuring that collaborators deliver as agreed.

Regular communication helps to foster commitment and ensure that deadlines are adhered to, as well as establishing trust between parties. The need to balance trust and openness with not releasing proprietary information can be a delicate balance to achieve. Flexibility and adaptability may mean that a highly structured relationship becomes more fluid and less structured over time as progress is made and trust is engendered between collaborators. Regular progress review meetings help to ensure that progress is made and that problems are aired and resolved.

ENSURING EQUALITY

Perceived equality between collaborators was mentioned by 42% of respondents. It relates to the balance of contribution during the venture and the benefits and contributions resulting from the collaboration. Dissatisfaction and resentment may ensue if one party feels that it is giving more to the collaboration than other parties, and can result in early termination. The level of contribution can be monitored during progress reviews to prevent this becoming a major issue leading to failure. Overdependence on a 'weaker' partner can mean that it directs its efforts to suiting the needs and demands of a 'stronger' partner, which may be detrimental to the 'weaker' partner. One respondent suggests that:

> The key to success in any collaboration must be to give added benefits to both parties on an equitable basis. At the end of the project you must have two winners not one.

PEOPLE FACTORS

The actions and commitment of the people involved are fundamental to the success of any venture, and 54% of respondents cited this factor. As one respondent stated:

You don't get collaboration between Company X and Company Y, you get a collaboration between people in Company X and people in Company Y.

Individuals can constructively shape the collaboration, or they can act to destroy it. The need for a collaboration champion was mentioned by 21% of respondents. The commitment of one or more key individuals marshalling support for the collaboration and taking the time and effort to resolve collaboration difficulties is important. Using the term 'mentor' to describe this role, one participant outlines the value of such a person, as follows:

Whilst humans are resourceful and will find solutions to problems given time, there is a need in collaborations for someone who will bang a spear on the ground and says follow me.

ENVIRONMENTAL FACTORS

These are generally factors beyond the direct control of management, such as market forces and customer preferences, changes to legislation and competitors' actions. In attempts to make the collaboration work, participants may ignore the wider context and its dynamics, which could have an important influence on the outcome. Interestingly enough, those respondents with more collaboration experience were more likely to refer to the effect of environmental factors. Frequent monitoring of the external environment carried out throughout the collaboration, along with some flexibility or response to any changes, is likely to be beneficial. The experiences of Telzone, a company involved in the research project, clearly illustrate this point.

Case 2: The Influence of the Environment

Telzone and Pace collaborated for 18 months on the development of Product Z. Company names have been changed for reasons of confidentiality. On Telzone's insistence, development teams were set up in both organisations to work on the project, composed of individuals with specific responsibility for 'making the relationship work'. Telzone's development team was a 'multi-disciplinary task force' of employees from the areas of marketing, technology and finance. Telzone placed considerable pressures on Pace to adopt a similarly multidisciplinary development team. Pace was keen to maintain amicable working relations with Telzone and attempted to set up such a team, although the Pace team was eventually based primarily around engineering expertise, since Pace was an engineering company.

The two development teams met regularly. While, in general, they were 'left to get on with it', there were also periodic meetings with the managing directors of the two organisations. Between formal meetings, according to both Telzone and Pace, considerable informal communication also took place.

Around a year after the collaboration began, Product Z, fully developed, was launched as part of a more comprehensive product package. Market response to the package was highly disappointing and, because of poor sales, it was withdrawn from the market within 18 months.

The influence of factors outside the scope of the collaborative process had a significant impact on the outcome of the collaboration. While considerable attention was paid to the internal management of the collaboration, it was only when Product Z was launched that some of its limitations became apparent to Telzone and Pace. The product did not conform to industry standards and was not offering potential customers appreciable advantages over products that were already available. There was an almost complete lack of attention to marketing considerations, which undoubtedly contributed to poor adoption. It may be that the collaboration processes concentrated too much on ensuring inter-organisational harmony and on preserving social interrelationships, rather than on the development of a marketable product. It is clear that considerable emphasis was placed on maintaining good working and personal contacts between the two organisations: neither party had any desire to 'rock the boat'. Little market research was carried out at Telzone into the design of Product Z. Pace was initially somewhat concerned about this, but did not pursue the issue, preferring to maintain the amicable relationship between the two organisations.

COLLABORATIVE PROCESS MODEL

Taking the key factors that have been identified as positively affecting product development collaboration, it is possible to draw up a schematic model of the collaborative process. The model is shown in Figure 8.1. It is not intended to be prescriptive, but simply to act as a guideline or checklist of the kinds of success factors that may aid the management process for collaborative product development.

CONCLUSIONS

Collaborative product development is typically regarded as a route to reducing the costs and spreading the risks of product development, reducing the time taken to develop products, sharing expertise and know-how, and

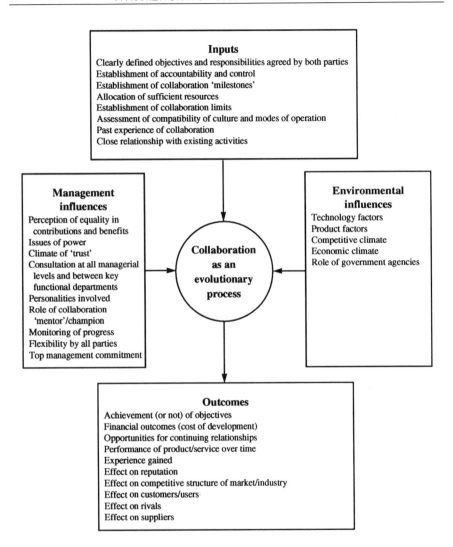

Figure 8.1 Factors affecting product development collaboration (Bruce et al. 1995); reproduced by permission

providing access to global markets. Such an approach to product development appears to be becoming somewhat prescriptive and part of the 'received wisdom' in ICT sectors.

As such, engaging in collaboration has been widely promoted as a means of improving the effectiveness of the new product development process. However, there is also a growing body of evidence charting the risks and high failure rates associated with collaborative ventures. It might be concluded that, in some sectors, the motivation to collaborate in product development is related less to a careful evaluation of the costs and benefits of such activity and more to 'softer' factors, such as an organisational or individual history of engaging in collaborative activity, or to 'strategic' factors, such as pressure to imitate competitors.

Those who have carried out collaborative ventures are more cautious in their perceptions of collaboration than the literature might suggest. The research reported here, involving UK ICT suppliers, highlights some of the potentially negative consequences of collaboration, such as lengthening the product development process, adding to costs and being difficult to control.

While recognising that the assessment of collaboration success is by no means straightforward, there is clearly a question of how the chances of achieving a positive collaboration outcome can be optimised. It is not our aim to present simple 'recipes for success', which so often results in statements that are so general as to be unhelpful, especially given the complexity and variety of environments in which new product development takes place. Rather, our aim was to identify items that should be on management's agenda for consideration when engaging in collaborative new product development. It is the combined influence of numerous and often complex factors that affects collaboration outcome. Thus, 'successful' collaboration is likely to result from blending a whole spectrum of influences. These involve putting in place agreed structures and processes that pay regard to both internal issues, such as those of accountability and control, and external issues, such as those of market developments, as well as attempting to maintain perceived equality of contributions and returns between partners. In addition, it is important to ensure that an effective 'collaboration champion' is in place and to pay attention to the cultural, social and psychological influences on the collaboration process. There is also a need for retaining flexibility, because collaborative arrangements, like any aspect of marketing strategy, will always be subject to the unpredicted. Above all, what is clear is that the factors affecting the 'success' of collaboration for new product development are diverse and often somewhat contradictory. It is important to achieve an appropriate balance between these influences for the particular collaboration in question.

ACKNOWLEDGEMENTS

The research reported here was undertaken by the authors and was financed by the Economic and Social Research Council's Programme on Information and Communication Technologies (PICT).

REFERENCES

Berg, S.V., Duncan, J. and Friedman, P. (1982). *Joint Venture Strategies and Corporate Innovation*, Oelgeschlager, Gunn and Hall, Cambridge.
Blonder, C. and Pritzl, R. (1992). Developing strategic alliances: A conceptual framework for successful co-operation, *European Management Journal*, **10**(4), 412–421.
Bruce, M., Leverick, F., Littler, D. and Wilson, D. (1995). Success factors for collaborative product development: A study of suppliers of information and communication technology, *R&D Management*, **25**(1), 33–44.
Burrill, G.S. and Ernst & Young High Technology Group (1989). *Biotech 90: Into the Next Decade*, Mary Ann Liebert, New York.
Collins, T.M. and Doorley, T.L. (1991). *Teaming Up for the 1990s*, Business One, Richard Irwin, Homewood, IL.
Cooper, R.G. and Kleinschmidt, E.J. (1987). Success factors in product innovation, *Industrial Marketing Management*, **16**, 215–223.
Crawford, C.M. (1987). New product failure rates: A reprise, *Research Management*, **30**(4), 20–24.
Dodgson, M. (1992). Technological collaboration, *Futures*, **24**(5), 459–470.
Dodgson, M. (1993). *Technological Collaboration in Industry*, Routledge, London.
The Economist (1993). The *Economist* survey of multinationals, 22, March.
Farr, C.M. and Fischer, W.A. (1992). Managing international high technology co-operative projects, *R&D Management*, **22**(1), 55–67.
Gugler, P. (1992). Building transnational alliances to create competitive advantage, *Long Range Planning*, **25**(1), 90–99.
Guy, K. and Georghiou, L. (1991). *The Alvey Programme on Advanced Information Technology*, HMSO, London.
Gyenes, L.A. (1991). Build the foundation for a successful joint venture, *Journal of Business Strategy*, **26**(6), 27–43.
Hamel, G., Doz, Y.L. and Prahalad, C.K. (1989). Collaborate with your competitors – and win, *Harvard Business Review*, **67**(1), 133–139.
Harrigan, K.R. (1986). *Managing for Joint Venture Success*, Lexington Books, Lexington, MA.
Hellan, P., Hovi, N. and Nieminen, J. (1992). Defining the concept of interim co-operation, presented at the 8th annual IMP Conference, Lyon, September.
Hlavacek, J.D. (1974). Towards more successful venture management, *Journal of Marketing*, **38**, 56–60.
Kent, D.H. (1991). Joint ventures versus non-joint ventures: An empirical investigation, *Strategic Management Journal*, **12**, 383–393.
Killing, J.P. (1982). How to make a global joint venture work, *Harvard Business Review*, May/June, 120–125.
Leverick, F. and Littler, D.A. (1993). *The Risks and Rewards of Collaboration: A Survey of Collaborative Product Development in UK Companies*, Manchester, Manchester School of Management, UMIST.
Leverick, F. and Littler, D.A. (1994). Developing Telepoint in the UK: A study of the role of marketing in new product development, in Biemans, W., Bruce, M. and Littler, D.A. (eds), *Proceedings of Workshop 'Meeting the Challenges of Product Development'*, 7–10 May, Manchester, Manchester School of Management, UMIST.
Littler, D.A., Leverick, F. and Bruce, M. (1995). Factors affecting the process of collaborative product development: A study of UK manufacturers of information and communications technology products, *Journal of Product Innovation Management*, **12**(1, January), 1–18.

Littler, D.A., Leverick, F. and Wilson, D.F. (1993). Collaboration in new technology based product markets, *Technology Analysis and Strategic Management*, **5**(3), 211–233.

Lorange, P. and Roos, J. (1991). Why some strategic alliances succeed and others fail, *Journal of Business Strategy*, January/February, 25–30.

Lynch, R.P. (1990). Building alliances to penetrate European markets, *Journal of British Strategy*, **11**(2), 4–8.

Lyons, M.P. (1991). Joint ventures as strategic choice: A literature review, *Long Range Planning*, **24**(4), 130–144.

Millson, M.R., Raj, S.P. and Wilemon, D. (1992). A study of major approaches for accelerating new product development, *Journal of Product Innovation Management*, **9**(1), 53–69.

Norburn, D. and Schoenberg, R. (1990). Acquisitions and joint ventures: Similar arrows in the strategic quiver, presented at the British Academy of Management conference, Glasgow, September.

Ohmae, K. (1989). The global logic of strategic alliances, *Harvard Business Review*, March/April, 143–154.

Rice, V. (1991). Why teaming up is so hard to do, *Electronic Business*, 8 April, 30–34.

Schaars, S.P. (1986). When entering growth markets, are pioneers better than poachers? *Business Horizons*, **29**(2), 27–36.

CHAPTER NINE

DEVELOPING CAPABILITIES FOR INNOVATIVE PRODUCT DESIGNS: A CASE STUDY OF THE SCANDINAVIAN FURNITURE INDUSTRY

Birgit Helene Jevnaker

Improvements to the designs of firms can be made by adopting new and superior product design competence and applying it to commercial ends. By investigating a long-term designer–client relationship, which led to new and unconventional product designs, processes for adopting design improvements in a Norwegian furniture firm are delineated. Inaugurating – that is, familiarising top managers with the new design practice – emerged as an essential contribution to changing the long-term strategic direction and competitiveness of the firm.

INTRODUCTION

The capacity of firms to recognise the value of external product design competence, assimilate it and apply it to commercial ends is one of the significant factors leading to increased competitiveness (Potter et al. 1991; Walsh et al. 1992). Nevertheless, it is not well understood how designers' contributions

Product Development: Meeting the Challenge of the Design–Marketing Interface.
Edited by M. Bruce and W.G. Biemans.   © 1995 John Wiley & Sons Ltd.

are actually integrated into business contexts. Earlier research indicates that design is fragmented and managed on an *ad hoc* and tacit, rather than planned, basis (Henderson 1991). This is particularly 'observable' in firms that do not have the formal position of a design manager (Dumas and Whitfield 1989).

Assuming a significant relationship between high design competence and a firm's capabilities in product design, the following question emerges as important: how may firms acquire, absorb and exploit new talents and competencies as represented by external design professionals? In earlier research on R&D, this kind of capability is labelled *absorptive capacity*. This construct is also suitable for investigating design capabilities, for reasons referred to in the next section. Viewed from this perspective, aspects that influence the firm's absorptive capacity in product design may be identified as:

- prior design-related knowledge
- individual and organisational design learning
- earlier design efforts

These features have also been observed or suggested in empirical research on design management and product development (Henderson 1991; Kircherer 1990; Walsh et al. 1992). What has received less attention is the relationship between the external professional designer and the client firm in building product design capabilities (see Bruce and Morris, Chapter 5, this volume). In other difficult fields of learning, as in most caring professions, a relational perspective is emphasised (Lauvaas and Handal 1990). Thus, instead of investigating either the designers or the clients, the focus of the research reported here is on designer–client relationships.

Earlier literature on design management, product development and industrial competitiveness has pointed to the value of *combining* new and existing knowledge and skills in order to provide quality for the customer. However, the issue of absorbing new design skills and blending these with existing competencies and capabilities has not been fully explored. In general, 'grafting' of new expertise to existing firms is not well understood (Huber 1991). Cognitive psychological theory, applied in both marketing research and research on absorptive capacity in R&D, points to the influence of prior knowledge, as well as relatedness and intensity of effort, in building new absorptive capabilities (Cohen and Levinthal 1990). However, the cognitive perspective may not capture how an innovation-seeking expert, in practice, may encounter clients with a different background and experience. By analysing in-depth and over time (more than 10 years) one dynamic designer–client relationship in a design-based competitive industry – the furniture industry – both the relational and absorptive aspects of building new design capabilities are explored.

The interactive experiences between product design, marketing efforts and business strategy highlight the need for improved design knowledge development in innovation-seeking firms. This chapter adopts a competence view of the firm, and deals with knowledge and competence building in relation to a new ergonomic design approach.

ABSORPTIVE CAPACITY: A NEW PERSPECTIVE ON DESIGN

The ability of a firm to exploit external knowledge – that is, to recognise the value of new, external and meaningful information, assimilate it and apply it to commercial ends – is considered critical to its innovative capabilities. Cohen and Levinthal (1990), as mentioned above, labelled this capability a firm's absorptive capacity. Their framework was developed for studying R&D, but is also highly relevant for design and product development because of similarities in these two fields (Walsh 1991). Interestingly, there are also differences between R&D and design, the latter typically not being institutionalised, often dependent on external competence-sourcing and related to ordinary, everyday product problems (Walsh et al. 1992).

Outside design experts may be a valuable source for upgrading products as well as for innovation designs. Industrial designers are trained to assimilate diverse information and sensory experiences, translate them into visual representations and synthesise these into physical forms and instructions (Borja de Mozota 1992; Kircherer 1990). The 'feeling' and 'seeing' based knowledge of design experts has been noted by many (e.g. Davies-Cooper 1994), although designers have also been critised for being insensitive to the needs of the user (Norman 1988). The ability to acquire *superior*, appropriate design competencies from independent designers may thus be a critical component of a firm's innovative capabilities. How the design competence is put to commercial use, weaving design-related business processes together with technological know-how and humanistic inputs to design, may be defined a 'design capability' (Jevnaker 1993a; inspired by Penrose 1968; Teece, Pisano and Shuen 1990).

In order to sustain and further develop the design expertise and competencies that are commissioned and/or experienced by the firm, the ability to 'absorb', or take in, and sustain (remember) the competencies are critical. The personal embodiment, embeddedness and distributive aspects of design expertise make this difficult, but not impossible (Jevnaker 1993a). Practical design knowledge may be distributed in one's notes, magazines for inspiration, contacts with model-makers, etc. The *non-routine* character of designers' expertise may make it difficult to grasp for clients or novice observers unfamiliar with the reflective practices of design professionals (Schön 1987).

Absorptive capacity refers not only to the acquisition of design resources by an organisation but also to the organisation's ability to exploit it (Cohen and Levinthal 1990). It does not simply depend on the organisation's direct interface with external designers; it also depends on transfers of knowledge across and within subunits of the organisation, some of which may be quite remote from the original point of entry (see Biemans, Chapter 7, this volume).

Cohen and Levinthal point to three aspects that may influence a firm's absorptive capacity:

1. the cognitive structures that a firm draws on
2. the individual and organisational absorptive capacity
3. the cumulative aspect of absorptive capacity

Cognitive Structures

Building absorptive capacity in new product design may depend on related knowledge, e.g. knowing the potential commercial applications of the design input. The premise of the notion of absorptive capacity is that the firm needs prior related knowledge in order to assimilate and use new knowledge (Cohen and Levinthal 1990).

Individual and Organisational Absorptive Capacity

The absorptive capacity of a firm is dependent on both individual and organisational absorptive capacities. Although it has not been studied much, learning at the organisational level is regarded as more complex than learning at the individual level (March and Olsen 1976). In product design, which has a high degree of innovative elements, both levels need to be addressed to allow for organisational adaptation and support.

Accumulation of Absorptive Capacity

Due to cognitive and learning factors, the ability of the firm to absorb new expertise is dependent on earlier acquisition, assimilation and deployment of the same or related types of expertise. Accumulating absorptive capacity in one period will permit its more efficient accumulation in the next. This represents a dynamic perspective suitable for analysing design capabilities, since designing is an iterative and cumulative process (Lawson 1990).

These three aspects affect a firm's ability to develop a new product design capability and, in particular, new and relatively unknown design competencies in product design may not be easily absorbed.

ABSORBING ERGONOMIC DESIGN COMPETENCE

One of the distinct advantages that industrial designers may develop is ergonomic design competencies (Blaich 1985; Freeze 1991; Green 1991). Ergonomics is the study of the relationships among human beings and the objects that surround them, providing information that can enable designers to avoid problems which can affect humans seriously, such as low back pain problems (Gross 1990). Ergonomic design(ing), then, may be defined as an approach and a course of action for the development of an artefact or a system of artefacts (Dumas and Whitfield 1989) that takes ergonomics into due consideration or as the *main* point of departure (Jevnaker 1993a). Ergonomic design opportunities exist in the Scandinavian environment because of the emphasis put on environmental issues at work.

A perspective that may help to shed light on the ergonomic design knowledge/skill acquisition of firms, is the resource-based or competence-based perspective of the firm (Nordhaug 1993; Teece, Pisano and Shuen 1990). In strategic management, sources of competitive advantage are resources that are heterogeneous and difficult to imitate, such as superior competence – in other words, talents, skills and knowledge that are potentially productive for particular business practices (Nordhaug 1993). The recent literature of business strategy stresses the development of core and complementary competencies and capabilities of firms (Itami and Roehl 1987; Teece, Pisano and Shuen 1990); competencies/capabilities are considered to be *core* if they differentiate a company strategically (Leonard-Barton 1992). Due to specialised, creative and integrative design competencies, professional designers' work may be a valuable source for developing attractive differentiated products in highly competitive environments. The professional design input is often supplied by a freelance designer. Even though it may be suggested that it takes time and talent to buy talent and develop design capabilities, very little is known about how firms learn about (new) design (Walsh et al. 1992).

APPROACH AND METHODOLOGY

The case study approach was chosen to explore the complexities of absorbing innovative product design competence in its natural context. The case selected represents both a new and long-term design effort. Burgelman (1991) proposes 10–15 years as a minimum for investigating strategic renewal processes. This pilot study started out with the client's initial working relationship with the designer, which originated in 1967–1970 and was strengthened from 1979 onwards. As the company is known industry-wide and in the design history (Jevnaker 1993a; Sparke 1986) for the launch of highly innovative pieces, it represents an 'extreme case', one in which the process of theoretical interest may be more transparent than it would be in other cases (Eisenhardt 1989).

The empirical material was first collected during the period 1991–1992 through focused, often repeated, telephone interviews with managers, designers and independent ergonomic/design experts. In addition, face-to-face conversations, searches for written documents, observation of managers' presentations to various audiences, and visits to the company, one dealer and the company's main design consultancy were conducted during the period 1991–1994, including lengthy follow-up face-to-face interviews with the former top manager and the most important external design expert. Data collection and analysis were done iteratively by the same researcher. Company folders, products and published information about the company were inspected, including a comparative study of the company's international distributors (Berg 1994). The main informants have read the case study reports and provided feedback and additional information on 'facts'.

CASE STUDY: ERGONOMIC FURNITURE DESIGN – 'STOKKE MAKES LIFE WORTH SITTING'

Company Background

Stokke Factories Ltd, specialising in seating furniture, has its main unit located at Sunnmöre on the western coast of Norway. In 1990 the operating revenue of Stokke Factories was 126 million Norwegian kroner, and the income before year-end appropriations was 15 million Norwegian kroner (three times as much as the previous year). Eighty-five per cent of the revenue was from exports. The company employed a staff of 140. Being a traditional furniture-making firm with a typical production-focused philosophy, the company, established in 1932, has changed its fundamental strategy during the past decade, primarily as a result of designer–company collaboration.

Product Design

Stokke's first encounter with what was later to become an entirely new philosophy of sitting came with designer Peter Opsvik and his chairs for children in

Figure 9.1   The Tripp Trapp® chair. Design: Peter Opsvik

the early 1970s. His Tripp Trapp chair for children, designed in 1972, is adjustable in both height and depth. With support for the feet and the back, the chair is intended to give the child an ergonomically good position no matter how young or old, big or small the child is. The Tripp Trapp chair (Figure 9.1) became an economic success for Stokke, creating a surplus for

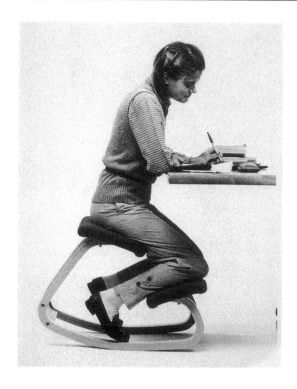

Figure 9.2   The Variable Balans® chair. Design: Peter Opsvik

further experimentation. In 1979, the designer–company relationship led to production of the first Balans chair (Figure 9.2). Subsequently, a design family of Balans chairs and other innovative products emerged, including a modern rocking chair, the Pendulum (1983). Not all of the ergonomically designed models have been successful; experimentation through 'failures' also occurred, according to top management. Innovative product design became one of the most significant activities of the company during the 1980s.

During the work with Opsvik and his experimental models, the new sitting philosophy was born. Balans (balance) means the body's self-regulated posture, giving freedom for dynamic uses of the muscles. The core of this philosophy was further developed by Opsvik into a philosophy of 'movement and variation'.

Other designers who were attracted by the movement and variation philosophy later started to cooperate with Stokke. During the early 1990s the company was working with five professional designers, all interior architects, on a freelance, commission basis, and its budget for design was 4–5 million Norwegian kroner per year (£1 is approximately 10.50 Norwegian kroner). However, Peter Opsvik remained the most important contributor to the company's product design.

Market Outlet

Initially Stokke tried to sell its innovative furniture through agents, chain distributors and volume retailers working in the furniture business. During the mid-1980s the company's strategy was changed completely because the distributional strategy did not work well. The chairs were bought as something new and exciting; later, the response fell drastically and cheaper copies emerged in the market, in particular in the US. The management of Stokke discovered that this approach was not suitable for the new products; the innovative message behind Opsvik's design did not reach the customer or the user.

In 1986 the company's marketing strategy was changed completely. More than fifty years of furniture sales experience was substituted with an entirely new strategy: a focus strategy (Porter 1980). Instead of 'selling', Stokke started to *focus* on information and awareness-raising in selected markets. Stokke has tried to educate the end users about their sitting needs. The target markets have been reached via seminars, brochures, carefully selected and committed retailers and personal contacts. From exporting via an export company (Westnofa), importers and a couple of joint ventures, the company, in the early 1990s, began to export through a range of sister companies in Europe, Scandinavia and Japan.

The main concern, over the past seven years, has been how best to organise the export outlet. According to the Stokke managers, the dealer's competence and motivation are very important, therefore many of them are 'hand-picked', thus building up an effective distribution network. In Germany around 250 dealers cooperate with the company, and, in addition, 900 distribute the Tripp Trapp chair (Berg 1994). The typical distributor of Stokke products in Europe is highly educated, believes in 'movement and variation' and tries to give the individual customer skilled assistance.

CASE ANALYSIS: ERGONOMIC FURNITURE DESIGN

The qualitative analysis is organised around four themes:

1. absorptive capacity in product design
2. absorptive capacity of top management
3. absorptive capacity in marketing
4. absorptive capacity in strategy

Absorptive Capacity in Product Design

Working with the ergonomically conscious designer, Opsvik, product development has been practised through the designer's continual design improvements and experimentation. The conceptual product design development is created on a long-term basis by the designer (Opsvik 1989; Westnofa undated). Activities and decisions concerning manufacturability, model-making and product testing have taken place in a designer–company cooperation, either 'in-house' (the designer spends one or two days in the factory) or in the designer's studio.

The links to ergonomic design competence started as a personal relationship (the designer and client were born in the same region), and the personal and social element is still very important for Stokke's competence-sourcing. The then 30-year-old owner of Stokke (Kaare Stokke) started to work with the designer Peter Opsvik during the 1970s, buying his design, which at that time was viewed as 'strange ideas' by the furniture business community. Opsvik also made a chair for Stokke in 1967, but this was not ergonomically designed. This designer–company relationship was *ad hoc* in the sense that it was not planned on the company side. Stokke did have prior knowledge of professional design but the company was not familiar with ergonomic design. Eventually, Stokke improved its absorptive capacity in ergonomic product design. No doubt, this evolution has transformed the design-related competencies and capabilities in product development and implementation. The absorptive design-related capacity has been improved by learning processes and path-dependent influence from the early product success (the Tripp Trapp chair). The improvement in product design capabilities is twofold; on both an individual and an organisational level. The design capabilities have developed as a result of learning and more strategic competence-sourcing in product design and product realisation; in other words, finding the interested potential customer, reaching the customer with the right product quality and identifying even subconscious and unrecognised user needs. No doubt – although this is not easily measured – management's ability to exploit external design competencies and apply design expertise to commercial ends has improved and an increasingly stronger connection has been made with the external designer.

Hence, in addition to organisational learning, a significant part of the company's increased capabilities seem related to the *continued input* from this particular designer. Even though Stokke has increased its design capabilities and is working with more than one design consultancy, more than 95% of the company's turnover is generated by models designed by the external designer Peter Opsvik. On the one hand, the interactive design management processes are embedded in the organisational substructures, such as the product development department, and do not belong only to the initial specific designer–manager relationship, although relational designer–manager aspects are still important. On the other hand, the continual ability of the designer and his co-workers to *expand* ergonomic design knowledge, and the company to 'absorb' the designer's competence is critical for Stokke's design capabilities and further product development, because its international relationship marketing seems dependent on a coherent system of leading-edge products. According to its Dutch distributor, Stokke does not sell furniture; it sells a concept (Berg 1994, p. 56).

How did this design capability emerge? As mentioned in the introduction, it is not self-evident that professional designers accumulate advanced and domain-related competencies in all fields. The designer was one of the major contributors to the innovative seating concept, *Balans* (Westnofa undated). The origins of the product concept lay in a collaboration between a technical inventor (Mengshoel) and three professional designers, one of whom was the design consultant, Opsvik (Jevnaker 1991, 1993a). The sources of the new designs, however, were influenced by a broader spectrum of personalities and ideas, such as a German ergonomic expert (Ulrich Burandt). Being an interior architect who had worked as an industrial designer at Tandberg Radio Factory and as a freelance furniture designer, Opsvik became deeply aware of ergonomic perspectives during a stay in Germany in 1970, where he met Burandt. His ergonomic design competence developed through personal relationships and practice (since the 1960s) in designing seating furniture that was inspired by, for instance, a Danish physician, A.C. Mandal, who strongly advocated a chair with a seat that tilts 15 degrees forward, to improve posture and diminish back strain (Westnofa undated). Interestingly, Peter Opsvik also works for other furniture producers, including a competitor of Stokke (Jevnaker 1993a). Ample evidence indicates that this particular designer has absorbed domain-specific competencies from multiple sources, which may allow for advanced cognitions and expressions as an expert in product design. For example, during a studio visit in 1994, a variety of journals and books on product life cycles, for instance, could be observed on his desk. According to Dreyfus and Dreyfus (1990), an 'expert' is able to respond intuitively and flexibly to new familiar but problematic situations by drawing on a vast body of embodied knowledge and skills. In this designer's work, the contrast between the familiar and the new is striking (Wildhagen 1987), such as his application of a familiar rocking principle to the unconventional Variable Balans (Jevnaker 1991). Central to this case is a design expert who is even reconfiguring his expertise by constant enquiry about users' daily sitting marathons. Rather than the conventional 'outside in' design, Opsvik has preferred:

> to be *in* the product models (as a potential user). Therefore, we build some models to accomplish this.   (interview, 1994)

The 'we' may include Stokke's product development team and Opsvik's co-designers working in his studio.

Transferring complex competencies from the design source to the company level may be difficult. Through personal explanations and demonstrations by the company's designer, managers, dealers, physiotherapists and other contacts of Stokke have been inaugurated or induced into the new design efforts. In addition, Opsvik has written down his ideas, as they relate to each of Stokke's products (Opsvik 1989). The use of both incorporating and inscribing practices has triggered and preserved design learning (Jevnaker 1993a).

Absorptive Capacity of Top Management

Stokke's top management team has repeatedly been inaugurated into the new product designing; in particular, narration of the design–philosophical perspective combined with concrete examples and demonstrations of the application of ergonomic knowledge played an important role, e.g. illuminating the alternative, dynamic practice by telling the story of how people sit when preparing food, working etc. in oriental cultures. This inauguration was often a *by-product* of a range of communicative efforts with dealers, physiotherapists and ergotherapists, an activity in which Stokke's managers or staff and the design consultant Opsvik took part. According to the designer, no one likes to be 'taught'. He stresses the participative, experiential aspect of learning:

> If people listen to someone else who is teaching other persons something, he/she will also incorporate it.   (interview, 1994)

This point is important, since research indicates the difficulties of learning new perspectives and values for already competent individuals or organisations (see Schön 1987, pp. 255–302).

Management's improved absorptive capacity in product design should also be considered in a broader situational context. The financial situation in the late 1970s was alarming. New managers with new ideas joined the company, one of whom had earlier work experience with Stokke and was appointed as the new chief executive (until May 1994). In addition, new managers and also management consultants with strong educational backgrounds in, for example, economics and business administration were recruited. Top management was influenced by theories of competitive strategy and international marketing, and became increasingly *receptive* to ergonomic design and user focus as a source of competitive advantage. Undoubtedly, the long-term designer and designer–manager relationship facilitated appreciation of the new designs, as acknowledged by both parties. Although tensions were also present, as in most open relationships (Lövlie 1982), and a new top management team was recently recruited (1994), the design expert is still closely linked to the company's product design and marketing development, as indicated by further commissioned product design projects and educational initiatives.

Absorptive Capacity in Marketing

As mentioned above, Stokke's initial attempts to sell its innovative furniture through conventional outlets – agents, chain distributors and volume retailers working in the furniture business – did not work well. Management discovered that this approach did not suit the new products; the innovative message behind Stokke's products and Opsvik's designs was not reaching the customer or the user. Thus, the company's marketing strategy and structure were radically changed. The product concept had to be clarified to educate the internal organisation and its distributors, as well as individual users, via seminars, brochures and hand-picked retailers. In some markets, as in Germany, this happened more or less 'naturally', i.e. without design-education initiatives from the Stokke company. According to Opsvik, this was due to committed and knowledgeable dealers who believed in the philosophy of movement and variation:

> . . . and it was only for me to *ask*: what do you think is wrong, what is right [of product qualities] and things like that. But when it comes to country X, it was only for me to pour out. Because they were so new, they hardly knew anything.

Although some distributors prefer more product-related knowledge and have received little training by the producer company (Berg 1994), a fairly unique European *network* of market relationships has been created by Stokke and its collaborating partners and sister companies. The increased absorptive capacity of marketing is illustrated in Stokke's fresh and coherent visual material for promotion, such as a narrative slides programme, brochures and product folders. The sister companies are governed in a manner that supports these goals and the local managers build their marketing message on the dynamic ergonomic design philosophy (Berg 1994 and key informant interviews).

This market network ('Stokke centres') is greatly appreciated by the design expert, Opsvik, as a crucial part of the company's competitive 'package', because he does not believe in single product initiatives and dispersed, fragmented outlets. The experience with Stokke's Variable Balans, designed by Opsvik, proved useful in this respect: this product was heavily copied by Far East producers. A coherent approach of product concepts and relationship marketing may not be as easily copied as single, successfully designed products, according to research on sustained competitive advantage (Williams 1992), although the designer must admit that Tripp Trapp, which is such a product, has generated a good part of the company's profit; see also Berg (1994). This fact may, however, be time-dependent – a first-mover advantage – because the Tripp Trapp principle has been copied recently (interview, 1994).

Absorptive Capacity in Strategy

The transformation of Stokke started in the late 1970s, but the implementation of the evolving business strategy was accelerated by the appointment of a new top manager in 1985, who was instrumental in bringing about a change in strategic direction. It is clear that the company's ergonomic design approach, initially driven by chance, became strategic. One indication of this is the increased number of new designs commissioned. Another indication is the creation of a coherent, innovative 'set' of ergonomically designed products. A range, or 'family', of new, innovative furniture designs was developed into a product programme to commercialise the innovative seating concepts of Balans and the movement and variation philosophy. The innovative product designs became a basis for a focused European strategy and relationship marketing.

This case illustrates a strategic renewal process originating in external product design expertise. As is often the case in innovation, the company's vision came afterwards – after the introductory efforts. However, the company's ergonomic design approaches, initially driven by chance, were taken up at the strategic corporate level by top managers. The new competitive strategy and company identity, or *ethos*, were immortalised in the new slogan: 'Stokke makes life worth sitting'.

FINDINGS AND INTERPRETATIONS

A number of factors contributed to the success of product design at Stokke. One aspect is the design expert's creative product concepts and his access to the firm's product development team to ensure that the concept design models and prototypes could be manufactured satisfactorily. More important is the marketing approach. The Variable Balans, designed by Opsvik and adopted by Stokke, was the first of ten Balans prototypes to succeed in the market. Notably, 'this goose had already laid one golden egg'. As the owner and chief executive explained at that time, 'we had to see if he had any more in him' (Westnofa undated). Further experimentation, knowledge creation, persistence and continuity in design efforts and product improvements were characteristic of the design process during the period 1979–1991. The empathic aspect of this design process is crucial. Empathic design comes out of understanding users' needs through empathy with their life-worlds, rather than from what users themselves tell developers they want and is highly significant (Rifkin 1994). This may be difficult for non-observers to grasp; recall the design expert's design development by mentally and literally being 'in' the product models. Hence, it is significant that Stokke's product development team spent some time in the designer's studio working with him in this process.

In addition to design competence, two other competence areas have been a major challenge for Stokke. Firstly, the process of change has required other managerial skills, including managing new relationships as well as implementing internal change. Secondly, the distribution system has been restructured, with the establishment of nine sister companies.

Three findings that influence competence-accumulation as drawn from the case study are:

1. inauguration of top management into the new design
2. mutual respect and acknowledgement between client and designer consultant
3. innovation, as well as continual design adaptation

INAUGURATIVE LEARNING

Top management level learning of the philosophy and application of ergonomics in the product design was achieved largely through explanations and demonstrations given by the designer.

The top management team's learning of the design competence does not imply that managers should learn to do designer's work, but rather that they should share design knowledge by *familiarity* (Johannessen 1988). The managers became familiar and well acquainted with the potential of the designers' services, and recognised why a design concept was used. This should not be taken for granted, because research suggests that management may not have absorbed this understanding (Jevnaker 1993b; Institute for Industrial Design 1994).

The case described here suggests that there are at least three aspects involved in the process of accumulating familiarity knowledge in design:

1. learning-by-doing
2. staying close to and being able to 'extract' knowledge from domain-specific experts ('learning-by-osmosis')
3. inaugurative learning (Jevnaker 1993a)

These aspects of learning are typically intertwined, but inaugurative learning may accelerate and deepen the learning process in significant ways, because the proficient design expert is reflecting first-hand practical knowledge 'loud' to the client. In this social learning process, also tacit knowing is articulated by words that explain complex connections supported by imaginative, often visual, examples and other means, such as demonstrations. The core of this process is the use of language in a broad sense, including, for instance, body language. According to a physiotherapist working with the designer Opsvik in another furniture firm, this designer is especially good at combining the verbal and the body language in his demonstrations for physiotherapists as well as lay persons. This social learning process has been neglected in strategic management literature, which wrongly refers to tacit knowledge as literally silent, and rethinking is needed. Hence, *inaugurative learning* is proposed as an activity typically involving interpersonal sharing and explaining of complex competencies, in which the experienced and knowledgeable person is initiating the other into his or her knowledge – even sharing (some of) his or her secrets – and the other person is activated by listening and participating in the learning process (Jevnaker 1993a). This can be achieved by *interpersonal relationships* and *skilled guidance*, and requires interactive learning to occur, often over time as in craft-based apprenticeships, professional and arts-based training and other reflective practices (Schön 1987). Evidence from Stokke indicates that learning-by-osmosis over time may be insufficient: *interpretants* were needed. One indication is that the designer provided his written insights linked to each product model after more than 10 years' collaboration (Opsvik 1989). Another driving force was the new top manager, who, according to Peter Opsvik, clearly defined what was happening to the company in the mid-1980s (Jevnaker 1991). When restructuring is necessary, as Stokke experienced in its marketing and distribution of the new product designs, this more complete learning, with new understanding, may be critical to avoid further risky failures.

ACKNOWLEDGEMENT

An interesting feature of this designer–client relationship is acknowledgement. In fact, both parties attribute a significant part of the commercial success to the other party. Acknowledgement may seem obvious, due to the early product success (see the Tripp Trapp chair), but research indicates that acknowledging relationships, including mutual respect and empathy, are not at all obvious in the furniture industry (Sparke 1986) or in client–design consultant relations (see Bruce and Morris, Chapter 5). Hence, the relationship between Stokke and Opsvik as one of *mutual* acknowledgement is significant. According to Bruce and Docherty (1993), 'it's all in the relationship', but what, exactly, is most significant in creating positive design development in the client firm? In the theory of dynamic relationships as developed in therapeutical and educational settings, acknowledging relations are suggested as preconditions of frame-breaking development (Bae 1992; Lövlie 1982). The design expertise may shape the client's responses by acknowledging, for example the client's need for a 'safe' design situation. Another case study, of the Lillehammer Olympic design programme, suggests that even experienced professional design users hesitate to explore new design opportunities (Jevnaker 1994). Acknowledgement is not regarded primarily as a communicative method. Its conception is linked to German philosophy (from Hegel, *anerkennen*); it is a theoretical construct to conceive aspects of dialectical relationships. Hence, acknowledgement is a relational, more than a personal, feature; it presupposes that both parties feel acknowledged; i.e. see the other party as separate, with an identity and integrity of its own, and its own rights, expertise, etc. Even though one might not always agree or approve of this expertise, acknowledgement is granted to the other party anyway (Bae 1992; Lövlie 1982).

Interestingly, Stokke's top manager recently stated (in a radio programme, March 1993) that it is the *designer* who creates the product. Even more surprisingly, the design expert argued (in a public meeting on design in business, October 1993) that it is the *selling* part that is most difficult, not the product design.

THE DESIGNER AS INNOVATOR AND ADAPTOR

Contrary to the innovator–adaptor theory (see Foxall, Chapter 13, this volume) the creativity of the new design exploited both innovative and adaptive design strategies, e.g. the Balans principles combined with back support.

In product designing, small-scale experimentation preceded strategic reorientation, and was followed by redesign and improvements to product families. This illustrates an individual as well as an organisational capacity to both innovate and adapt, which is consistent with recent research into the individual innovator (see Foxall, Chapter 13, this volume) and entrepreneurial organisations (Burgelman 1991; Burgelman and Sayles 1986). The empathic design approach and continuous exploration of users' life-worlds may constitute one explanation behind the designer as innovator and adaptor.

MANAGEMENT IMPLICATIONS

Building up a design capability that can absorb and recreate new design is advantageous to firms, given that their rivals may be locked in old methods and approaches (Jevnaker 1993b; Lahti 1990; Sparke 1986). Competitive capabilities may be obtained by a continued input of product design expertise, while a designer–client relationship characterised by acknowledgement and a shared design direction is valuable. Indeed, the absorptive capacity concept has certain one-way, passive connotations (like a sponge), and it may not fully capture the interactive dynamism of a relational approach in product design practices. As illuminated in this case, both the client and the designer created essential knowledge and reflection-in-action (Schön 1987), through relations with other experts, dealers, distributors, etc. The client–designer relationship was part of a larger network, but a *core* part that differentiated the company strategically with positive commercial results. If sustained competitive advantages are dependent on relative differences in leading-edge products, then the difference that 'makes the difference' may be such a superior design capability. Creativity in product design, at least in furniture, is often associated with endless variation; in this case, thoughtful product differentiation and focus on user needs and ergonomics have been of particular importance. This strategic capability may be developed from 'outside-in'; i.e. in collaboration with an external competence source. As design protection may be difficult via patents, competing on ergonomic product design has critical implications for investments in (continued) absorptive capacity and knowledge creation, through client–designer consultant relationships. Moreover, the design expertise may be successfully included in the marketing and distributional networks, as this case suggests, creating knowledge and relationship dynamics that are unique and therefore less imitable than single products.

CONCLUSIONS

The recognition and appreciation of design may be increasing in some business contexts, as illustrated by this optimistic, but fairly uncritical, statement:

> Around the globe, CEOs are depending more and more on product designers to make greater headway in the marketplace. That makes sense. The designer is the one who conceives what form the original product should take, the one who renews an aging product line. Without designers, neither engineers nor marketers can do their magic. So, in the end, it is the American, European or Japanese designer whose creations define what a corporation is – what image it will have among the people who buy its products.
>
> (*Business Week* 1990, p. 171)

What is less focused, however, is the knowledge improvement of firms to absorb and exploit design competence. This chapter indicates that inaugurative design learning may be one missing link in generating absorptive capacity for new competencies and a new direction in product design. In this particular case, inauguration was grounded in a designer–client relationship characterised by an emerging mutual acknowledgement. Moreover, product design contributed to marketing and distribution activities in building up cross-functional capabilities for product realisation. The particular firm's design capability was improved by both influencing the absorptive capacity for design and the continued input of the designer, a capability that even transformed the company's strategy and self-understanding. Hence, the following proposition should be explored further:

A long-term expertise-based innovative product design strategy is strongly associated with acknowledging relations between design expertise and their clients.

ACKNOWLEDGEMENTS

The author would like to thank the Norwegian Design Council, who commissioned this research, and the Norwegian Research Foundation, the Ministry of Industry and Oil, the NHO and SNF for additional financial support. In particular, thanks to Stokke Factories Ltd and independent design expert Peter Opsvik, for their openness, valuable insights and rich descriptions.

REFERENCES

Bae, B. (1992). Acknowledging children's experiences – Focus on the quality of the teacher–child relationship, in ETEN Conference, Viborg College, Denmark, 3–5 May, College of Early Childhood Education, Norway.

Berg, H. (1994). A comparative analysis to explore critical success factors linked to establishment of a sales and distributional company in a foreign market, confidential student report, Norwegian School of Economics and Business Administration, Bergen (in Norwegian).

Blaich, R. (1985). *Natural Design: The Search for Comfort and Efficiency*, Boilerhouse, Victoria and Albert Museum, London.

Borja de Mozota, B. (1992). Design education and research: A theoretical model for the future, *Design Management Journal*, **3**(4), 19–25.

Bruce, M. and Docherty, C. (1993). It's all in a relationship: A comparative study of client–design consultant relationships, *Design Studies*, **14**(4), 402–422.

Bruce, M. and Morris, B. (1994). *Strategic Management of UK Design Consultants: Policy and Practice*, Manchester School of Management, UMIST, Manchester.

Burgelman, R.A. (1991). Intra-organisational ecology of strategy making and organisational adaptation: Theory and field research, *Organisation Science*, **2**(3), 239–262.

Burgelman, R.A. and Sayles, L.R. (1986). *Inside Corporate Innovation*, Free Press, New York.

Business Week (1990). Design, the new buzzword of the corporate world in the nineties, Innovation Issue, 15 June, 171.

Cohen, W.M. and Levinthal, D.A. (1990). Absorptive capacity: A new perspective on learning and innovation, *Administrative Science Quarterly*, **35**, 128–152.

Davies-Cooper, R. (1994). Marketing and design: A critical relationship, in Wilson, I. (ed.), *Marketing Interfaces: Exploring the Marketing and Business Relationship*, Pitman, London, pp. 127–162.

Dreyfus, H. and Dreyfus, S. (1990). What is morality? A phenomenological account of the development of ethical expertise, in Rasmussen, D. (ed.), *Universalism versus Communitarism: Contemporary Debates in Ethics*, MIT Press, Cambridge, MA, pp. 237–264.

Dumas, A. and Whitfield, A. (1989). Why design is difficult to manage: A survey of attitudes and practices in British industry, *European Management Journal*, **7**(1), 50–56.

Eisenhardt, K.M. (1989). Building theories from case study research, *Academy of Management Review*, **14**(4), 532–550.

Freeze, K.J. (1991). Design management lessons from the past: Henry Dreyfuss and American business, Design Management Institute, Boston, MA.

Green, B. (1991). *Ergonomics and Design*, Rainbow/Danish Design Centre, Copenhagen.

Gross, G.A. (1990). Preventing low back pain, in Goldbloom, R. and Lawrence, R. (eds), *Preventing Disease*, Springer-Verlag, New York.

Henderson, R. (1991). Architectural innovation as a source of competitive advantage, *Design Management Journal*, **2**(3), 43–47.

Huber, G. (1991). Organisational learning: The contributing processes and the literatures, *Organisational Science*, **2**, 88–115.

Institute for Industrial Design (1994). Design management in practice, confidential student papers on the design management course (course director: B.H. Jevnaker), IFID, National College of Art and Design, Oslo (in Norwegian).

Itami, H. with Roehl, T.W. (1987). *Mobilising Invisible Assets*, Harvard University Press, Cambridge, MA.

Jevnaker, B.H. (1991). Make the world a better place to sit in! *Design Management Journal*, **2**(4), Fall, 48–54.

Jevnaker, B.H. (1993a). Inaugurative learning: Adapting a new design approach, *Design Studies*, **14**(4), 379–401.

Jevnaker, B.H. (1993b). Competence in practice, in Nordhaug, O. with others, *Governance of Competence*, TANO, Oslo (in Norwegian).

Jevnaker, B.H. (1994). Building organisational capabilities in design, lessons from the 1994 Olympic Games, presented at the 6th International Forum in Education and Research on Design Management, Paris, June.

Johannessen, K.E. (1988). Thoughts on tacit knowledge, *Dialoger*, No. 6, 13–28 (in Swedish).

Kircherer, S. (1990). *Olivetti, A Study of the Corporate Management of Design*, Trefoil Publishers, London.

Lahti, A. (1990). *The Competitive Position of the Scandinavian Furniture Industry*, Furniture Excellence Club, Helsinki.

Lauvaas, P. and Handal, G. (1990). *Supervision and Practical Theory of Professions*, Cappelen, Oslo (in Norwegian).

Lawson, B. (1990). *How Designers Think*, Butterworth Architecture, London.

Leonard-Barton, D. (1992). Core capabilities and core rigidities: A paradox in managing new product development, *Strategic Management Journal*, **13**, 111–125.

Lövlie(-Schibbye), A.L. (1982). *The Self of the Psychotherapist: Movement and Stagnation in Psychotherapy*, Norwegian University Press, Oslo.

March, J.G. and Olsen, J.P. (1976). *Ambiguity and Choice in Organisations*, Norwegian University Press, Bergen.

Nordhaug, O. (1993). *Human Capital in Organisations*, Scandinavian University Press and Oxford University Press, London.

Norman, D.A. (1988). *The Psychology of Everyday Things*, Basic Books.

Opsvik, P. (1989). Some thoughts about sitting, in general, and about my products at Stokke, in particular, unpublished paper, Oslo (in Norwegian).

Penrose, E. (1968). *The Theory of the Growth of the Firm*, 4th impression, Basil Blackwell, Oxford.

Porter, M. (1980). *Competitive Strategy*, Free Press, New York.

Potter, S., Roy, R., Capon, C.H., Bruce, M., Walsh, V and Lewis, J. (1991). The benefits and costs of investments in design: Using professional design expertise in product, engineering and graphics projects, report DIG-03, Design Innovation Group, Open University and UMIST, Milton Keynes/Manchester.

Rifkin, G. (1994). Product development, empathic design helps understand users better, briefings from the editors, *Harvard Business Review*, April/May, 10.

Schön, D.A. (1987). *Educating the Reflective Practitioner*, Josey-Bass, San Francisco, CA.

Sparke, P. (1986). *Furniture, 20th Century Design*, Bell and Hyman, London.

Teece, D.J., Pisano, G. and Shuen, A. (1990). Firm capabilities, resources, and the concept of strategy, economic analysis and policy working paper EAP-38, The Regents of the University of California.

Walsh, V. (1991). Managing design programmes to achieve high levels of innovation, presented at the Design Management Conference, Chatham, Massachusetts, 9–13 October, Design Innovation Group, Manchester School of Management, UMIST, Manchester.

Walsh, V., Roy, R., Bruce, M. and Potter, S. (1992). *Winning by Design*, Basil Blackwell, Oxford.

Westnofa (undated). Balans seating – The story of its discovery, company literature.

Wildhagen, F. (1987). Three in one museum, from exhibition Göteborg, Röhsska Konstslöyd-museum, *Norsk Design og Kunsthaandverk*, Norsk Form, Oslo.

Williams, J.R. (1992). How sustainable is your competitive advantage? *California Management Review*, **34**(3), 1–23 (special reprint).

LAUNCH STRATEGIES

INTRODUCTION

Wim G. Biemans

The final stage of the product development process is the launch of the new product onto the market, where customers decide about its level of success. The chapters in this section discuss new product announcements and new product launch strategies.

Before new products are launched onto the market, companies will typically issue new product announcements. Although the primary objective of such an announcement is to inform customers, other objectives include getting customers to postpone the purchase of competitive products, informing suppliers and discouraging competitors. While the product development literature has largely ignored the role of new product announcements, the effective management of new product announcements is emerging as a critical factor in successful product development. In Chapter 10, Biemans and Setz distinguish between internal (within the firm) and external (to the market-place) announcements, and illustrate these concepts and processes with examples from the Dutch telecommunications industry. The results of their empirical investigation outline the role of new product announcements, the various parties involved, and the major managerial issues. The chapter closes with detailed guidelines for the management of new product announcements.

Although launch strategy decisions are important for a new product's success or failure, there is little research on how specific elements of the launch strategy relate to new product success. In Chapter 11, Hultink and Robben present a simple model showing the various factors influencing launch strategies. The model shows that launch strategies consist of strategic launch variables and tactical marketing-mix decisions. These launch strategies are influenced by both company and personal characteristics. In addition, Hultink and Robben discuss a number of methods to investigate new product launch strategies. Based on this discussion, they suggest the use of conjoint analysis as one research method, and illustrate its use by describing the findings of an empirical study using conjoint measurement to investigate successful launch strategies.

CHAPTER TEN

MANAGING NEW PRODUCT ANNOUNCEMENTS IN THE DUTCH TELECOMMUNICATIONS INDUSTRY

Wim G. Biemans and Henriette J. Setz

Despite the increasing strategic relevance of new product announcements, the existing product development literature has largely ignored this important subject. This chapter addresses this issue by presenting the results of a study of new product announcements in the Dutch telecommunications industry. In-depth interviews with manufacturers, distributors, dealers, consultants and industrial customers demonstrate that announcing new telecommunications equipment is a complex and multifaceted process, involving many parties. Manufacturers can increase their chances of successfully developing and launching new products by effectively linking into existing networks.

INTRODUCTION

Researchers and practitioners alike increasingly recognise that a continuous stream of new products is of strategic importance, and they try to formulate

Product Development: Meeting the Challenge of the Design–Marketing Interface.
Edited by M. Bruce and W.G. Biemans.   © 1995 John Wiley & Sons Ltd.

practical guidelines for improving the process of new product development (NPD) on the basis of extensive empirical research (Craig and Hart 1992). However, the role of new product announcements is generally ignored, even though such announcements strongly influence the eventual success of the new product, both internally (support for the product within the organisation) and externally (success in the market-place). Firms increasingly recognise that the announcement of new products is an important part of their communication strategy:

- The number of new products, and thus the number of new product announcements increases.
- The growing number of new product announcements makes it imperative for a firm to reach the target audiences with the right message.
- The ever-increasing costs of NPD enhance the need for a successful market launch.

While the issue of investigating and improving launch strategies is covered in Chapter 11, this chapter describes the results of a study in the Dutch telecommunications industry designed to address the much neglected issue of managing new product announcements.

THE ROLE OF NEW PRODUCT ANNOUNCEMENTS IN THE NPD PROCESS

The process of NPD has been described in various ways (Saren 1984; Hart, Chapter 1, this volume). Most models depict the process as consisting of a series of consecutive activities, which are sometimes connected by evaluation points, at which the critical *go/no go* decisions are made (Balachandra 1984). Perhaps the best-known representation of the NPD process is the model developed by Booz, Allen and Hamilton (1968), which shows the NPD process as consisting of six consecutive stages:

1. exploration
2. screening
3. business analysis
4. development
5. testing
6. commercialisation

This has inspired a large number of similar models. However, the announcement of the new product as a distinct activity within the NPD process is not mentioned. Even the very comprehensive model by Crawford (1983) refers to announcement as a 'self-explanatory' part of the commercialisation stage, despite the fact that, as Rabino and Moore (1989) recently noted:

> product announcements and the planning that leads up to product announcements have become increasingly formalized as part of the pre-launch activities of a new-product introduction. This is particularly true in the high-technology sector.

The strategic role of new product announcements is also acknowledged by Wind and Mahajan (1987), who introduced the concept of *marketing hype*, a set of pre-launch activities leading to the creation of a supportive market environment, which includes distribution channels, providers of support products and services, and media and opinion leaders. They stated that the success of high-tech products greatly depends on the support of multiple stakeholders: 'the introductory pre-launch marketing program of an innovative new product should be geared to all these actors and not just the consumer'. Finally, Chaney, Devinney and Winer (1989) showed that the announcement of new products increases the market value of the firm.

Empirical evidence supporting the view that new product announcements should be regarded as a distinctive part of the NPD process, which needs to be managed carefully to ensure successful product launch, is scarce. From a study of new product development within Dutch firms (Biemans 1992) the following conclusions can be distilled, regarding new product announcements:

- The *timing* of new product announcements is crucial: premature announcements followed by production or shipping problems can lead to serious problems and can strain inter-firm relations.
- An *extensive internal communication programme* is an essential part of the new product announcement process. One of the firms investigated, working through operating companies in various countries and through dealers in others, distinguished the following internal announcements: at company headquarters, to sales staff at the holding company, to directors of operating companies, to sales staff at operating companies, and to dealers in other countries.
- A difference exists between planned and realised new product announcements: premature disclosure of information about a new product by sales representatives is basically a new product announcement. Similarly, the testing of prototypes by potential users may result in the new product no longer being confidential. Testing in the market is a means by which information is disseminated as well as gathered (Foxall 1984). This is also recognised by Rabino and Moore (1989), who mention that 'beta tests . . . serve the important function of alerting selected users to an imminent product launch'.

Rabino and Moore (1989) conducted an exploratory study to 'examine the extent to which new-product announcements emerge as part of the formalized process in keeping with management's strategic objectives'. Based on a study of new product announcements in the US market for mainframe computers, they arrived at the following conclusions:

- The formal announcement of a new product introduction is not an isolated communication, but rather the culmination of a multifaceted process, comprising informal as well as formal components.
- The nature and length of the announcement process is determined by product-related variables and may vary not only from company to company, but from product to product within a single company.
- An announcement may be targeted to any of a number of different constituencies in keeping with specific strategic objectives.
- The precise content of an announcement, as well as the medium and timing of its communication, is determined in keeping with the target audience.

DEFINITION OF A NEW PRODUCT ANNOUNCEMENT

For the purpose of the study of Dutch firms a new product announcement was defined as *all communication from which it can be deduced that a specific new product is coming*. (Cf. Spence (1974), who discussed the broader concept of 'signalling' as a means to more efficient market behaviour and defined it as 'any communication which provided information to the market and allowed for more informed decision making'.) The two main elements of our definition are explained briefly in the following subsections.

'All Communication'

The announcement of a new product not only refers to the external announcement in the market-place, but also includes the internal announcement within the organisation (Dundas and Krentler 1982). In addition, new product announcements have both a formal and an informal component. These two dimensions lead to the matrix depicted in Figure 10.1.

As new product announcements were considered as a part of the firm's marketing policy, the investigation focused on external announcements. After all, it is only through external announcements that the relevant parties in the market are informed about the advent of a new product. The realised external announcement is a combination of the formal, external announcement, which

	Internal	**External**
Informal	Informal, internal planning of product development projects, including implicit announcements to various departments and individuals	Informal communication with external parties, e.g. during sales presentations with customers and informal conversations during distributor meetings
Formal	Formal, internal announcements to inform various departments and individuals, e.g. Production and Sales, about the coming of the new product	Formal, external market introduction, directed at various target audiences, by using various communication channels and media

Figure 10.1 The various kinds of announcements

is carried out as part of the firm's marketing strategy, and possible informal, external announcements that are not planned by the organisation, but may nevertheless occur, e.g. through informal communication between a sales representative and customers. This distinction between formal and informal is summarised in Table 10.1, where both situations should be regarded as the extremes of a continuum.

Formal, internal announcements are also included in the investigation because they may substantially influence informal, external announcements. For instance, information disclosed during a sales presentation may prematurely inform customers about a pending new product introduction and thus result in unintended order cancellations. Such undesired effects can be prevented by using procedures (formal, internal announcements) that clearly state what information may be provided to whom and when.

A second example is more complex. Large manufacturers of telecommunications equipment maintain relationships with various parties, including consultants. These parties are usually informed informally through personal relationships about the latest developments (*informal* leakage). Sometimes, the formal, internal announcement explicitly mentions that consultants are allowed to be informed informally, knowing that the information will

Table 10.1   Characteristics of formal and informal announcements

Formal announcement	Informal announcement
Planned by the organisation	Not planned by the organisation
Part of the firm's strategy	Opportunistic
Public	Not public
Mass communication	Personal communication
Usually put in writing	Usually orally transmitted

eventually reach the general market. Thus, the network of personal relationships is used as a means of informing the market without making a formal, external announcement (*controlled* leakage). The formal, internal announcement is used to direct the informal, external announcement.

Finally, informal, internal announcements refer to the fact that even the most informal planning of a product development project implies an internal announcement. However, although all kinds of interesting communication processes are involved, these announcements are so implicit and elusive as to make the term 'announcement' too far-fetched.

'Communication from which It Can Be Deduced that a Specific New Product Is Coming'

Although new product announcements are typically quite explicit, information about new products may also reach the market in ways that are much more subtle. For instance, a product manager may unwittingly disclose too much information during a trade show, while enthusiastically trying to win a new customer. When the information leads the customer to believe that the new product is coming, it may influence his or her behaviour, and the effect may be identical to that of a formal announcement. Another example concerns a firm's announcement that it will participate in state-of-the-art technological developments that are of strategic importance. Even though no products may be mentioned, knowledgeable customers may be able to deduce such information from the technology involved.

In particular cases, new products may be announced long before the NPD process nears its completion. Strategic considerations may lead a firm to announce specific new products even before the required technology is developed. A good example is provided by the continuing commotion and lobbying around high definition television (HDTV), where specific new products are announced prematurely to influence regulating (government) agencies and public opinion, and to persuade suppliers to make the required investments in the new technology.

OBJECTIVES AND TARGET AUDIENCES OF NEW PRODUCT ANNOUNCEMENTS

The HDTV example illustrates that new product announcements may serve several objectives, apart from the primary marketing objective of informing potential customers. The most important objectives, and the accompanying target audiences, of new product announcements are discussed below.

INFORMING POTENTIAL CUSTOMERS

The primary objective of new product announcements is to inform (potential) customers about the advent of a new product. In many industrial markets, customers are informed at an early stage (i) to give them sufficient time to prepare for the new product (e.g. when using the new product requires investments in the existing infrastructure) and (ii) to postpone the purchase of competing products. In order not to disturb relationships with existing customers, the firm should make sure that the announced products are subsequently introduced with no or only minimal delays!

DISCOURAGING (POTENTIAL) COMPETITORS

Sometimes the announcement of a new product may serve the strategic goal of discouraging competitors. In the computer industry, IBM has traditionally enjoyed the dubious reputation of frequently resorting to the practice of *preannouncing*; that is, announcing a product long before it can actually be delivered. In the software industry such products are being referred to as *vapourware*. When such an early announcement is made by the market leader, it can have a paralysing effect on the market. Take the case of Adobe Systems Inc., maker of software that controls how computer printers produce typefaces. In September 1989, Microsoft and Apple Computer Inc. announced that they would jointly develop a rival product. Adobe's stock fell by 20% in one day, and for the next nine months the company spent 90% of its time answering customer's questions and 'fighting vapourware', according to Chairman John E. Warnock. As it turned out, Apple backed off and Microsoft did not ship its competing product, TrueImage, for two years. Announcing nonexistent products is one of the charges that led to the lengthy investigation by the Federal Trade Commission into Microsoft's competitive tactics (Rebello et al. 1993).

STIMULATING DEVELOPMENT ACTIVITIES AND INVESTMENTS BY SUPPLIERS AND MANUFACTURERS OF COMPLEMENTARY PRODUCTS

New product announcements may also serve the purpose of initiating development activities by suppliers and manufacturers of complementary products. For instance, manufacturers of hardware sometimes inform suppliers of software at an early stage, so that they can start the development of the necessary compatible application programmes.

ESTABLISHING OR CONFIRMING AN INNOVATIVE CORPORATE IMAGE

This objective of new product announcements is aimed at stockholders, potential investors, industry watchers, the business press and the general public. For start-up companies in high-tech industries, the new product announcement may be closely tied to the firm's strategic positioning and one or more high-profile individuals. For instance, by announcing very innovative computers and stressing the involvement of Steven Jobs (one of the founders of Apple), NeXT Inc. was able to generate a high degree of interest and capital. In addition, this strategy may give the firm several benefits of being a pioneer in the market, such as establishing a favourite position in the most profitable market segment (Eliashberg and Robertson 1988).

SPEEDING UP DIFFUSION

The early announcement of a new product may also be directed at developing initial levels of opinion-leader support and favourable word-of-mouth needed to accelerate the diffusion of the innovative product. In this context, a change agent is defined as 'an individual who influences clients' innovation decisions in a direction deemed desirable by a change agency' (Rogers 1983). Examples of change agents, whom it is crucial to identify and characterise, include trade associations, private and government industry consultants and architects/engineers. If the change agents can be convinced of the merits of the new product, they can speed up diffusion through expert testimonies, testimonies of participants in demonstration programmes and articles in the trade literature (Harrer, Weijo and Hattrup 1988).

DEVELOPING A SUPPORTIVE DISTRIBUTION SYSTEM

Frequently, new product announcements are aimed at distribution partners in order to create access to efficient distribution systems and develop the required levels of knowledge (product benefits, applications, installation, maintenance) and product support.

MOTIVATING PERSONNEL

Finally, the periodic announcement of innovative new products, particularly by means of extravagant events that are extensively covered by the trade press, may serve to motivate a firm's own personnel, especially its sales staff.

RESEARCH METHODOLOGY

The study of new product announcement practices in the Netherlands focused on the telecommunications industry because of the present rapid pace of technological development, leading to the introduction of a large number of new products. The rate of growth of the market for telecommunications is approximately 10% per year, while the average firm spends around 4–5% of total costs on new telecommunications products. In order to obtain a detailed and complete picture of new product announcements, all relevant parties were investigated – manufacturers, distributors, dealers, consultants and customers.

A total of 21 people within 14 firms were interviewed, mostly marketing managers, engineers, general directors, division managers, product managers and senior consultants. The in-depth semi-structured interviews, lasting two to three hours, were based on a detailed checklist. The nature of the questions differed for each category of firm. The most important issues covered were:

- formal and informal announcements
- external and internal announcements
- the existence of procedures and guidelines
- experiences with announcements
- trends and developments
- knowledge about announcements by competitors
- the role of distributors and dealers
- the role of consultants
- the customer's perspective
- the perceived relevance and independence of distributors, dealers and consultants

In addition, a limited number of case histories were studied in depth. The interviews were conducted by two researchers and the respondents were provided with the opportunity to comment on detailed case descriptions and tentative analyses.

This methodology allowed for a comparison of answers, while maintaining the required flexibility to address unexpected relevant issues.

NEW PRODUCT ANNOUNCEMENTS IN THE DUTCH TELECOMMUNICATIONS INDUSTRY

The announcement of new products in the Dutch telecommunications industry appears to be a complex process. The specific content of a new product announcement strongly depends on the characteristics of the situation, and a number of different parties appear to be involved. Although in specific cases the situation may become quite complex, the relevant parties can be categorised into manufacturers, distributors/dealers, consultants and customers. The parties exchange information and make up the general network shown in Figure 10.2.

The network depicted in Figure 10.2 greatly simplifies the complexity of the real world, as is illustrated by the following example. In the Dutch telecommunications industry, PTT Telecom is a major player and, because of its size and dominant market position, is generally regarded by customers in a similar

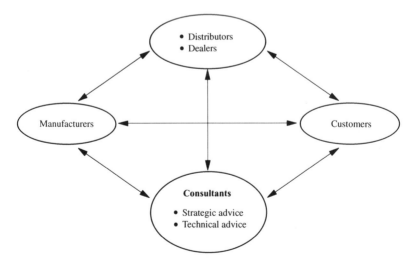

Figure 10.2   The major parties involved in announcing new telecommunications products

way to major manufacturers such as Alcatel, Siemens and Motorola. However, PTT Telecom does not manufacture anything itself, but distributes the products of a large number of manufacturers. In distributing its products, PTT Telecom uses its own distribution outlets (the Primafoons, retail stores aimed at consumers, and the Business Centres, directed at industrial customers), as well as independent outlets (like autodealers). PTT Telecom, together with its own distribution system, belongs to the category 'distributors' in Figure 10.2. However, many customers do not make this careful distinction, and use the more general term 'suppliers' instead. The roles of the various parties in announcing new telecommunications products will now be discussed.

MANUFACTURERS

The manufacturers are mostly large, multinational corporations, such as Philips, Alcatel, Ericsson, Siemens, Motorola and AT&T, which produce various products, ranging from simple handsets to complex telephone switches and systems for mobile communications. Manufacturers supply their customers mainly with information about products and the firm, while good manufacturers emphasise the product's function rather than its characteristics. The information is provided through sales visits and supplemented by brochures, mailings and advertisements. In addition, some manufacturers inform their customers through newsletters, and participation in specialised trade shows, conferences and seminars. These means of communication are typically used to provide customers with strategic information: the latest technological developments and market trends, as well as the firm's strategic vision. PTT Telecom supplies both strategic and operational information through regular (mostly monthly) meetings with large customers.

Manufacturers increasingly recognise that customers obtain their information through many different channels. For instance, rapid technological developments result in customers being increasingly dependent on consultants, who are being hired to select suppliers for the shortlist, to draw up contracts etc. The growing importance of consultants means that manufacturers will be confronted with an additional party in the decision making process, one that has extensive specialised knowledge and is able to see through exaggerated promises that can never be fulfilled. On the other hand, the use of consultants leads to the faster formulation of better product specifications.

The emerging role of consultants is capitalised upon by manufacturers, e.g. by organising tailor-made seminars. British Telecom recently started a toll-free telephone service for consultants, with the telephone number included in advertisements and publications. PTT Telecom is considering the idea of offering consultants access to a specialised Videotex service, providing up-to-date general information about products and prices, as well as the telephone numbers of the individuals to contact for additional information. Such an approach is regarded by PTT Telecom as faster, cheaper and easier to control than the use of written information, and is also more closely tuned to the needs of consultants for actual information.

Earlier in this chapter, the danger of unwanted informal, external announcements by sales representatives was mentioned. This may lead manufacturers (and distributors) to inform their sales representatives as late as possible, to prevent them from prematurely disclosing information that may harm the company's image, e.g. by informing customers about a product that does not exist as yet. However, the sales force need to be well informed in order to be a credible partner for their customers. In addition, an uninformed sales force may result in missed opportunities. For example, one of the distributors revealed that it once lost a major project, which could have been obtained with a new product that would be introduced in the very near future, because the sales representative was unaware of the product. Theoretically, these problems can be resolved by issuing detailed guidelines that spell out the desired behaviour of sales representatives.

In practice, however, managers hold varying opinions with regard to the extent to which new product announcements can be structured and guided by procedures. One marketing executive felt that the formulation of general guidelines was hardly useful, because the content of a specific announcement strongly depends on the characteristics of the situation: 'It would be nice if it was more structured, but that is not really possible'. The only thing one can do is learn from experiences with previous announcements. Other suppliers, on the other hand, try to formulate clear-cut guidelines that explicitly mention when customers may be informed, which customers may be informed and what information may be provided. For instance, PTT Telecom in 1992 introduced its Assortment Information Procedure, which includes detailed guidelines to structure the announcement of new products. The procedure specifies the individuals and departments involved, their responsibilities, the activities to be performed, the time schedule, the departments to be informed, the information to be provided and the individuals responsible for providing the information. This formal, internal announcement serves to guide the external announcements.

DISTRIBUTORS AND DEALERS

The distinction between a distributor and a dealer refers to whether or not substantial value is added to the product. This essential difference concerning their role is accompanied by differences in the products sold. *Distributors* sell all kinds of complex telecommunications equipment (such as PABX) and add substantial value (mostly installation, maintenance, advice and technical support), and consist of a large number of medium-sized firms operating in the Netherlands (e.g. Koning & Hartman, Geveke Electronics), as well as PTT Telecom, which does not manufacture any of the products it distributes. *Dealers* sell a broad range of standard equipment that is less expensive, can be installed by the user and does not require technical support (e.g. telephones, fax machines, answering machines and small telephone switches for the home). They mostly consist of small, locally operating firms carrying a large number of different products.

Distributors and dealers are primarily used to pass on product information provided by manufacturers. In so doing, distributors especially are able to tailor the information to the specific local situation. Dealers only provide product information, through advertisements in local newspapers, catalogues that are distributed regionally and advice provided by salespeople in the showroom. They do not employ their own sales representatives who visit customers. Distributors, on the other hand, provide both product information and more general additional information, employ their own sales representatives and technical staff, and communicate through advertisements and participation in trade shows and seminars. Sometimes, manufacturers and distributors jointly announce a new product, e.g. when the manufacturer supports the distributor in participating in a trade show or during a meeting organised for distributors and potential customers.

In general, manufacturers only have very limited influence on a distributor's advertisements. Distributors have a broad knowledge of the market, wish to profile their own firm and prefer to take care of their own advertisements. At the most, a manufacturer is allowed, in exchange for a contribution to the costs, some very general influence, but never about issues like the selected positioning or the pictures used. Typically, a manufacturer will demand that the advertisement does not include any competitive products. With dealers, the opportunities for exerting influence are considerably greater. Dealers are less knowledgeable about the market, while advertisements are the most important means of informing their customers. Therefore, it is common practice for a manufacturer to determine the content of an advertisement, while the dealer takes care of its lay-out and style, so that the dealer can make it consistent with its corporate style. Needless to say, in this situation the manufacturer will also pay part of the costs involved. For dealers, the brand's power and image are usually important reasons for adding a product to their range.

For many manufacturers, distributors and dealers are a very important channel for (indirectly) communicating with their customers, and they are also the primary means of feedback about customer requirements. Because of this mutual dependency, manufacturers are able to exercise some measure of control. This is in strong contrast with consultants, whose independent position precludes the exertion of control.

CONSULTANTS

Consultants advise customers about their telecommunications policy and intended purchases. They include both firms that have traditionally specialised in telecommunications (such as Intercai) and small, new departments within large, established accounting and consulting firms (e.g. KPMG) that are increasingly advising customers about their telecommunications problems. Several changes contribute to the increasing importance of consultants:

- Rapid technological developments and an ever-growing number of new products cause customers to lose track.
- Customers increasingly focus on their core activities and source out everything else.
- For many customers, information technology is growing in importance, and decisions about it are increasingly being taken by functional managers.
- Many customers consider intervening product announcements to be disturbing ('Did we make the right decision?').

Because customers, in the study, regard consultants as being independent and trustworthy, most manufacturers supply them with relevant information. As one of the managers remarked, 'It is the consultant's job to combine the coloured information provided by suppliers into more or less objective information'. Therefore, a recommendation by a consultant can be considered to be more valuable than one given by a distributor or manufacturer. It is interesting to note that most large manufacturers employ their own internal consultants, who provide customers with advice that is relatively inexpensive. Nevertheless, one of the managers interviewed remarked that consultants typically have detailed knowledge of only a limited number of suppliers, thus making them no more objective than distributors.

Manufacturers and distributors increasingly acknowledge the significance of maintaining good relationships with the most important consultants, which are best realised by establishing and maintaining a network of informal personal relationships. However, in so doing one should beware of establishing relationships that are too close, because they may compromise the consultant's independent position. As one of the distributors put it, 'Relationships with consultants that are too good may harm the position on the shortlist'.

Naturally, consultants are also very much aware of the need to maintain an independent position. One consultant remarked that some customers may have a problem with the fact that another part of the consulting firm has a business relationship (e.g. an alliance or financial interest) with a major manufacturer of telecommunications equipment.

Consultants provide customers with technical advice (a large number of predominantly small firms) and strategic advice to assist customers in establishing telecommunications policy (a limited number of larger firms, as well as newly founded specialised departments at large, established accounting and consulting firms). Naturally, there are also consultants that offer a mix of both strategic and technical advice.

Manufacturers provide consultants with information about products and prices, as well as with general information about their organisation. In addition, consultants would like to receive more strategic information and the manufacturer's view on present and future developments. Some manufacturers already comply with this request: apart from sending brochures and manuals, they periodically organise tailor-made seminars and informal meetings. Especially large manufacturers maintain good relationships with consultants, although the information mostly concerns systems and networks rather than individual products. Although consultants place large demands upon the information provided by manufacturers, they realise that it is impossible to comply with all of their wishes. One of the consultants explained that the ideal information package contains detailed and up-to-date intelligence about products, prices, discounts and delivery times, as well as information of a strategic nature that displays the manufacturer's view of present and future developments. Such an ideal information package can never become a reality: 'In a specific situation, concerning a specific project, you always need to contact the manufacturer to obtain the most recent information'. In order to stay fully informed, a high-quality network of personal relationships is essential. However, the time-consuming nature of maintaining such contacts immediately reduces the time available for short-term consultancy projects. Therefore, every consultant needs to carefully balance the short-term costs and long-term benefits of maintaining a network of personal relationships, and focus on the most profitable ones.

CUSTOMERS

Finally, the role of the customers, at whom all information about new products is ultimately directed. Although every firm needs telecommunications equipment, in our investigation only large firms were examined. These firms needed telecommunications for conducting traffic between various locations, or operated in industries where telecommunications can be expected to be critical in carrying out core business activities (such as financial services and transportation).

Most customers limit their contacts with suppliers to periodic meetings with one or two *preferred suppliers* (remember that these suppliers include the distributor PTT Telecom). These regular meetings are used to discuss all aspects of telecommunications. Other suppliers provide customers with product information through mailings and visits by sales representatives. Although most customers use preferred suppliers, they typically follow the policy of requesting proposals from several (usually three) suppliers. Large differences between price/performance ratios may lead to the decision to select another supplier! Because the potential of obtaining an order is always present, it remains useful for out-suppliers to provide the customer with relevant information regularly. At the same time, it keeps the preferred suppliers alert and competitive.

The extent to which customers are willing to change suppliers depends strongly on the nature of the product and the number of units already installed. For instance, Van Gend & Loos, a major Dutch transportation firm, relies heavily on a smoothly functioning telecommunications system supplied mainly by IBM and PTT Telecom. To prevent problems and incompatibility, Van Gend & Loos is unlikely to switch to other suppliers. However, products that are not critical to the core network (e.g. modems and fax machines) and are more or less standard products are bought from local distributors/dealers, with price being an important criterion. However, even with these products, bearing in mind possible future integration of products and systems, the number of potential suppliers is kept to a minimum.

In addition to the information provided by manufacturers directly, customers keep abreast of the latest developments through trade shows, trade journals and distributors. Distributors are considered to be more objective than manufacturers because they generally offer products from various manufacturers. Nevertheless, the information provided by them is mostly at the level of individual products. When a customer needs additional information or objective advice, a consultant may be called in to provide strategic advice (market trends, technological developments, vision) or technical advice (product specifications, installation). Sometimes, a customer needs both kinds of advice, and hires a consultant that can also take care of project management, and thus implement the solution suggested. Just as with suppliers, many customers maintain good relationships with consultants. The government and large firms, in particular, generally work with *preferred consultants*. The status of preferred consultant is typically based on the consultant's market position and the customer's experiences with previous projects.

In general, the rapid pace of technological development makes it increasingly difficult for customers to keep up with all of the changes and increases their dependence on consultants, especially when it concerns projects involving large investments. The extent to which customers allow themselves to depend on consultants is greatly determined by the role of telecommunications within the firm. When telecommunications is strongly connected to the firm's core business, the customer will want to keep the required expertise in-house. One manager of Van Gend & Loos stated that they did not work with consultants: 'For us, telecommunications is too important to delegate to external parties.'

MANAGERIAL IMPLICATIONS

Most suppliers in the Dutch telecommunications industry do not pay very much attention to the announcement of new products. Manufacturers do not approach new product announcements in a structured way, frequently leaving the planning and implementation to advertising agencies and/or distributors. Distributors limit their efforts to the use of standard means of communication (advertisements in trade journals and participation in trade shows) in traditional ways. Dealers, finally, look upon new products as a promotional vehicle to increase the attention value of advertisements.

In addition, the announcement of a new product is mostly interpreted as informing customers and distributors, with consultants rapidly becoming a third relevant party, while 'informing or misleading competitors' is generally not considered to be an important objective for these kinds of products. This is in sharp contrast to the computer industry, where new product announcements as a rule are employed as an important strategic weapon to influence competitors. Increasing competitive pressures in the telecommunications industry, combined with the growing integration of data communications and telecommunications, will cause managers in the telecommunications industry to realise that the effective management of new product announcements is becoming a prerequisite for the successful development and launch of new telecommunications products. In this study, these changing conditions were foreshadowed by the respondents' increasing awareness of both the complexity and strategic importance of new product announcements. The results of the investigation in the Dutch telecommunications industry suggest several relevant implications that may assist managers in more effectively managing future new product announcements (see Table 10.2).

Table 10.2   The 'do's and 'don't's of managing new product announcements

1. DO treat the announcement of new products as a series of complex, related decisions and activities. Aim at establishing a balanced mixture of communication means and messages.
2. DON'T treat all products the same, but make a distinction between useful categories and determine the right announcement process for each category.
3. DO make a well-considered trade-off between announcing new products yourself and hiring specialised agencies to take care of specific communication tasks.
4. DON'T ignore parties that are involved in communication with your customers. Develop and maintain a network of personal relationships with all relevant parties and provide them frequently with pertinent information about products and strategies.
5. DO register significant developments in the market-place, analyse their consequences for the announcement of new products and take appropriate action.
6. DON'T be a passive actor, but take the initiative in providing customers and change agents with information about new products and combine it with query systems that they can use to gain quick access to relevant additional information.
7. DO determine for each relevant party the optimal mix of general information tailored to their specific needs and circumstances.
8. DON'T neglect the influence of organisational idiosyncrasies on the new product announcement process, but benchmark your process with that of other companies, identify bottlenecks and potential areas for improvement and take action.
9. DO put the basic principles of new product announcements in writing and communicate them clearly to all people involved.
10. DON'T ignore the role and relevance of external contacts. Inform those of your employees who interact with external parties about company policy concerning the dissemination of information about new products.

MANAGING NEW PRODUCT ANNOUNCEMENTS AS A COMPLEX PROCESS

The problems and issues discussed here serve to emphasise the complexity of managing new product announcements, and may assist managers in structuring the most relevant decisions and evaluating possible consequences. The presented framework linking the formal/informal and internal/external components of new product announcements stresses the underlying relationships between the various activities. For instance, it demonstrates that unwanted informal, external announcements may be prevented by careful planning of the formal, internal announcement. Managers need to realise that the announcement of new products is a very complex process, consisting of several interdependent elements. Achieving the right balance between internal and external announcements is critical to success, and requires careful orchestration.

STRATEGIC AND OPERATIONAL COMPONENT

The complex process of announcing new products consists of both a strategic and an operational component. The *strategic* component concerns the management of new product announcements and the relationship with the firm's strategy. Announcements are a result of the formulated strategy, while they may also contribute to determining the firm's perceived strategy. After all, one or more new product announcements may be interpreted as indicators of the strategy followed by the firm. The *operational* component refers to the decisions regarding the execution of new product announcements and raises questions such as: do we bring in a specialised communication agency or do we use our own marketing or PR department? Although an external agency may provide the necessary expertise and objective perspective, both the complexity of many telecommunications products and the numerous and vastly different applications generally require a careful briefing and close involvement in developing the best approach.

INVOLVEMENT OF VARIOUS PARTIES

The announcement of new telecommunications products clearly involves much more than a one-way flow of information from manufacturer to customers. Distributors, dealers and consultants all play their own roles in the announcement process. The manufacturer should be aware of:

- the various parties involved in the announcement of new products
- the roles played by the individual parties
- the customer's perception of the various parties and their roles
- possible changes in the factors mentioned above (e.g. the increasing role of consultants)

The involvement of various parties, each of them with its own individual role and idiosyncratic information needs, implies that a manufacturer must target its information about new products carefully. The manufacturer's decision about the extent to which information is targeted to individual parties is based on a trade-off between the importance of the party involved and the costs of providing tailor-made information.

The available communication channels (distributors, dealers and consultants) have very different characteristics. Communication through consultants has the major advantage that consultants add information that is of critical importance to customers (such as a broader perspective, strategic vision, technological developments, market trends, organisational issues concerning implementation, exploitation costs and comparable information about various applications). In addition, the consultant is generally perceived as being relatively independent. Distributors, on the other hand, provide the manufacturer with a communication channel that can be controlled to a certain extent, but customers clearly view distributors as representing a number of manufacturers, and thus as less independent. Finally, while a manufacturer may have a strong hand in dealers' advertisements, their role in announcing new products is quite limited.

INFLUENCE OF PRODUCT AND ORGANISATION

Rabino and Moore (1989) concluded that the length and nature of a new product announcement is determined by the product, rather than by the organisation involved. This is only partly confirmed by the results of our study. Naturally, new product announcements are strongly determined by the product involved, with the nature of the product and its relative newness being the most important variables. For instance, the announcement of a new handset is limited to the dissemination of specification sheets, including the new model in the catalogue and perhaps displaying it prominently in one or two advertisements. More complex products, such as telephone switches, require a more extensive and targeted announcement to distributors, consultants and a number of selected customers. Yet, examples from the study were found where the nature of the organisation strongly influenced both the content of new product announcements and the way in which they were managed. In particular, the firm's market position, policy/strategy and culture may be strongly related to the announcement process. For instance, PTT Telecom has experienced major restructuring processes in order to change from being a product-orientated firm to a market-orientated one. This strong emphasis on the customer's perspective resulted in the formulation of various manuals and guidelines, including extensive procedures to direct the formal, internal announcements. These procedures will ultimately result in more standardised external announcements as well.

PROCEDURES OR MADE-TO-MEASURE?

The various suppliers do not agree about the extent to which the complex process of new product announcements can be standardised by means of detailed procedures. Nevertheless, they acknowledge the benefits of introducing structure, e.g. based on experiences with previous announcements. Such a learning process could eventually result in the formulation of very general guidelines to be followed. In our opinion, even though the complex process of announcing new products cannot be directed by extensive procedures accounting for all possible eventualities, a supplier should nevertheless formulate some guidelines to lay down the basic principles. These principles should address such basic issues as:

- the individuals/departments to be informed
- when one needs to be informed
- who needs to provide the required information
- the activities that need to be undertaken
- the division of responsibilities
- the general time schedule involved

Laying down these basic principles reduces uncertainty and misunderstandings, provides guidance for action and prevents *ad hoc* decision making. Subsequently, each individual firm can decide whether it wants to translate these basic principles into more detailed procedures and manuals.

NEW PRODUCT ANNOUNCEMENTS AND RELATIONSHIP MANAGEMENT

The discussion in this chapter has clearly demonstrated the importance of personal relationships in announcing new products. For instance, developing and maintaining a network of personal relationships was found to be of critical importance to consultants. Nevertheless, the emphasis on personal relationships in announcing new products involves two problems as well.

The first revolves around the issues of credibility and perceived objectivity. Even though personal relationships may play a crucial role in announcing new products, the study showed that relationships that are perceived as being too close may turn out to be a liability rather than an asset.

The second problem refers to the frequently mentioned danger of a sales representative inadvertently providing too much information to a customer, thus resulting in a premature announcement. Although this will lead suppliers to inform their sales representatives as late as possible, they are also aware of the potential negative consequences of an uninformed sales force. The suppliers' responses to these considerations vary from (i) formulating detailed guidelines that spell out the desired behaviour of the individuals involved in external contacts to (ii) leaving the management of external relationships to the discretion of the people involved. This second strategy is also implied by management guru Peter Drucker (1988), when he writes that the increasing importance of relationships 'will require greater self-discipline and even greater emphasis on individual responsibility for relationships and for communications'.

TRACING NETWORKS AND SPEEDING UP DIFFUSION

The results presented in this chapter emphasise the need to trace the existing network structure, with all of its constituent members and roles (Woodside and Wilson 1994). Identification of the relevant parties, their roles, wants and needs can contribute to the formulation of a coherent communication strategy. One of the primary aims of announcing a new product is to assist its adoption and speed up the rate of diffusion. The key parties in this respect are change agents. In this particular study of the Dutch telecommunications industry, consultants are an obvious example of change agents and their growing role needs to be capitalised upon by manufacturers. As Harrer, Weijo and Hattrup (1988) concluded, 'once the key change agents have been identified and characterised, appropriate methods need to be developed to inform them of the relative merit of the new product.' How this functions in practice is illustrated by the example of PTT Telecom, which is considering the introduction of a Videotex service aimed at consultants. Harrer, Weijo and Hattrup (1988) mention a number of other methods, and stress that, once the change agents are convinced of the merits of the new product:

> they can be used in information dissemination through expert testimonies, testimonies of participants in demonstration programs, articles in the trade literature, and any other methods that can tap into their ability to influence product adoption decisions.

CONCLUSION

While the NPD processes has been investigated from various angles, the relevance of new product announcements has generally been overlooked. The present study intended to remedy this situation by investigating in detail announcement practices in the Dutch telecommunications industry. The knowledge thus gained may assist managers in enhancing the effectiveness of NPD efforts by effectively linking into existing networks.

REFERENCES

Balachandra, R. (1984). Critical signals for making go/no go decisions in new product development, *Journal of Product Innovation Management*, **2**(2), 92–100.

Biemans, W.G. (1992). *Managing Innovation within Networks*, Routledge, London.

Booz, Allen and Hamilton (1968). *Management of New Products*, Booz, Allen and Hamilton Inc., New York.

Chaney, P.K., Devinney, T.M. and Winer, R.S. (1989). The impact of new product introductions on the value of firms, Report 89-105, Marketing Science Institute, Cambridge, MA, January.

Craig, A. and Hart, S. (1992). Where to now in new product development research? *European Journal of Marketing*, **26**(11), 2–49.

Crawford, C.M. (1983). *New Products Management*, Richard Irwin, Homewood, IL.

Drucker, P.F. (1988). The coming of the new organisation, *Harvard Business Review*, January/February, 45–53.

Dundas, G.R. and Krentler, K.A. (1982). Critical path method for introducing an industrial product, *Industrial Marketing Management*, **11**, 125–131.

Eliashberg, J. and Robertson, T.S. (1988). New product preannouncing behaviour: A market signalling study, *Journal of Marketing Research*, **XXV**, 282–292.

Foxall, G.R. (1984). *Corporate Innovation: Marketing and Strategy*, Croom Helm, London.

Harrer, B.J., Weijo, R.O. and Hattrup, M.P. (1988). The role of change agents in new product adoption: A case study, *Industrial Marketing Management*, **17**, 95–102.

Rabino, S. and Moore, T.E. (1989). Managing new-product announcements in the computer industry, *Industrial Marketing Management*, **18**, 35–43.

Rebello, K., Schwartz, E.A., Verity, J.W., Lewin, M. and Levine, J. (1993). Is Microsoft too powerful? *Business Week International*, 1 March, 48–55.

Rogers, E.M. (1983). *Diffusion of Innovations*, 3rd edn, Free Press, New York.

Saren, M.A. (1984). A classification and review of models of the intra-firm innovation process, *R&D Management*, **14**(1), 11–24.

Spence, M.A. (1974). *Market Signalling*, Harvard Business School Press, Cambridge, MA.

Wind, Y. and Mahajan, V. (1987). Marketing hype: A new perspective for new product research and introduction, *Journal of Product Innovation Management*, **4**(1), 43–49.

Woodside, A.G. and Wilson, E.J. (1994). Tracing emergent networks in adoptions of new manufacturing technologies, presented at the 1994 research conference on relationship marketing, Emory Business School, Emory University, 11–13 June, Atlanta, GA.

CHAPTER ELEVEN

SUCCESSFUL LAUNCH STRATEGIES: NEW AND FUTURE RESEARCH EFFORTS

Erik Jan Hultink and Henry S.J. Robben

New product launch strategies are critical for new product success. This chapter shows how launch strategies consist of strategic launch variables and tactical marketing-mix decisions, both of which are influenced by company and personal characteristics. All of these variables interact and influence the eventual level of new product success. The chapter describes the different variables and their interactions, as well as different research methods for investigating successful launch strategies. Because of the methodological problems involved in measuring success in hindsight, the authors suggest conjoint analysis as an alternative method, and illustrate its use by presenting the results of an empirical study.

INTRODUCTION

New product launches have been acclaimed as vital for the commercial health and survival of companies (e.g. Dwyer and Mellor 1991). Much has already been written about the determinants and correlates of new product success or failure (see, for example, Hart, Chapter 1 and Johne, Chapter 2, this volume). Obviously, new products must have an excellent score on one or more critical performance parameters, a favourable price–performance ratio, and be

Product Development: Meeting the Challenge of the Design–Marketing Interface.
Edited by M. Bruce and W.G. Biemans.   © 1995 John Wiley & Sons Ltd.

reliable. Not only does a product need these qualities, but the market also has to be convinced as well.

There are differences between successful and unsuccessful products in terms of launch strategy components. In general, firms handle their launch activities better for successful than for unsuccessful products (Cooper and Kleinschmidt 1986), and managers have cited poor execution of a new product's launch as a major reason for failure (Cooper 1979). Although, evidently, launch strategy decisions are important for a new product's success or failure, there has been little research on how specific elements of the launch strategy relate to new product success. For instance, how do launch strategy choices like pricing and promotion influence new product success? Such variables are under managerial control and thus manipulable. Managers would benefit from analysis of the relationship between launch strategy variables and new product success.

For the present purposes, a launch strategy is regarded as consisting of those strategic and tactical marketing choices that the firm makes in launching the new product and that the firm follows in the first year after introduction to position the product in the market-place (Green and Ryans 1990). This launch strategy contributes to the firm's long-term success or market failure.

Launch strategies can best be described according to a small number of strategic launch variables and several marketing-mix decisions (Biggadike 1979). Strategic launch variables are, for example, relative product innovativeness, production entry scale and order of entry. The marketing-mix elements touched upon in this analysis are pricing, promotion and product assortment strategy.

In Figure 11.1, the above variables and their relationships with new product success are presented in a theoretical model. This model shows a direct influence of the launch strategy elements on new product success. In addition, company and personal characteristics influence the launch strategy elements. Following Biggadike (1979), it is assumed that strategic launch variables precede the tactical marketing-mix decisions. Strategic launch variables therefore create the conditions in which the firm has to operationalise the marketing-mix.

In this chapter, the theoretical model is discussed in conjunction with a literature review. The necessity of obtaining reliable data on launch strategies is addressed and it is suggested that conjoint analysis may be helpful. A study is described that highlights the usefulness of the conjoint analysis methodology for investigating launch strategies. Finally, research consequences are delineated for studies on launch strategies and new product success.

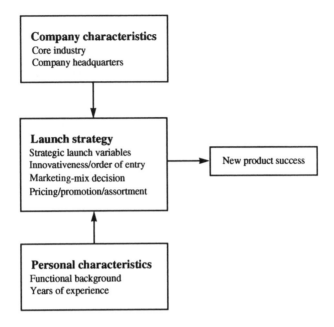

Figure 11.1   A theoretical model of successful launch strategies

THE MODEL FOR INVESTIGATING LAUNCH STRATEGIES

This section discusses both the strategic launch variables and the tactical marketing-mix decisions which make up the launch strategy. In addition, company and personal characteristics are shown to influence launch strategies.

STRATEGIC LAUNCH VARIABLES

Relative innovativeness and order of entry are pertinent strategic launch variables (Kleinschmidt and Cooper 1991; Lambkin 1988). Strategic launch variables for products commercialised by firms frequently change along these two dimensions. Firms continually try to introduce new and better versions of products that will allow them to maintain their competitive market positions. These two strategic variables are examined in more detail to ascertain how they interact with marketing-mix decisions made in launching new products.

Relative Innovativeness of New Products

New products differ in their degree of innovativeness (Kleinschmidt and Cooper 1991; Yoon and Lilien 1985). The literature shows mixed results on the relationship between product innovativeness and new product success. Kleinschmidt and Cooper (1991) report a U-shaped curve, with products low or high in terms of their innovativeness being commercially more successful than moderately innovative products. Increased product complexity probably contributes to increased customer resistance because of higher perceived risks (Rogers 1983). When customers face a product demanding substantial changes in their usual behaviour, the likelihood of adoption decreases (Frambach, Chapter 12, this volume; Gatignon and Robertson 1991). Innovativeness also moderates companies' pricing strategies. Companies tend to use penetration pricing for new-to-the-world products, whereas for incremental innovations they rely more on skimming strategies (Choffray and Lilien 1984).

Order of Entry

Market entrants can be divided into pioneers, early entrants and late entrants. A pioneer is the first company to launch a new product, and is often the first to develop the new technology necessary for the product's performance. An early entrant is a quick follower in a new and dynamic market. A late entrant enters when the speed of market growth slows down. The order of a firm's entry into markets is not only relevant in preventing the introduction of underdeveloped products in the market, or sacrificing sales in deferring the launch too long; it also involves the type of innovation concerned. For original new products, being an early follower appears more beneficial than being a pioneer (Yoon and Lilien 1985). Pioneers need more time, money and effort to develop a market and make customers aware of the product's benefits. Also, risks of liabilities and unsatisfactory product performance are higher for highly innovative products than for other products. Order of entry can also moderate the impact of the marketing-mix decisions on new product success; for example, the promotion strategy of pioneers should create awareness of the new product or category. When early entrants enter the market, customers are already aware of the new product. Under such circumstances, several product alternatives are available. This situation may imply that 'pull promotion' is more effective for pioneers, whereas 'push promotion' may be more effective for early and later entrants. Followers have to convince dealers that their new products have a relative advantage over pioneers' products.

MARKETING-MIX DECISIONS

The marketing-mix decisions included in the model are pricing, promotion and product assortment. According to Kotler (1994), pricing and promotion are key elements in product launch strategies. Traynor and Traynor (1989) mention product assortment as one of the most important marketing tools. More tactical launch variables, such as distribution decisions and branding, can also be included in the model.

Pricing Decisions

It is difficult to draw firm conclusions about the relationship between specific pricing strategies and new product success. Price is not only seen as one of many concepts in models describing new product success, but there is also a growing consensus about the role played by non-financial ideas in attaining new product success. Studies show different effects of price (Biggadike 1979; Cooper 1979; Dolan and Jeuland 1981). Dolan and Jeuland (1981) relate skimming and penetration strategies to the demand curve. When the demand curve is stable over time and production costs decrease with accumulated volume, then initial high prices can be followed by low prices. Penetration pricing can be used as the principal instrument for highly innovative new products when the long-term positive effect of cumulative production on costs (the experience effect) is important (Choffray and Lilien 1984).

Promotion Decisions

Important promotion decisions entail the level of marketing expenditures and the choice between emphasising pull or push promotion. Promotion and distribution expenditures are positively related to new product success (Green and Ryans 1990). It seems obvious that for highly innovative products more elaborate market preparation is necessary than for reformulated products. The latter typically capitalise on existing market infrastructure and customer needs and awareness. The marketing literature usually divides promotion strategies into push and pull promotion. A push strategy directs marketing activities at channel intermediaries, inducing them to carry the product and promote it to end users. Pull promotion is directed at end users, with the aim of encouraging them to 'pull' the product through the distribution chain. The literature is inconsistent about the impact of the different promotion strategies on new product success. There is, however, some evidence that marketing managers prefer pull promotion to push promotion in order to communicate directly with the end user of the product (Hultink and Schoormans 1995).

Product Assortment Strategy

Product assortment strategy refers to the breadth of the product line, meaning the number of models one year after introduction. Traynor and Traynor (1989) reported that the breadth of the product line was among the marketing tools most frequently cited as being important by high-technology marketers. Breadth of product line may be associated with market share of new firms (Lambkin 1988). Hisrich and Peters (1991) argue that offering many versions of the same product to a single segment might actually confuse the customer. However, by differentiating an innovative product and targeting the alternatives at different market segments, firms can increase their competitive space. Pioneers and early entrants may even pre-empt the competition.

COMPANY AND PERSONAL CHARACTERISTICS

Figure 11.1 shows the direct influence of company and personal characteristics on the strategic and tactical launch decisions that managers make. Examples of company characteristics are the core industry of the company and the geographical location of the company's headquarters. It is likely that managers from, for instance, Japanese companies make different launch decisions to managers from American companies. Hayes and Abernathy (1980) criticise the focus of American managers on short-term goals instead of on long-term growth, which may influence launch decisions.

Personal characteristics refer to the functional background and the marketing experience of the manager, so, for example, a marketing manager is likely to make different launch decisions to an R&D manager. Hultink, Robben and Griffin (1994) found that preferred launch strategies depended on the years of experience a manager has in a marketing-related position.

In sum, the launch variables mentioned above have a direct relationship on new product success and can be influenced by managerial decisions. The theoretical model summarises salient ideas that have been identified as contributing to the understanding of new product success. Yet, many specific relationships cannot be predicted unequivocally. For instance, it cannot be established that pricing strategy affects new product success in a straightforward manner because of the potentially confounding influences of promotion strategies. It is therefore necessary to investigate launch strategies in more detail.

HOW TO INVESTIGATE SUCCESSFUL LAUNCH STRATEGIES

It may be difficult to obtain valid objective data on launch strategies. Some aggregate information can be derived from annual reports, but the available information is not always at a project or product level (Hart 1993).

It is difficult to discover a company's appraisal of new product launch strategies before launch occurs. Few companies allow academics access to their decision making and implementation meetings. In addition, unequivocal hard data are notoriously difficult to obtain. Therefore, empirical studies have measured launch strategies in hindsight. Typically, researchers asked managers to pick successful and failed new products that their companies had launched some years ago (Choffray and Lilien 1984; Cooper 1979; Yoon and Lilien 1985). Managers had to indicate which launch strategy their company followed for the product, or were asked to rate the importance of selected launch decisions and activities.

This method, which relies on managerial hindsight, may not be the most valid because measuring success in hindsight has some serious problems and drawbacks. Firstly, managers often do not remember exactly what strategy their company used for the product (Golden 1992). Secondly, it is uncertain whether success or failure of the new product is the result of the chosen launch strategy or due to external factors that occurred between the launch and the measurement of success (Green and Ryans 1990). Thirdly, asking people in hindsight for the reasons for success or failure, as is done frequently in this kind of research, is sensitive to attribution errors (Curren, Folkes and Steckel 1992). Psychological research has shown that people may construct their answers at the time of being asked, or retrieve them from memory using an availability heuristic. Also, using methods in which individuals are approached directly may evoke disturbing processes, such as ingratiation, self-presentational concerns, impression management and evaluation apprehension (Robben 1991, pp. 66–67). The data delivered by individual managers in personal interviews or questionnaires may be compromised by these psychological reactions to the interviewer or the research instrument or setting.

How can we satisfy the need for valid data? Firstly, such a procedure requires systematic observation of new product launches in terms of recording the number and nature of the strategic launch variables involved and the marketing instruments used. The current pervasiveness of new product launches in consumer and industrial markets would yield a potentially sufficient database. Such an observation strategy does require significant participation from researchers.

For instance, when the national and global manufacturer Philips launches a new product, this would be easy to observe given Philips' substantial marketing communication efforts. But when national Dutch manufacturer BNS introduces a new hi-fi speaker, this would almost certainly go unnoticed. Only if the new system attained substantial market share would marketing efforts be clearly visible. Considerations like these call for a research instrument that objectively, and preferably automatically, records vital data of new product launches. Complementary to this ideal research route, a different research option is described below.

It is possible to gain insight into an individual manager's decision strategies by having him or her systematically evaluate or rank alternative launch strategies in a controlled setting. A promising method employed to investigate launch preferences given certain personal or company conditions is *conjoint analysis*. Conjoint analysis received academic interest long ago, and it has also been put to commercial use (Wittink, Vriens and Burhenne 1994). The next section reports the major findings of a study in which conjoint analysis was used to investigate the impact of selected launch elements on new product success.

A CONJOINT ANALYSIS APPROACH TO INVESTIGATE SUCCESSFUL LAUNCH STRATEGIES

Hultink and Schoormans (1995) asked 28 product and marketing managers to evaluate eight launch strategies in a conjoint analysis design. The participants all had experience in launching new high-tech products. The managers had to imagine that they were advising a medium-sized Dutch consumer electronics company, which was the third entrant on the market for photo-cd players, on these launch strategies. The eight strategies can be characterised by a combination of four launch variables:

- pricing strategy (skimming versus penetration pricing)
- product assortment (small versus large)
- promotion strategy (push versus pull promotion)
- the product's competitive advantage (higher quality, better design and more innovative)

To simplify the participants' task, they responded to only eight launch strategies. For each of these strategies, the managers rated the chances of success on a nine-point rating scale. Besides these estimates, they provided information on firm background characteristics.

The general results of the conjoint analysis study of Hultink and Schoormans (1995) led to an additional cluster analysis that revealed two conceptually meaningful clusters. The first cluster was characterised by emphasis on a penetration pricing strategy, the second by a skimming price strategy. Members of the first cluster emphasised penetration pricing, pull promotion and a small assortment. In the second cluster, a skimming price strategy and a small product assortment were chosen. The major difference between the two strategies is the choice of the pricing strategy.

From the information obtained in qualitative follow-up interviews, the authors derived a tentative interpretation with respect to the managers' pricing preferences. Managers in the *penetration* cluster rated the different strategies more according to market share and sales objectives, while managers in the *skimming* cluster were more interested in financial success objectives, such as return on sales and profitability. Either pricing strategy can be successful. This preference for a certain strategy, however, may depend on the objectives for the new product launch, for instance, attaining market share or yielding profit.

The strategies preferred by members of the clusters were significantly different in terms of a rank-order correlation: managers in the first cluster attached different values (in terms of utilities) to launch strategies than those in the second cluster. This finding, although statistically significant, does not suggest that the preferred strategies in either cluster were each other's mirror images. Instead, strategies that were valued highly in one cluster received moderate evaluations in the other cluster, and vice versa. This means that although the authors statistically differentiated two pricing strategy clusters, the conceptual differences between the clusters were not that large. This interpretation may hint at some confusion on the part of the managers as to which strategies may be successful in the task at hand, or may indicate that they think that it does not really matter which strategy is actually employed.

By cross-tabulating company characteristics such as the firm's core industry and the geographical location of its headquarters with the derived clusters, Hultink and Schoormans investigated the possible relationships between these variables and cluster membership. Although they did not find any statistically significant effects, some of their findings are conceptually relevant for investigating new product launches. Firstly, there is a trend for managers in the non-consumer electronics industry to be more likely to belong to the penetration cluster. Secondly, the findings suggest a weak relationship between membership of the penetration cluster and the location of the company's headquarters in the USA.

The last set of findings suggests that firm characteristics are in one way or another associated with managers' evaluations of the possible success of hypothetical launch strategies (see Figure 11.1).

The value of the study by Hultink and Schoormans (1995) is that it showed that a conjoint analysis approach to managers' perceptions of new product launches revealed relevant data. Although their sample size was small, they obtained interpretable and significant differences in the success estimates of each launch strategy.

LIMITATIONS, SCOPE AND OPPORTUNITIES

Hultink and Schoormans (1995) measured *expectations* about success instead of measuring success in hindsight. This choice was important because, in this way, the impact of launch strategy variables on new product success was not contaminated by other factors that typically occur between the launch of a new product and the measurement of success, when success is measured in hindsight. Although persuasive in terms of results, it is possible to enhance the generalisability of the reported findings.

Firstly, a fractional factorial design made it possible to collect data from respondents who had a tight time schedule. This data collection procedure inhibited the testing of interaction effects, however. A full-factorial design allows for testing interaction effects as well. Future research should explore this possibility. Secondly, Hultink and Schoormans (1995) only used expectations about successful launch strategies. Therefore, a comparison with actual results was not possible. In a more refined longitudinal research design, an assessment of actual results should follow the expectations about the impact of different launch strategies.

Furthermore, the respondents gave their opinions almost in a business vacuum, i.e. without a *psychologically* realistic environment. A possible enrichment of the conjoint analysis method is to embed the conjoint analysis task in a *business management simulation*. Robben (1991) has shown in a different setting that participants in his simulations became involved in what is basically a computerised business management task. This task required participants to act like an entrepreneur; in a simulated small supermarket, for instance, people made decisions about product prices, advertising strategy, investment strategy and fiscal requirements. The main advantage of this simulation method is that respondents become involved in the situation, enhancing the realism of the task *and* the quality of the data obtained. One could systematically vary the factors of interest in launch strategies, such as the maturity of the market, perceived or expected competitor reactions, and type of pricing strategies. Such investigations allow for causal inferences to be drawn, instead of relying on correlational evidence obtained in questionnaire or econometric studies. It is advisable to have the simulation followed by a qualitative debriefing session to assess company and individual characteristics and respondents' appreciation of the research setting and their reactions. Although it is interesting to know what causes lead to a certain launch strategy, the correlates of such a decision are also relevant in that they might hint at other possibly promising variables to be included in such simulation studies. Having established causal directions in new product launch decisions through the experimental methodology described above, it is possible to subject the acquired knowledge to more extensive structural modelling. The number of independent factors in such a simulation may be limited, but the methodological improvement in terms of internal validity of results compensates for this relative imperfection.

Apart from these problems relating to the methodology employed in such investigations, the quality of the dependent variable requires additional conceptualisation. The empirical study by Hultink and Schoormans (1995) employed a *single* general expected success measure of new product success. This procedure referred to Cooper's (1982) definition of the degree to which one expects the product's total profits to exceed or fall short of the firm's acceptable profit criteria. However, many different measures of new product success are available (Griffin and Page 1993). Therefore, several authors have stressed the usefulness of a multidimensional view of new product success (Griffin and Page 1993; Hart 1993). Robben and Hultink (1993) conducted a survey of new product success measures among Dutch general and marketing managers, starting from Griffin and Page's (1993) inventory. This study showed that not all new product success measures are equally important. Furthermore, it was found that the importance of new product success measures depended on the time perspective. The results of that survey, in combination with other relevant studies, should lead to a set of measures that can be used unequivocally to determine and identify new product success. In this respect, future research should also clarify how 'successful' launch strategies depend on the chosen success measure.

CONCLUSION

In developing a launch strategy, marketing managers formulate explicit or implicit expectations about the contribution of the various launch elements to the future success of the new product. In the case of, for example, high-tech new-to-the-world products it is almost impossible to formulate reliable and numerically specified expectations. Market, technological and organisational uncertainties dominate the introduction of such products (Moriarty and Kosnik 1989). Given such circumstances, *qualitative* expectations have to be formulated. Product, company and personal characteristics influence this process of formulating qualitative evaluations (Figure 11.1). In the empirical study described, the influence of product characteristics was kept to a minimum because all respondents launched the same new product. Salient respondent characteristics are experience with the product category and experience with launching new products. The influence of these respondent characteristics on preferred launch strategies should be explored further in future research.

The study investigated such expectations in a controlled fashion. It showed that marketing managers have outspoken ideas about the direction of the effects and the relative importance of the various marketing-mix elements. An additional research question, addressed by Hultink, Robben and Griffin (1994), focused on the question as to whether managers have different marketing-mix preferences when the company is a pioneer instead of an early entrant. Surprisingly, the impact of company and personal characteristics on preferred launch strategies was larger than the impact of the order of entry variable. Only the preferred pricing strategy varied with the order of entry. Pioneers preferred skimming whereas followers opted for a penetration pricing strategy. This finding is consistent with the product life cycle literature (Kotler 1994).

In this chapter, suggestions have been made to extend research on launch strategies in the following ways:

1. To systematically record internal and external company variables to assess companies' actual commitment to those strategies.
2. To examine these decisions at an individual managerial level to encompass both individual and perceived company characteristics.
3. To systematically collect data in a more controlled environment to enhance the reliability and validity of the data.

By including data at both the company and the individual level, a complete picture will emerge of how new product launch decisions come about and to which results these will lead. By relating such data to several success measures of new products, companies might learn where and how to improve or innovate their launch strategies.

ACKNOWLEDGEMENTS

The authors appreciate the constructive comments of Jan P.L. Schoormans and Walle M. Oppedijk van Veen on an earlier version of this chapter.

REFERENCES

Biggadike, E.R. (1979). *Corporate Diversification: Entry, Strategy and Performance*, Harvard University Press, Cambridge, MA.

Choffray, J.M. and Lilien, G.L. (1984). Strategies behind the successful industrial product launch, *Business Marketing*, November, 82–95.

Cooper, R.G. (1979). The dimensions of industrial new product success and failure, *Journal of Marketing*, **43**, 93–103.

Cooper, R.G. (1982). New product success in industrial firms, *Industrial Marketing Management*, **3**(11), 215–223.

Cooper, R.G. and Kleinschmidt, E.J. (1986). An investigation into the new product process: Steps, deficiencies and impact, *Journal of Product Innovation Management*, **3**, 71–85.

Curren, M.T., Folkes, V.S. and Steckel, J.H. (1992). Explanations for successful and unsuccessful marketing decisions: The decision maker's perspective, *Journal of Marketing*, **56**, 18–31.

Dolan, R.J. and Jeuland, A.P. (1981). Experience curves and dynamic demand models: Implications for optimal pricing strategies, *Journal of Marketing*, **52**, 52–62.

Dwyer, L. and Mellor, R. (1991). New product strategies of high technology firms, *Asia Pacific International Forum*, No. 16, 4–11.

Gatignon, H. and Robertson, T.S. (1991). Innovative decision processes, in Robertson, T.S. and Kassarjian, H.H. (eds), *Handbook of Consumer Behaviour*, Prentice Hall, Englewood Cliffs, NJ, pp. 316–346.

Golden, B.R. (1992). The past is the past – Or is it? The use of retrospective accounts as indicators of past strategy, *Academy of Management Journal*, **35**(4), 848–860.

Green, D.H. and Ryans, A.B. (1990). Entry strategies and market performance: Causal modelling of a business simulation, *Journal of Product Innovation Management*, **7**, 45–58.

Griffin, A.J. and Page, A.L. (1993). An interim report on measuring new product development success and failure, *Journal of Product Innovation Management*, **10**(4), 291–308.

Hart, S. (1993). Dimensions of success in new product development: An exploratory investigation, *Journal of Marketing Management*, **9**(1), 23–41.

Hayes, R.H. and Abernathy, W.J. (1980). Managing our way to economic decline, *Harvard Business Review*, **58**(4), 67–77.

Hisrich, R.D. and Peters, M.P. (1991). *Marketing Decisions for New and Mature Products*, Macmillan, New York.

Hultink, E.J. and Schoormans, J.P.L. (1995). How to launch a high-tech product successfully: An analysis of marketing managers' strategy choices, *Journal of High Technology Management Research*.

Hultink, E.J., Robben, H.S.J. and Griffin, A.J. (1994). Predicting successful launch strategies: An easy prediction? Well, maybe . . ., working paper, Delft University of Technology, The Netherlands.

Kleinschmidt, E.J. and Cooper, R.G. (1991). The impact of product innovativeness on performance, *Journal of Product Innovation Management*, **8**, 240–251.

Kotler, P. (1994). *Marketing Management: Analysis, Planning, Implementation and Control*, 8th edn, Prentice Hall, Englewood Cliffs, NJ.

Lambkin, M. (1988). Order of entry and performance in new markets, *Strategic Management Journal*, **9**, 127–140.

Moriarty, R.T. and Kosnik, T.J. (1989). High-tech marketing: Concepts, continuity and change, *Sloan Management Review*, Summer, 7–17.

Robben, H.S.J. (1991). *A Behavioural Simulation and Documented Behaviour Approach to Income Tax Evasion*, Kluwer, Deventer, The Netherlands.

Robben, H.S.J. and Hultink, E.J. (1993). The importance of new product success and failure measures in the Dutch industry, in Cardozo, R.N., Roering, K.J. and Shocker, A.D. (eds), *Teamwork: Keystone for Getting High Quality Products to Market Quickly*, The Product Development and Management Association, Indianapolis, IN, pp. 92–104.

Rogers, E.M. (1983). *Diffusion of Innovations*, 3rd edn, Free Press, New York.

Traynor, K. and Traynor, S.C. (1989). Marketing approaches used by high tech firms, *Industrial Marketing Management*, **18**, 281–287.

Wittink, D.R., Vriens, M. and Burhenne, W. (1994). Commercial use of conjoint analysis in Europe: results and critical reflections, *International Journal of Research in Marketing*, **11**(1), 41–53.

Yoon, E. and Lilien, G.L. (1985). New industrial product performance: The effect of market characteristics and strategy, *Journal of Product Innovation Management*, **3**, 134–144.

ADOPTION AND DIFFUSION

INTRODUCTION

Wim G. Biemans

The ultimate test of the new product will be its performance in the market-place. Information about adoption and diffusion processes can be used by companies to increase their chances of successfully developing and launching new products. This section contains two chapters about the adoption and diffusion of new products.

In Chapter 12, about the diffusion of innovations in business-to-business markets, Frambach presents a survey of the most relevant literature. Based on this survey, he concludes that diffusion theory strongly focuses on the characteristics of both the product and the adopter, and fails to give sufficient attention to supply-side variables. After having demonstrated the relevance of supply-side variables, he goes on to provide a survey of the literature with respect to supply-related issues, such as the development process, interaction between buyer and supplier and the supplier's marketing strategy. Subsequently, Frambach combines all variables into an integrated model of innovation diffusion in business-to-business markets. The model offers insights into the determinants of market acceptance of new products and can be used by companies to improve their marketing strategy and, ultimately, their products' performance.

In studying adoption and diffusion processes, companies and researchers have displayed great interest in identifying the first or early adopters of new products. In Chapter 13, about 'consumer innovativeness', Foxall concludes, firstly, that the literature on adoption of innovation uses confusing terminology, and, secondly, that the relationship between innovativeness and personality characteristics is based on weak evidence. He proposes a different approach to investigating the personality profiles of early adopters and illustrates its use with the results of five empirical investigations. The results demonstrate that the issue of 'consumer innovators' is more complex than the existing literature seems to suggest, because no direct relationship between consumer behaviour and innovative personality profiles is apparent. Foxall concludes his chapter with a discussion of the implications of this for marketing practice.

CHAPTER TWELVE

DIFFUSION OF INNOVATIONS IN BUSINESS-TO-BUSINESS MARKETS

Ruud T. Frambach

In this chapter a comprehensive model of innovation adoption and diffusion in business-to-business markets is discussed. It is argued that the speed and rate of acceptance of innovations in the industrial market is determined by factors related to both the potential adopter of the innovation and the supplier of the new product. Adopter-side variables influencing innovation adoption include the perceived characteristics of the innovation, the characteristics of the potential adopter, the degree to which the potential adopter is socially active and the competitive environment of the potential adopter. Supply-side variables include the innovation development activities undertaken by the supplier, the marketing strategy pursued by the supplier and the degree to which interaction with potential adopters has taken place during the innovation development process. Finally, the availability of information about an innovation influences its probability of adoption in the market-place.

INTRODUCTION

Diffusion theory aims to provide insight into the factors affecting the rate of acceptance of innovations (Rogers 1983). Shanklin and Ryans (1984) state that:

Product Development: Meeting the Challenge of the Design–Marketing Interface.
Edited by M. Bruce and W.G. Biemans.   © 1995 John Wiley & Sons Ltd.

the concept of diffusion of technological innovations . . . is the basis for developing useful high-tech marketing insights, for effectively researching high-tech markets, and for formulating consequent marketing strategies that prove capable of achieving the company's goals.

By identifying the variables underlying the individual adoption decision, one can gain understanding of the diffusion process of new products.

This chapter focuses on adoption and diffusion in business-to-business markets. A comprehensive literature review is undertaken, which identifies weaknesses with the received wisdom of adoption/diffusion. The variables influencing adoption/diffusion in business-to-business markets are identified and integrated into a coherent framework that serves to explain the adoption/diffusion process.

THE CURRENT DIFFUSION PARADIGM

Research on the diffusion of innovations has enjoyed the interest of many scientific disciplines over the last few decades. As Rogers (1986, 1992) points out, innovation diffusion has emerged as one of the most multidisciplinary research topics in the social sciences today.

The main elements of the diffusion paradigm have been described by Rogers (1983, p. 5) as '(1) an innovation, (2) which is communicated through certain channels, (3) over time, (4) among the members of a social system'.

At the heart of the diffusion paradigm lies the adoption process of a decision making unit and the way it is influenced. The innovation adoption process is defined by Rogers (1983, p. 163) as:

the process through which an individual or other decision-making unit passes from first knowledge of an innovation, to forming an attitude toward the innovation, to a decision to adopt or reject, to implementation of the new idea, and to confirmation of this decision.

Other research (see, for example, Robertson 1971) has outlined the adoption process in a similar way. In the case of the adopting unit being an organisation, the adoption decision will often be made by a 'buying centre' (Johnston and Bonoma 1981). This is a decision making unit consisting of people who each play a different part in the buying process, and therefore exert a definite influence on the adoption decision. Depending on the buying situation ('new-task buy', 'modified re-buy', 'straight re-buy'; see Robinson, Faris and Wind 1967), the adoption process will involve more people, will take longer and will therefore be more complex altogether. In this respect, the innovation adoption decision is the most complex one that an organisation will be faced with, because little experience of the buying process exists for that particular product.

The variables influencing innovation adoption in business-to-business markets will be considered as identified in diffusion theory. As such, characteristics of the innovation, characteristics of the adopting organisation, the information-processing characteristics of the (potential) adopter, network participation and the competitive environment of the adopter will be discussed.

PERCEIVED INNOVATION CHARACTERISTICS

Research has revealed a number of innovation characteristics, as perceived by potential adopters, that influence rate of adoption (Rogers 1983; Tornatzky and Klein 1982). Although no standard classification of innovation characteristics, influencing the process of adoption, has yet been derived in the literature, the influence of several innovation characteristics has found empirical support on a larger scale.

Rogers (1983) identified five innovation characteristics that are related to the rate of adoption. The *relative advantage* of an innovation, defined as 'the degree to which an innovation is perceived as being better than the idea it supersedes', has been found to be one of the best predictors of the rate of adoption of an innovation (Rogers 1983, p. 218; also see Robinson 1990). The innovation adoption decision in the business-to-business market in particular will be a result of the search for and prospects of relative advantages (i.e. improved profitability; Chisnall 1989, p.83; Webster 1969, p. 37). The *compatibility* of an innovation, defined as 'the degree to which an innovation is perceived as consistent with the existing values, past experiences, and needs of potential adopters', is positively related to adoption (Rogers 1983, p. 226). The more an innovation is compatible with the current situation of a potential adopter and his or her needs, the less his or her switching costs and uncertainties will be and the more probable it is that the innovation will be adopted. As regards the *complexity* of an innovation, defined as 'the degree to which an innovation is perceived as relatively difficult to understand and use', Rogers (1983, p. 231) argues that this is negatively related to its rate of adoption. The *trialability* of an innovation and its *observability*, respectively defined as 'the degree to which an innovation may be experimented with on a limited basis' and 'the degree to which the results of an innovation are visible to others', are positively related to the rate of adoption (Rogers 1983, pp. 231–232).

The innovation characteristics put forward by Rogers do not take account of considerations of *uncertainty* (Nooteboom 1989a). Uncertainty is related to the perceived risk of an innovation. The level of perceived risk is found to be negatively related to the speed of adoption (Gatignon and Robertson 1985, p. 862). Considerations of uncertainty are, in several major ways, involved in the adoption process of an innovation. Firstly, the potential adopter is uncertain as to whether advantages of the innovation (e.g. concerning cost savings or quality improvement), as promised by the supplier, will be realised. The extent of the relative advantage of the innovation is not known before adoption has taken place. Secondly, the potential adopter faces uncertainty regarding the implementation of the innovation in its organisation. In order to bring the performance of the innovation up to the required or expected level, additional efforts, unknown prior to adoption of the innovation, may have to be made. Therefore, the uncertainty surrounding an innovation might cause a potential adopter to postpone the decision to either adopt or reject the innovation. Furthermore, *expectations* of rapid technological development among potential adopters of a certain technological innovation may preclude its adoption. Potential adopters may be uncertain about the emergence of technology standards and the length of the technology life cycle (Gatignon and Robertson 1991). When this is the case, such expectations inhibit the process of adoption and diffusion of the innovation, because the potential adopter may consider the postponement of adoption of the innovation to be the most profitable strategy (Nooteboom 1989b; see also Butler 1988, p.20).

Conclusion

The relative advantage, compatibility, trialability and observability of a technological innovation, as perceived by potential adopters, are positively related to its rate of adoption; the complexity of an innovation, the uncertainty surrounding its adoption and expectations of fast technological development among potential adopters are negatively related to the rate of adoption.

ADOPTER CHARACTERISTICS

In the discipline of marketing, diffusion research has tended to focus on individuals as the adopters of innovations. Nowadays, however, there is a growing interest in industrial diffusion (Gauvin and Sinha 1993; Robertson and Gatignon 1986).

Some characteristics of organisations have been found to influence the innovation adoption decision. The variable most often found to be positively related to the adoption of innovations is the *size* of an organisation (Kennedy 1983). Due to the size of an organisation a certain critical mass may be present, which justifies the adoption of particular innovations. Also, for larger organisations there may be a greater necessity to adopt some innovations than for smaller ones (Kimberley and Evanisko 1981). Furthermore, several variables concerning the *organisational structure* influence the innovativeness of an organisation. A higher level of *complexity* of an organisation, being a function of the number of specialists in the organisation and their professionalism (Hage and Aiken 1970, p. 33), may facilitate adoption of an innovation. The diversity in the backgrounds of the members of the organisation may increase the number of information sources by means of which an organisation may become aware of the existence of an innovation (Cohn and Turyn 1984; Zaltman, Duncan and Holbek 1973, p. 135). The same argument holds for the degree of *specialisation* in an organisation, which refers to the degree of division of labour (Moch and Morse 1977, p. 717). Other variables, such as the degree of *formalisation* (the emphasis placed within the organisation on following rules and procedures in performing one's job) and *centralisation* (the degree to which power and control in a system are concentrated in the hands of relatively few individuals), have been found to be negatively related to its degree of innovativeness (Rogers 1983; Zaltman, Duncan and Holbek 1973).

Conclusion

The probability of an organisation adopting an innovation (sooner) increases with its size, and/or level of complexity and/or degree of specialisation, and decreases with its degree of formalisation and/or centralisation.

INFORMATION PROCESSING CHARACTERISTICS

In a recent empirical study, Gatignon and Robertson (1989, p. 45) conclude that 'the decision-maker's information-processing characteristics contribute significantly in separating adopters from non-adopters' of an innovation. The more willing a potential adopter is to receive information about innovation and the greater the capability of the recipient to process the information received, then the greater the probability of the innovation being adopted. This all depends on the *absorption capacity* of the potential adopter, which refers to the knowledge and ability of an organisation to judge and process certain information in order to make as efficient as possible use of the information within the organisation (Baldwin and Scott 1987, p. 117; Jevnaker, Chapter 9, this volume).

Conclusion

The higher the information absorption capacity of an organisation, the more receptive it will be to innovation.

NETWORK PARTICIPATION

The interaction between members of a social system can play an important role in the rate of the adoption and diffusion process (Zaltman, Duncan and Holbek 1973). The participation of organisation members in informal networks facilitates the dissemination of information on a certain innovation, which may positively influence the probability of an organisation adopting the innovation ('interaction effect'). Such an informal network may consist of either the industry in which the organisation operates or organisations in other industries.

Conclusion

The probability of an organisation adopting an innovation (sooner) increases with the intensity of its members' participation in informal networks.

COMPETITIVE ENVIRONMENT

Robertson and Gatignon (1986) propose to incorporate competitive effects among organisations in the diffusion model. They take account of the competitive effects on technology diffusion of both the suppliers and the adopters. However, empirical research does not always give clear support to the proposed relations. In most cases, unambiguous support is only found for the relation between the competitiveness of a market (competitive environment adopter-side) and the rate of diffusion of an innovation in that market (Baldwin and Scott 1987, p. 143; Kamien and Schwartz 1982, p. 102). A high level of competition among firms in a certain industry may enhance the pressure on an individual firm to adopt a certain technological innovation. If the firm chooses not to do so, it may find that the adoption of that specific innovation by other firms results in a competitive disadvantage (see, for example, Stoneman 1983, p. 95).

Conclusion

The speed and rate of adoption of an innovation by organisations in a certain industry will be positively related to the degree of competitiveness of that industry.

EXTENDING THE DIFFUSION PARADIGM: SUPPLY-SIDE FACTORS

It is the case that the influence of supply-side variables on organisational adoption behaviour has not been given sufficient attention, although the relevance of such variables has been pointed out by a number of researchers (Brown 1981; Clark and Staunton 1989; Robertson and Gatignon 1986; Rogers 1983). In the field of consumer diffusion, Brown (1981) has developed a 'market and infrastructure perspective', which focuses upon the process by which innovations and the conditions for adoption are made available to individuals and households (p. 7), thus recognising the supply aspect of diffusion. Based primarily on the industrial marketing literature, Brown supports the view that supply-side variables influence the diffusion of technological innovations, and stresses the importance of the development of a conceptual framework of the diffusion of technological innovations in the business-to-business market (p. 169). Preliminary empirical research in this regard supports such a view: 'Supply-side factors . . . are found to be particularly important in explaining adoption' (Gatignon and Robertson 1989, p. 46).

In this section, determinants of innovation adoption related to the supply-side are presented. For this purpose, the literature on innovation management and industrial marketing is drawn upon. First of all, the innovation development process that precedes the diffusion of the innovation is discussed. Research on innovation management has identified several pre-diffusion factors that can hinder or accelerate the diffusion process. Secondly, the influence on diffusion of interaction between the supplier and (potential) customers during the development process of an innovation is considered. Thirdly, the industrial marketing literature makes it clear that the supplier of an innovation can exercise significant influence on the diffusion process of the innovation by means of marketing activities.

INNOVATION DEVELOPMENT PROCESS

In the innovation management literature, a relatively large body of research has emerged investigating the determinants of new industrial product performance (Calantone and Cooper 1981; Cooper 1979, 1983, 1988; Cooper and Kleinschmidt 1987; Maidique and Zirger 1984; Zirger and Maidique 1990). Lilien and Yoon (1989) have given an overview of empirical research on this subject. Based on this, they drew up a summary of the main determinants of industrial product performance. Four categories of variables are identified, which determine the success of an innovation in the market-place:

1. Business strategic and organisational factors, including general management's support and involvement, business–project fit and R&D–manufacturing–marketing interaction. These factors are controllable by management at the corporate level in the long run.

2. R&D and production factors, including the relative superiority or uniqueness of the innovation, experience and synergy effect in R&D and production, user benefit or economic advantage of the innovation ('relative advantage' of the innovation), the role of product champion and patent protection. These factors are controllable by management through internal decisions and allocation of resources.
3. Marketing factors, including experience and efficiency in marketing and interaction with potential customers. These factors are also controllable through internal marketing decisions and allocation of resources. Interaction with potential customers can be given form in several ways.
4. Market and environmental factors, which include the degree of competition in the market ('competitive environment') and the market's size and growth rate. These factors cannot be controlled by the decisions made by the management of the individual firm.

Determinants of industrial product performance that are controllable by management are dependent on the way in which the innovation development process is organised within the firm. The innovation development process consists of several stages. It is defined by Rogers (1983, p. 135) as:

> all of the decisions, activities and their impacts that occur from recognition of a need or problem, through research, development, and commercialization of an innovation, through diffusion and adoption of the innovation by users, to its consequences.

Based on research into product success and failure, both Cooper (1983) and Zirger and Maidique (1990) have set up models of new industrial product development, incorporating the critical factors necessary to develop successful new industrial products. The model proposed by Cooper (1983) is a normative seven-stage process model, which describes the activities a firm has to undertake to create successful industrial products. Cooper distinguishes the following stages:

1. idea
2. preliminary assessment
3. concept
4. development
5. testing
6. trial
7. launch

The model proposed by Zirger and Maidique (1990) provides less detail. It describes the innovation development process in terms of the organisational and external entities that influence product outcome. Organisational entities include the three primary groups involved in product development: R&D, manufacturing and marketing (see also Gupta, Raj and Wilemon 1986). The competencies of the functional groups, their planning of the development process and the cooperation between the groups are considered in the model. External entities included in the model comprise market characteristics, such as degree of competitiveness, market size and growth. An empirical test of the model underlined the importance of variables comparable to the ones summarised by Lilien and Yoon (1989). The commitment of a capable organisation to the development of an innovation, offering significant value to the potential adopter, is crucial in innovation development (Zirger and Maidique 1990, pp. 879–880). An important instrument for accomplishing this is understanding the needs of the customers by interacting with them during the process of development.

Conclusion

The speed and rate of adoption of a technological innovation by organisations will be positively related to the extent that the supplier firm:

- has given more support to the development of the innovation, and/or
- has given more attention to the incorporation of the innovation project in its overall strategic posture, and/or
- has given more attention to the creation of an innovative climate within the organisation, and/or
- has given more attention to the development of a unique and superior product from the perspective of the potential adopter, and/or
- can take advantage of past experiences or synergy more easily than its competitors.

SUPPLIER–BUYER INTERACTION

The degree to which an innovation offers significant value to potential customers and the degree of compatibility with their needs and wants are important determinants of the success of an innovation. In order to avoid problems, the supplier of an innovation may cooperate with potential adopters during the process of innovation development. Urban and Von Hippel (1988) conclude that 'lead user analysis' can improve the productivity of new product development in industrial markets (p. 579). Lead users of a novel product are defined as:

> those who display two characteristics with respect to [the novel product]: (1) lead users face needs that will be general in a marketplace, but face them months or years before the bulk of that marketplace encounters them, and (2) lead users are positioned to benefit significantly by obtaining a solution to those needs.
> (Urban and Von Hippel 1988, p. 569)

Cooperation can be referred to as the 'interaction approach' to innovation development (Hakansson 1982). An important condition for interaction between suppliers and buyers is the existence of an explicit (long-term) relationship between them. The existence of long-term relations with customers also facilitates diffusion of a new product among them. The relationship reduces the risk of adoption.

Conclusion

The rate of adoption of a technological innovation by organisations will be positively related to the extent that the supplier firm has interacted with potential adopters of the innovation during the innovation development process.

MARKETING STRATEGY AND ACTIVITIES OF THE SUPPLIER

The most fundamental choice a supplier will have to make when marketing a new product is whether to be a 'market pioneer' or a 'follower', i.e. *when* to enter the market. This decision will concern a trade-off between the risks of premature entry and the problems of missed opportunities (Lilien and Yoon 1990). Within this broad framework, a firm has to decide *how* to enter the market. Easingwood and Beard (1989) have identified four main groups of market launch strategies for new industrial products aimed at accelerating the rate of early adoption.

The first alterative to consider is the possibility of *working with other producers* in order to educate potential users and expand total primary demand. The cooperation can take two major forms. One is to share the technology with others so as to increase total demand and prevent users from being confronted with competing and incompatible technologies (by setting a technology standard). The other is to educate a target audience (i.e. other producers of similar technologies – the target market) as to the workings of the new technology. This can provide the basis to an accelerated diffusion of the innovation.

The second marketing strategy concerns the *positioning of the innovation in the market-place*. By identifying the potential 'early adopters' in the market, marketing efforts can be concentrated on these groups in order to accelerate the initial rate of adoption of the innovation. This can be accomplished by approaching innovative adopters, heavy users of the product category or heavy users of the preceding technology. Innovative adopters are those early buyers of new products who are undeterred by the risk of early adoption. Other groups of early adopters include heavy users of the general product category from which the innovation comes and heavy users of the technology that the new product is intended to replace. Early adopters of innovation can influence the adoption decision of others in the market, and this is important for the diffusion process to take off ('contamination effect'). Another possibility of achieving a fast market penetration is to pursue a *rapid-penetration strategy*, which consists of launching the new product at a low price and spending heavily on promotion (Kotler 1991, p. 355).

The third group of marketing strategies were directly intended to *reduce the risks associated with early adoption*. The supplier of the innovation can use several approaches to reduce the risk of adoption. For example, the innovation may be given to the customer 'on trial' for a certain period of time ('perceived trialability').

Ultimately, the success of an innovation depends on the reputation it gathers in the market-place. Therefore, *winning market support* can be identified as another major category of marketing strategies. A supplier can try to gain market support in several ways. The first approach is to win the endorsement of opinion leaders. In the business-to-business market one may think of approaching key people in decision making units of firms, or people from outside the firm who may influence the adoption decision (e.g. consultants, accountants; see Biemans and Setz, Chapter 10 and Hultink and Robben, Chapter 11, this volume). The second approach is to establish a 'winner' image in the market-place by creating instant success by investing substantial resources into launching the new product. The final approach is to 'legitimise' the product by corporate endorsement.

Conclusion

The speed and rate of adoption of an innovation by organisations will be positively related to the extent that the supplier firm has pursued a marketing strategy of:

- cooperation with other suppliers by sharing the technology or educating some target audience (including other producers), and/or
- positioning the innovation in the market by approaching innovative adopters, heavy users of the product category, heavy users of the preceding technology and/or setting a penetration price, and/or
- reducing the risk of adoption by offering a trial period or absorbing all of the risk involved for the potential adopter, and/or
- winning market support by gaining the endorsement of opinion leaders, establishing a 'winner' image, or legitimising the product in the market-place.

ADOPTER'S INFORMATION

The probability of an organisation adopting an innovation over a certain period of time may be influenced by the *quantity*, *quality* and *value* of the available *information* (Webster 1969). The availability of information depends considerably on the level of communication activity of the supplier of the innovation, on the one hand, and on the extent to which potential adopters communicate with 'third parties' (e.g. adopters of the innovation, advisors), on the other. The role of the latter has already been addressed as part of network participation. The former is part of the marketing activities undertaken by the supplier of an innovation. Clark and Staunton (1989, p. 131) point out that diffusion research has focused on the influence of available information on the adoption decision without considering the question of whether information is supplied actively to potential adopters in the first place. In this respect, postponement of adoption of an innovation, in some cases, may not be attributed to factors related to the potential adopter, but to the lack of information. It is clear that the supplier of the innovation plays an important role in making information available. The quality of the available information refers to its ability to reduce uncertainty for the potential adopter. The value of the information concerns the relative advantage that the information offers to the potential adopter. Chapters 10 and 11 on launch strategies reinforce this point.

Conclusion

The probability of an organisation adopting an innovation (sooner) increases with the availability of information, the quality of the available information and the value of the available information.

A MODEL OF INNOVATION DIFFUSION IN BUSINESS-TO-BUSINESS MARKETS

Table 12.1 summarises the relations between the main elements of the diffusion model and the innovation adoption decision in the business-to-business market. These elements are integrated in Figure 12.1. From this framework, it becomes clear that, in addition to adopter-side variables, other factors influence, either directly or indirectly, adoption behaviour. It is evident that the supplier of an innovation can play an important role in shaping the diffusion process of the innovation. Therefore, it should be pointed out that the diffusion process is not a deterministic one, shaped by uncontrollable factors only (Lambkin and Day 1989). Organisations certainly can – and do – influence the underlying process of innovation adoption.

Table 12.1   Determinants of innovation diffusion in business-to-business markets

Variable	Relation to diffusion	Variable	Relation to diffusion
Innovation characteristics:		Innovation development:	
relative advantage	+	management support	+
compatibility	+	incorporation in strategic posture	+
complexity	−	innovative organisational climate	+
trialability	+	superior product	+
observability	+	experience and synergy effects	+
uncertainty	−	organisation/execution of	+
expectations technology	−	development	
Adopter characteristics:		Marketing strategy:	
size	+	cooperation with other suppliers	+
complexity	+	positioning innovation in the market	+
specialisation	+	reducing the risk of adoption	+
formalisation	−	winning market support	+
centralisation	−		
Information processing characteristics:		Information:	
absorption capacity	+	availability	+
Network participation:		quality	+
level of interaction	+	value	+
Competitive environment:			
competitiveness industry	+		

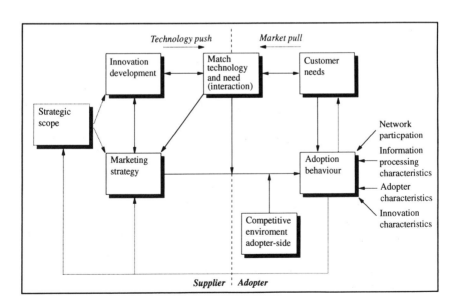

Figure 12.1   An integrated framework of innovation diffusion in business-to-business markets

CONCLUSIONS AND MANAGERIAL IMPLICATIONS

In this chapter a model of innovation diffusion in business-to-business markets is presented. Research findings about the influence of suppliers of innovations on the process of diffusion of new products, drawn from the literature on innovation management and industrial marketing, are integrated with the current diffusion paradigm. The need for such an integration is twofold. Firstly, it has been recognised by diffusion researchers that the influence of the supply-side on processes of adoption and diffusion of innovations has received little attention in previous research. This is surprising, because the importance of supply-side variables has been acknowledged by several researchers in the field of diffusion, and because of the observation that research findings from areas such as innovation management and industrial marketing can be used to enhance the understanding of innovation diffusion in the business-to-business market. Secondly, the main points of criticism of diffusion research, in particular 'individual blame' (i.e. in diffusion research individuals, instead of the system they are part of, are blamed for not adopting an innovation), can be addressed by taking an integrative perspective that considers the factors involved in the diffusion of innovations.

The framework of organisational diffusion of innovations presented in this chapter integrates research findings on factors influencing processes of adoption and diffusion from several sources. By gaining insight into the determinants of the market acceptance of new products, companies can more adequately formulate their marketing strategy, and, therefore, improve the marketing performance of new products.

Consequently, managerial implications of the presented model of innovation diffusion can be derived. Firstly, the model shows that the supplier can play an important role in shaping the diffusion process of an innovation. Although giving explicit attention to the development process of an innovation and formulating a marketing strategy for the new product may seem logical, the impact of these activities on the success of the innovation in the market-place is often underestimated or even ignored entirely (Lilien and Yoon 1989). Secondly, this chapter has made it clear that the success of an innovation in the market-place is dependent on a large number of factors. In particular, suppliers of an innovation should be aware of their potential impact on the process of adoption and diffusion. Applying the integrated framework of innovation diffusion can enhance such an understanding.

ACKNOWLEDGEMENTS

Part of this chapter is based on 'An integrated model of organisational adoption and diffusion of innovations', *European Journal of Marketing*, **27**(5), 22–41, and is reproduced here by permission of MCB University Press.

REFERENCES

Baldwin, W.L. and Scott, J.T. (1987). *Market Structure and Technological Change*, Harwood, Chur, Switzerland.

Brown, L.A. (1981). *Innovation Diffusion*, Methuen, London.

Butler, J.E. (1988). Theories of technological innovation as useful tools for corporate strategy, *Strategic Management Journal*, **9**, 15–29.

Calantone, R. and Cooper, R.G. (1981). New product scenarios: Prospects for success, *Journal of Marketing*, **45**(2), 48–60.

Chisnall, P.M. (1989). *Strategic Industrial Marketing*, Prentice Hall, Englewood Cliffs, NJ.

Clark, P. and Staunton, N. (1989). *Innovation in Technology and Organisation*, Routledge, London.

Cohn, S.F. and Turyn, R.M. (1984). Organisational structure, decision-making procedures, and the adoption of innovations, *IEEE Transactions on Engineering Management*, **31**(4), 154–161.

Cooper, R.G. (1979). The dimensions of industrial new product success and failure, *Journal of Marketing*, **43**, 93–103.

Cooper, R.G. (1983). A process model for industrial new product development, *IEEE Transactions on Engineering Management*, **30**(1), 2–11.

Cooper, R.G. (1988). Predevelopment activities determine new product success, *Industrial Marketing Management*, **17**, 237–247.

Cooper, R.G. and Kleinschmidt, E.J. (1987). Success factors in product innovation, *Industrial Marketing Management*, **16**, 215–223.

Easingwood, C.J. and Beard, C. (1989). High technology launch strategies in the UK, *Industrial Marketing Management*, **18**, 125–138.

Gatignon, H. and Robertson, T.S. (1985). A propositional inventory for new diffusion research, *Journal of Consumer Research*, **11**, 849–867.

Gatignon, H. and Robertson, T.S. (1989). Technology diffusion: An empirical test of competitive effects, *Journal of Marketing*, **53**, 35–49.

Gatignon, H. and Robertson, T.S. (1991). Diffusion of innovation, in Robertson, T.S. and Kassarjian, H.H. (eds), *Handbook of Consumer Theory and Research*, Prentice Hall, Englewood Cliffs, NJ.

Gauvin, S. and Sinha, R.K. (1993). Innovations in industrial organisations: A two-stage model of adoption, *International Journal of Research in Marketing*, **10**(2), 165–183.

Gupta, A.K., Raj, S.P. and Wilemon, D. (1986). A model for studying the R&D–marketing interface in the product innovation process, *Journal of Marketing*, **50**, 7–17.

Hage, J. and Aiken, M. (1970). *Social Change in Complex Organisations*, Random House, New York.

Håkansson, H. (ed.) (1982). *International Marketing and Purchasing of Industrial Goods: An Interaction Approach*, John Wiley & Sons, Chichester.

Johnston, W.J. and Bonoma, T.V. (1981). The buying centre: Structure and interaction patterns, *Journal of Marketing*, **45**, 143–156.

Kamien, M.I. and Schwartz, N.L. (1982). *Market Structure and Innovation*, Cambridge University Press, Cambridge.

Kennedy, A.M. (1983). The adoption and diffusion of new industrial products: A literature review, *European Journal of Marketing*, **17**, 31–88.

Kimberley, J.R. and Evanisko, M.J. (1981). Organisational innovation: The influence of individual, organisational, and contextual factors on hospital adoption of technological and administrative innovations, *Academy of Management Journal*, **24**(4), 689–713.

Kotler, P. (1991). *Marketing Management: Analysis, Planning, Implementation and Control*, 7th edn, Prentice Hall, Englewood Cliffs, NJ.

Lambkin, M. and Day, G.S. (1989). Evolutionary processes in competitive markets: Beyond the product life cycle, *Journal of Marketing*, **53**(3), 4–20.

Lilien, G.L. and Yoon, E. (1989). Determinants of new industrial product performance: A strategic re-examination of the empirical literature, *IEEE Transactions on Engineering Management*, **36**(1), 3–10.

Lilien, G.L. and Yoon, E. (1990). The timing of competitive market entry: An exploratory study of new industrial products, *Management Science*, **36**(5), 568–585.

Maidique, M.A. and Zirger, B.J. (1984). A study of success and failure in product innovation: The case of the US electronics industry, *IEEE Transactions on Engineering Management*, **31**(4), 192–203.

Moch, M.K. and Morse, E.V. (1977). Size, centralisation and organisational adoption of innovations, *American Sociological Review*, **42**, 716–725.

Nooteboom, B. (1989a). Diffusion, uncertainty and firm size, *International Journal of Research in Marketing*, **6**, 109–128.

Nooteboom, B. (1989b). Inhibition of progress and risk of introduction: Two problems in the marketing of new technology, in Industrial and new technologies marketing, proceedings of the XVIth international research seminar in marketing, IRET La Londe les Maures, 17–19 May, pp. 230–246.

Robertson, T.S. (1971). *Innovative Behaviour and Communication*, Holt, Rinehart and Winston, New York.

Robertson, T.S. and Gatignon, H. (1986). Competitive effects on technology diffusion, *Journal of Marketing*, **50**, 1–12.

Robinson, P., Faris, C. and Wind, Y. (1967). *Industrial Buying and Creative Marketing*, Allyn and Bacon, Boston, MA.

Robinson, W.T. (1990). Product innovation and start-up business market share performance, *Management Science*, **36**(10), 1279–1289.

Rogers, E.M. (1983). *Diffusion of Innovations*, 3rd edn, Free Press, New York.

Rogers, E.M. (1986). Three decades of research on the diffusion of innovations: Progress, problems, prospects, presented at the conference on innovation diffusion, Venice, Italy, 18–22 March.

Rogers, E.M. (1992). The diffusion of innovations model, presented at the NATO advanced research workshop on modelling the use and diffusion of geographic information technologies, Sounion, Greece, 8–11 April.

Shanklin, W.L. and Ryans, J.K. (1984). *Marketing High Technology*, Lexington Books, Lexington, MA.

Stoneman, P. (1983). *The Economic Analysis of Technological Change*, Oxford University Press, Oxford.

Tornatzky, L.G. and Klein, K.J. (1982). Innovation characteristics and innovation adoption-implementation: A meta-analysis of findings, *IEEE Transactions on Engineering Management*, **29**(1), 28–45.

Urban, G.L. and Von Hippel, E. (1988). Lead user analyses for the development of new industrial products, *Management Science*, **34**(5), 569–582.

Webster, F.E. (1969). New product adoption in industrial markets: A framework for analysis, *Journal of Marketing*, **33**, 35–39.

Zaltman, G., Duncan, R. and Holbek, J. (1973). *Innovations and Organisations*, John Wiley & Sons, New York.

Zirger, B.J. and Maidique, M.A. (1990). A model of new product development: An empirical test, *Management Science*, **36**(7), 867–883.

CHAPTER THIRTEEN

CONSUMER INITIATORS: ADAPTORS AND INNOVATORS

Gordon R. Foxall

Studies of consumer behaviour are currently beset by two problems: (i) a proliferation of confusing and inexact terms referring to innovativeness, and (ii) a mass of weak evidence relating to consumer innovativeness and behaviour. This chapter presents a more coherent set of terms to designate the behavioural and psychological dimensions of innovative consumer behaviour. It illustrates the new concepts by presenting the results of five empirical studies. The findings suggest a more complicated psychographic composition of consumer innovators than is generally appreciated in managerial prescriptions for new product development and marketing and in theoretical explanations of consumer behaviour that rely on conceptual abstractions such as 'innate' or 'inherent' innovativeness.

INTRODUCTION

Consumer researchers have shown an interest in the first adopters of new products and brands that exceeds their concern for almost any other aspect of purchase and consumption. Both theoretical and practical studies have sought to locate these 'consumer innovators' and to establish the role they play in the creation of markets and the communication of innovations. This chapter argues that, for all its popularity among investigators, 'consumer innovativeness' remains a field of enquiry beset by confusion over basic terminology and

Product Development: Meeting the Challenge of the Design–Marketing Interface.
Edited by M. Bruce and W.G. Biemans.   © 1995 John Wiley & Sons Ltd.

characterised by an inability to come to terms with the weak evidence on which its generalisations about the personality profiles of 'consumer innovators' are based.

The chapter begins by briefly summarising why consumer innovativeness has become a central topic in both new product marketing and the explanation of early adoption. In doing so, it comments on the elusive nature of the personality traits assumed to be associated with consumer innovativeness. Although the conventional terminology is necessarily employed thus far, a solution can now be proposed to the confusion it has engendered. Next, the chapter argues that the personality profiles of early adopters can be usefully investigated by the Kirton Adaption–Innovation (KAI) inventory, which measures both the cognitive/personality styles generally associated with consumer innovativeness and those that are, by implication, diametrically opposite. Five empirical studies of 'innovative' consumer behaviour employing the KAI are described. The first three concern consumers' early adoption of new food products and brands, i.e. with 'purchase innovativeness'; the latter two, consumers' use of personal computers to solve a range of problems, i.e. with 'use-innovativeness'. The revolutionary nature of the findings is apparent in that in no case is the consumer behaviour uniquely associated with an innovative personality profile: both the innovators identified by Kirton's measure and the adaptors who exhibit the obverse personality profile are found among both groups. Finally, the implications of these findings for marketing practice and the explanation of early adoption are discussed, and directions for further research are suggested.

CONSUMER INNOVATORS IN MARKETING PRACTICE AND CONSUMER THEORY

The marketing literature imputes one or other of two strategies to consumers according to the stage in the product life cycle. The first adopters of new products, who differ socially and economically from later adopters, are portrayed as more involved in the product field and are said to engage in extended problem solving prior to purchase (Howard 1977). These so-called 'consumer innovators' are socially independent, requiring little or no personal communication before adopting (Midgley 1977). By contrast, later adopters need other people to 'legitimate' the purchase and use of new products: the product life cycle may have progressed well into its maturity stage before the last of them buy for the first time. Later purchasers are said to be less involved in the product field; by the time they adopt, pre-purchase decision making has become safe and routine.

The expected patterns of behavioural and psychographic difference between early and later adopters form the basis of a strategic prescription for product development, according to which marketing mixes should be tailored to the distinctive requirements of successive adopter categories. The resulting temporal market segmentation is described as leading to the profitable development of both new and established products (Baker 1983; Wind 1981; Wind, Mahajan and Cardozo 1981). If potential initial and later adopters of new products can be identified at early stages of the new product development process, the tailoring can begin that much earlier and can be incorporated into the market testing of alternative prototypes. Non-product elements of the marketing mix, notably persuasive communications, can be directed specifically towards the needs and vulnerabilities of the homogeneously-conceived primary market. Numerous attempts have been made to differentiate these adopter categories psychographically, on the basis of links between early adoption and such traits as risk taking, impulsiveness, dominance, inner-directedness, flexibility and venturesomeness, and perception of innovative product characteristics (Foxall 1984; Foxall and Goldsmith 1988; Gatignon and Robertson 1991; Midgley 1977; Rogers 1983).

Identification of the personality characteristics of these initial adopters has also excited intellectual curiosity. One of the more sophisticated theoretical quests for the nature of 'the innovative personality' is that of Midgley and Dowling (1978), who draw attention to the situational influences that facilitate or impede early adoption. However, the principal explanatory element in their model is a hypothetical construct, 'innate innovativeness', mediated by product field interest. They argue that, in order to account for different levels of 'actualised innovation' – the single act defined by time elapsed from launch, the adoption of several new products in the same field measured by a cross-sectional method and the adoption of new products across product fields measured by a generalised cross-sectional method – it is necessary to posit increasingly abstract concepts of 'innovativeness', an abstract personality trait assumed to be possessed in some degree by everybody but actually existing only in the mind of the investigator. The extent of an individual's early adoption is ultimately explained by a reference to his or her degree of innate innovativeness, which is 'a function of (yet to be specified) dimensions of the human personality' (Midgley and Dowling 1978, p. 235). Hirschman (1980) speaks similarly of 'inherent' innovativeness and 'inherent' novelty seeking without specifying the traits with which they might be associated.

Both managerial and theoretical views of the personality profiles of these consumers anticipate a relationship between the behaviours of interest and the psychographics of the people who perform them. But empirical confirmation of their expectations has been elusive. The quest for operationally measurable traits of personality related to innovative behaviour has a long history in marketing and consumer psychology, but has produced nothing more than a mass of weak, if positive, correlations. The most that can be said is that these weak findings constitute a body of consistent evidence linking innovative behaviour with several cognitive–behavioural traits: category width, flexibility, tolerance of ambiguity, self-esteem and sensation seeking (Foxall 1984, 1989; Goldsmith 1989; Horton 1979; Midgley 1977; Mudd 1990; Rogers 1983; Schiffman and Kanuk 1987). The implication is that if the personality traits that explain actualised innovativeness (and which, by implication, are the 'yet to be specified' dimensions of personality of which innate innovativeness is a function) are to be identified, then these cognitive–behavioural variables must define the area in which we should look.

As the effects of personality traits on behaviour are cumulative, it would be desirable to employ a composite measure of these cognitive–behavioural variables if a theoretically-grounded instrument were available.

The KAI, which provides an operational measure of the adaptive and innovative cognitive styles posited by Kirton (1976), appears to be a suitable instrument. 'Cognitive style' refers to an individual's way of processing information; his or her preferred approach to decision making and problem solving as distinct from his or her cognitive level, ability or complexity (Guildford 1980). The adaption–innovation theory, which originated in the context of organisational behaviour, proposes a continuum of such styles and relates them to the individual's characteristic manner of approaching change. The extreme adaptor prefers order and precision, and is concerned with the accuracy of details, prudence, soundness, efficiency and a degree of conformity. The adaptor is happiest working within a well-established pattern of rules and operating procedures. By contrast, the innovator prefers to think tangentially, challenges rules and procedures and is uninhibited about breaking with established methods and advocating novel perspectives and solutions. The innovator is easily bored by routine and seeks novelty and stimulation in discontinuous change; he or she tends towards risk taking, exploration and trial (Kirton 1976, 1989). The KAI's suitability for research in consumer innovativeness is confirmed by its positive correlation with validated measures of category width, tolerance of ambiguity, flexibility, self-esteem and sensation seeking.

As relatively narrow categorisers, adaptors are more likely than innovators to seek to avoid mistakes, even if this means missing some positive opportunities (Foxall 1988). Their need for structure (Gryskiewicz 1982) and reluctance to change (Goldsmith 1989) leads them to take a more cautious view. Adaptors tend, therefore, in making decisions, to be conservative, usually confining their search for information within the frame of reference dictated by their direct personal experience. Since adaptors are more intolerant than innovators of change and disruption, unwilling to accept ambiguity, and more dogmatic and inflexible (Goldsmith 1989; Gryskiewicz 1982; Kirton 1976, 1989), they are predictably less amenable to new product trial. Their consequent lack of experience of new products further reinforces their unwillingness to explore. Innovators, who by contrast are broad categorisers, risking errors and costs to take advantage of potentially positive chances, are more likely to try new products, accepting the risk of buying an unsatisfactory item. They use more environmental stimuli, taking in more of the data that impinge on them and using them more actively to find a solution. Their more abstract thinking leads them to ask more questions, search widely for information and investigate more relationships. Seeing products as more alike than adaptors, they are less brand loyal.

The KAI requires respondents to estimate on 32 five-point ratings how easy or difficult they would find it to sustain particular adaptive and innovative behaviours over long periods of time. The measure is scored in the direction of innovativeness from an adaptive extreme (32) to an innovative extreme (160), and with a theoretical mean suggested by the scale midpoint (96). Three general population samples, for the UK, the USA and Italy, have observed means of 95 ± 0.05, about which scores are approximately normally distributed within the restricted range of 45–146. The KAI shows high levels of internal reliability and validity (Foxall and Hackett 1992; Kirton 1989).

OVERCOMING TERMINOLOGICAL CONFUSION

The scope for confusion in the use of terms such as 'innovator' and 'innovativeness' will already be apparent to the reader. At its simplest, it takes the form of quite distinct conceptual levels being described in similar terms, from the hypothetical and abstract 'innate innovativeness' and 'inherent innovativeness', to the concrete and observable 'actualised innovativeness'. To use the same term in each case, while claiming that the former provides an explanatory basis for the latter, is to prejudge the issue of whether innovative behaviour is attributable to an underlying personality trait or system. At the intermediate level, there is a plethora of terms to refer to measurable intervening variables: 'sensory innovativeness', 'cognitive innovativeness', 'hedonic innovativeness', 'adaption–innovation', etc. (Hirschman 1984; Kirton 1976). Finally, at the level of consumption rather than purchasing, the term 'use-innovativeness' refers to the deployment of a product that has already been adopted to solve a new problem of consumption (Hirschman 1980).

Foxall (1989) proposed the substitution of 'market-initiators' for 'purchase innovators'. The term emphasises that such adopters are initial purchasers but also that they have an initiating role in the communication and diffusion of new brands and products. The diffusion literature ascribes to this group the functions of earliest adoption of an innovation, plus its communication to the later adopters who comprise the bulk of the market. This usage is in line with that found in both marketing studies of adoption and diffusion and in the wider analysis of these phenomena in a broad range of other fields (Foxall and Bhate 1993a; Rogers 1983). A synonym is 'initial adopters'. Both designate an observable level of analysis, the relationship of which to a personality trait or group of associated traits that predisposes a consumer towards innovative behaviour is an empirical question rather than a matter of preordination. Market-initiation also covers consumers' reactions to the range of newness available in new brands and products more successfully than the blanket term 'innovators'. The word 'innovation' describes an entire spectrum of new products, from the discontinuous, which has highly disruptive consequences for consumer behaviour, to the continuous, which requires almost no accommodation on the part of the consumer (Robertson 1967). Compare the adoption of television in the 1950s with the more recent adoption of fluoride toothpaste. To refer to the earliest purchasers of both types of new product as 'innovators' is misleading and requires constant clarification of the degree of innovativeness exhibited in each case (and the many cases that lie between these extremes). However, to define the behaviour of these first adopters functionally, as initiation, removes this confusion, separating the specification of the degree of continuity/discontinuity possessed by the innovation itself from the consumer's subjective reaction to it.

Similarly, the term 'use-initiation' might cover the phenomena of so-called 'use innovativeness'. Again, it describes the behavioural level on which the consumer initiates novel functions for an accepted product, without confusing this observable action with any underlying personality trait or system that might account for it. But it again has the advantage of covering uses of an already-adopted product that range from radically inventive, qualitative changes to the more quantitative deployment of a product in a number of more mundane alternative functions (Foxall and Bhate 1991). An example of the former is consumers' using household bleach as a germicide (which involves a high degree of discontinuity and dissimilarity); the latter is exemplified by the use of a home computer for spreadsheet analysis in addition to word processing (a more continuous re-application that involves much greater similarity of behaviour). Once again, the continuity/discontinuity of the product function is conceptually separate from the consumption behaviour of the consumer.

These terms are used in the following description of a research programme concerned with both market-initiation and use-initiation, which incorporated as explanatory cognitive/personality variables the adaptive–innovative cognitive styles defined by Kirton. In the following account, the first purchasers of a new brand/product are called *market-initiators* or *initial adopters*; consumers who turn a product they already own to novel uses are called *use-initiators*. The generic term to cover both types is consumer initiators. Only those who score appropriately on the KAI are called *innovators*, and this term is used to refer to consumers whose cognitive style is innovative, as defined by Kirton.

METHOD

Five studies have employed the KAI in consumer research with the intention of relating a pattern of personality traits to market- and use-initiation. The first three concern the initial adoption of food brands/products; the fourth, use-initiation in the context of home computer use; and the last, computer use-initiation in organisations. Data for the food studies were collected by an independent market research firm, which recruited convenience samples of respondents, administered the measures, and advised on the selection of new products/brands and their availability at sampling points. Sampling points were selected supermarkets in the south of England. For the fourth study, the same organisation obtained a systematic sample and responses but the products were selected by the respondents. The last study involved students on graduate courses in a university business school, specialising in either marketing, business information technology or legal studies. Methodological details can be found in the original reports (Foxall 1988; Foxall and Bhate 1991, 1993a, 1993c).

RESULTS

STUDY 1: NEW FOOD BRANDS

This exploratory study tested the broad proposition that innovators would evince a greater volume of market-initiation than adaptors, i.e. buy more new brands of food products. This hypothesis was not confirmed, but the results pointed to a more complicated pattern of initial adoption than either the researchers or the literature of adoption and diffusion had assumed (Foxall and Haskins 1986). The KAI mean of the 101 female respondents was 95.06. The observed range of new-brand purchases was 1–8. The sample mean was significantly more innovative than that of the general UK female population:

$z = 2.27$, $p < 0.025$. A positive but extremely weak and non-significant correlation was found between the number of new brands purchased and KAI: $r = 0.09$, $p = 0.22$. Purchasers of 4 or 5 brands (m_{c}an $= 99.31$, sd $= 15.96$, $n = 29$) scored more innovatively than purchasers of 1–3 ($m = 93.83$, sd $= 14.25$, $n = 60$). However, purchasers of the highest number of new brands (6–8) scored unexpectedly adaptively ($m_{can} = 90.75$, sd $= 19.48$, $n = 12$). One-way analysis of variance (ANOVA) gives an F ratio of $F_{2,98} = 1.76$, $p = 0.18$. The mean of purchasers of 4 or 5 new brands was notably higher than those of the other two groups; it alone differed significantly from that of the general female population ($z = 2.67$, $p < 0.01$). Moreover, the sample contained 40 adaptors (whose KAI mean was equal to or less than the female general population mean) and 61 innovators.

STUDY 2: NEW 'HEALTHY' FOOD PRODUCTS

The first study produced weak evidence of a tendency for the heaviest purchasers of innovations to be adaptive rather than innovative. The second study pursued this possibility by investigating innovative product purchase within a coherent product field, namely 'healthy' food products. The KAI mean of the 345 female respondents, 95.01, was significantly higher than that of the general female population: $z = 3.20$, $p < 0.001$. Purchasing innovativeness was again not linearly related to KAI: $r = 0.04$, $p = 0.26$. The sample consisted of 142 adaptors and 203 innovators. The range of products purchased was 0–19, although only four respondents reported not having purchased any of the items (Foxall and Haskins 1987). Neither the KAI mean of purchasers of up to 2 new products, nor that of purchasers of 16–19 differs significantly from the general female population mean. Means of both of these groups are distinctly adaptive. However, means of the purchasers of intermediate quantities of new products are significantly higher than that of the general female population. Moreover, in this study stronger evidence of the adaptive cognitive styles of members of the group of purchasers of the highest number of new products is apparent. One-way ANOVA gave an F ratio of $F_{5,339} = 3.35$, $p = 0.006$. A *post hoc* Sheffé procedure indicates that the means of the extreme groups (purchasers of 0–2 and purchasers of 16–19) differ significantly from that of purchasers of intermediate levels ($p < 0.05$).

STUDY 3: NEW 'HEALTHY' FOOD BRANDS

The third study provided an opportunity to refine the research in two ways (Foxall and Bhate 1993a). Firstly, it was expected (Foxall 1988) that adaptors who had become committed to the cause of healthy eating, and therefore to this product field, would indeed be more likely than innovators or other, less involved adaptors to seek out assiduously not a few but as many as possible relevant food items. This was operationalised in terms of personal involvement with healthy eating, which was measured by the Zaichkowsky Personal Involvement Inventory (PII). This instrument consists of ten 7-point scales on which the individual indicates the degree of interest as opposed to boredom and other aspects of ego involvement with the product field (Zaichkowsky 1987). These instruments and a questionnaire with respect to recent food brand purchasing, representing the second focusing of the research, were administered to 151 female grocery shoppers; the KAI sample mean at 93.1 (sd = 16.06) was not significantly different from that of the general UK female population, $z = 1.4$. Purchase innovativeness was not linearly related to adaption–innovation: $r = 0.04$. Two-way ANOVA, with the number of 'healthy' food brands purchased as the dependent variable and KAI and PII as the independent variables, showed no significant main effects for either adaption–innovation ($F_{1,47} < 1$) or for personal involvement ($F_{1,147} = 1.88, p > 0.17$). A significant interaction effect was observed, however: $F_{1,147} = 4.27, p < 0.05$). A *post hoc* Sheffé procedure indicated a significant difference between the mean volume of purchase of the more involved adaptors (3.10, sd = 1.53, $n = 40$) and that of the less involved adaptors (2.20, sd = 1.30, $n = 44$) ($p < .05$). The means of the less involved innovators (2.83, sd = 1.83, $n = 24$) and that of the more involved innovators (2.65, sd = 1.54, $n = 43$) fell between those of the adaptor groups but were not significantly different.

STUDY 4: SOFTWARE APPLICATIONS IN HOME COMPUTING

This study extended the research in several ways (Foxall and Bhate 1993b). It investigated use-initiation. The research design was developed at this stage to include products that were intrinsically more involving than foods, namely computing software applications. Sample KAI means for 151 male home computer users were 99.05 (sd = 17.90) and 49.69 (sd = 10.02). This KAI mean did not differ significantly from that of the general male population sample for the UK (98.12, sd = 16.75, $n = 290$): $z = 0.52$. Respondents used between 1 and 7 software applications. KAI is not linearly related to use-innovativeness: $r = -0.01$. Following the example of Mudd (1990) the KAI and PII means of users of up to 4 applications were compared with those of users of 5–7. The KAI mean of the latter group (111.00, sd = 18.69, $n = 7$) was significantly more innovative than that of the users of 1–4 (98.47, sd = 17.72, $n = 143$): $z = 1.82, p < 0.05$. While the KAI mean of the group of users of 5–7 applications was significantly more innovative than that of the general male population ($z = 1.81, p < 0.05$), that of the users of only 1–4 applications was not ($z = 0.20$). The PII mean of users of 5–7 software applications (56.00, sd = 9.1) was significantly higher than that of the users of 1–4 (49.40, sd = 10.00): $z = 1.72, p$ < 0.05. In the sample, there were 71 adaptors (47.3%) and 78 (52.7%) innovators. Two-way ANOVA revealed no significant main effects or significant interactions among the independent variables (KAI × PII) on the number of computer applications used ($F < 1$). Two sources of situational influence significantly affected the number of applications to which the computer had been put. The length of time the current computer had been owned correlated significantly with use-initiation ($r = 0.23, p < 0.01$). In addition, the degree of use-initiation varied with the make of computer owned.

STUDY 5: SOFTWARE APPLICATIONS IN ORGANISATIONAL CONTEXTS

The final study developed the theme of situational influence on use-initiation (Foxall and Bhate 1991). The Business Information Technology Systems (BITS) programme simulated situations of required use of computers; the Marketing programme, situations of discretionary use; and the Legal Practice programme, situations of minimal use. The sample KAI mean at 98.56 (sd = 13.39) did not differ significantly from that of students (c. 100) or managers (c. 97). The PII mean was 44.65 (sd = 15.26). KAI scores were skewed towards the innovative pole (range 70–138) while the range of PII scores covered the entire theoretical range. The sample contained 57 adaptors and 50 innovators. Multiple regression analysis was used since the standardised ßs allow the influence of different independent variables to be assessed directly. The dependent variables studied were programming experience, frequency of computer use, number of packages used, length of computing experience and a weighted index of all of these, called overall computer use. When situational factors are ignored – i.e. KAI and PII are the independent variables – overall computer use correlates with both KAI (ß = 0.17, $p < 0.05$) and PII (ß = 0.24, p < 0.01), although these relationships are rather low. The number of packages used correlates with KAI (ß = 0.17, $p < 0.05$) and PII (ß = 0.34, $p < 0.001$). PII correlates with programming experience (ß = 0.33, $p < 0.001$), and with frequency of computer use (ß = 0.56, $p < 0.001$). Neither independent variable is related significantly to duration of computing experience. When organisational influence is included (as three dummy variables representing course affiliation), this factor assumes greater explanatory significance than either cognitive variable. (The full results are available in Foxall and Bhate 1991.) However, PII remains significantly correlated with overall computer use (ß = 0.29, $p < 0.001$) and KAI is marginally correlated with this variable (ß = 0.14, $p < 0.1$). Neither cognitive variable is related to programming experience, although each shows a unique relationship to one other dependent variable: KAI with the number of packages used (ß = 0.27, $p < 0.01$), PII with the frequency of computer use ($ß = 0.33$, $p < 0.001$). Both cognitive variables correlate with duration of computing experience (in both cases, $ß = 0.19$, $p < 0.05$).

The sample was divided into four 'style/involvement' groups based on whether their KAI and PII scores exceeded or fell short of the sample means. One-way ANOVA was used to examine the relationship of each group's KAI and PII scores to each of the dependent variables. Significant F ratios were found for overall computer usage ($F_{3,103} = 8.38$, $p = 0.000$), programming experience ($F = 3.16$, $p = 0.027$), frequency of computer use ($F = 11.13$, $p = 0.000$) and number of packages used ($F = 5.03$, $p = 0.002$). In the case of duration of computing experience, $F = 0.53$, $p = 0.66$. For each dependent variable where F was significant, *post hoc* Sheffé tests indicate that highly involved groups, whether innovative or adaptive, have a group mean that differs from each of the low involved group means ($p < 0.05$).

IMPLICATIONS

The findings resolve the problem of low correlations between measures of personality and consumer behaviour, which were frequently a feature of early research. Low correlations were presumably the outcome of researchers' measuring the traits of personality embodied by innovators, and overlooking those of the adaptors who are also substantially represented among consumer initiators. Low correlation of KAI and consumer initiation would be a problem for this measure only if it operationalised innovativeness alone; however, as a bipolar measure of adaptiveness as well as innovativeness, it has consistently produced results that are intelligible once the coexistence of adaptors and innovators among market-initiators is recognised. This finding has several important implications: for the conceptualisation of 'consumer innovativeness', for the depiction of the adoption decision process, for the psychographic segmentation of new product markets and for further research.

■ The view that the behaviour of consumer initiators can be explained by a set of personality traits that define 'innate' or 'inherent' innovativeness is untenable.

The theoretical import of the results is that consumer initiators may manifest either adaptive or innovative personality characteristics rather than the profile suggested by research in marketing and cognitive/personality psychology. Although psychometric techniques will continue to improve, it seems infeasible that traits other than those investigated in the five studies will emerge as related to 'innate innovativeness'. In any case, the failure of the investigated traits to correlate with 'actualised innovativeness' would still have to be explained. The notion that consumer initiators' behaviour can be explained by reference to an underlying trait of innate or inherent innovativeness is, therefore, unconfirmed. Far from indicating that actualised innovativeness is a function of an underlying personality configuration, the results show that adaption–innovation, a dimension of cognitive style that correlates reliably with traits generally associated with initial adoption, is only weakly – and usually non-linearly – related to market-initiation (operationally measured as the number of new brands purchased or as use-innovativeness). Moreover, in the case of food innovations, the cognitive style profiles of market-initiators were approximately evenly divided between the adaptive and the innovative, while a subset of the adaptors were responsible for the highest level of purchase. In the case of use-initiators for software products, both adaptors and innovators were again well represented. Although, in the organisational context, personal involvement in computing played a dominant role in determining the extent of use-initiation, both adaptors and innovators were present in substantial proportions. The results also suggest that Midgley and Dowling (1978) were right in calling attention to the mediation of innovative behaviour by situational events, but do not confirm those authors' preoccupation with an ultimately trait-based explanation of observed early adoption.

Further research should concentrate on the paradoxical finding that both systematic buyers and systematic non-buyers may be the same kind of people, *adaptors* who differ according to their personal involvement with the product field. This result, since replicated by Mudd and McGrath (1988) for the adoption of educational innovations by college professors in the United States, flies in the face of conventional adoption theory. It emphasises the need, which further research should recognise, to treat adaption–innovation as a continuum rather than as the dichotomy that work to date has assumed in order to simplify analysis. Since a unique configuration of personality traits can no longer be expected to characterise initial adopters, researchers should finally turn their attention to the situational influences on consumer initiation. These have been especially powerful explicators of use-initiation where further research might, for instance, profitably refine the sources of contextual pressure inherent in different task orientations.

- Accounts of consumers' information processing must recognise the differences in cognitive style and personal involvement that distinguish adaptors and innovators at each stage of the decision making sequence.

By confirming that market-initiators may have one of two diametrically opposed personality profiles, only one of which is predicted by adoption theory, the results have profound implications for the understanding of consumers'

Table 13.1 Decision styles of market segments based on adaption–innovation and personal involvement

Adoption decision process stage	Less-involved adaptors	Innovators	More-involved adaptors
Problem recognition	Passive, reactive	Active	Proactive
Search	Minimal, confined to resolution of minor anomalies caused by current consumption patterns	Superficial but extensively based within and across product class boundaries	Extensive within relevant product category; assiduous exploration of all possible solutions within that framework
Evaluation	Meticulous, rational slow and cautious; objective appraisal using tried and tested criteria	Quick, impulsive, based on currently-accepted criteria; personal and subjective	Careful, confined to considerations raised by the relevant product category: but executed confidently and (for the adaptor) briskly within that frame of reference
Decision	Conservative selection within known range of products, continuous innovations preferred	Radical: easily attracted to discontinuously-new product class and able to choose quickly within it. Frequent trial, followed by abandonment	Careful selection within a product field that has become familiar through deliberation, vicarious trial, and sound and prudent pre-purchase comparative evaluation
Post-purchase evaluation	Meticulous, tendency to brand loyalty if item performs well	Less loyal; constantly seeking novel experiences through purchase and consumption	Loyal if satisfied but willing to try innovations within the prescribed frame of reference; perhaps tends towards dynamically-continuous innovations

Source: Foxall and Bhate (1993c); reproduced by permission of MCB University Press

cognitive processing. They disconfirm the widely-held view that initial buyers are inevitably highly involved and engaged in extended problem solving, while low involvement, manifesting in routine decision making and purchasing, is characteristic of later adopters. Both high- and low-involved consumers have been identified at the earliest stage of the diffusion process. Moreover, in the case of new foods, while involvement makes no difference to the purchase level of innovators, for adaptors it marks a crucial distinction. The problem solving behaviours of consumer initiators can be expected to differ at each stage of the adoption decision process, depending on their adaptive–innovative cognitive style and, in the case of adaptors, their level of involvement with the product field (Foxall and Bhate 1991, 1993a, 1993b, 1993c).

Table 13.1 illustrates the differences by reference to the decision styles of the three segments found in innovative food markets.

Further research should seek to elucidate the behavioural implications of the coexistence of adaptive and innovative segments within markets for new brands and products. Adaptors' narrow category width, relative inflexibility, intolerance of ambiguity, lower self-esteem and sensation seeking suggest that they are more likely to be attracted to relatively continuous new products (artificial innovations) than to genuine (discontinuous) ones. Foxall (1989) reported evidence that consumers' perceptions of the degree of continuity/discontinuity of new food brands were reflected in the predominance of adaptors and innovators, respectively, among their purchasers. This result, if replicated by further work, would explain why more-involved adaptors bought the highest numbers of food brands/products, items which at their most radically new tend still to be fairly continuous. By comparison, the more discretely new software applications could be expected to be used in the largest volumes by more-involved innovators. The use of innovative products in alternative functions is, however, more likely to be determined by involvement and situational imperatives. Research aimed at testing these propositions is not only relatively straightforward to carry out but capable of clarifying the place of adaptive–innovative cognitive style in models of adoption.

■ The post-launch market for new products includes both adaptors and innovators whose reactions to marketing communications and other elements of the marketing mix are likely to be diametrically opposed.

The research has identified not only market segments whose coexistence at the beginning of the product life cycle may be inimical to the successful introduction of a unified launch marketing mix, but also the psychographic basis on which they differ. The practical import of the five studies lies not in the weak correlational relationships between KAI and consumer behaviour but in the reason for their prevalence, which the adaption–innovation theory makes clear. The consistent finding that both adaptive and innovative market segments must be addressed at the launch stage of the product life cycle raises obvious questions for marketing strategy. According to the received wisdom of the product development and marketing texts, the initial market for new products consists of innovators. Yet, Table 13.1 suggests that the market for new 'healthy' foods can be psychographically segmented three ways, while that for computing applications software contains both adaptive and innovative subsegments for both more- and less-involved consumer segments. It is essential, therefore, to consider the probable differences in decision making styles for adaptors and innovators as they influence product perceptions and responses to persuasive marketing communications. Advertising, for instance, plays a crucial role in the persuasion of initial adopters since it is virtually the sole means by which new brands and products can be communicated to this primary market. Yet adaptors and innovators will probably respond quite differently to new product advertising.

Further research at the managerial level should seek solutions to the problem of accommodating marketing strategy for new products to the psychographic segments revealed in the research. One possibility is that the new product development process may produce innovations that are tailor-made for one segment – on the conventional wisdom, this would be the innovative segment – but that are simply ignored as inappropriate by the other. At worst, persuasive appeals aimed towards one segment may simply alienate the other. Authoritarian appeals, likely to appeal to extreme adaptors, might stimulate antipathetic feelings in innovators that preclude their trying the innovation; more 'freewheeling' appeals aimed at innovators that stressed the novelty and radical difference of an innovation could similarly alienate adaptors. However, the extent to which these considerations actually influence market take-up of specific innovations remains to be empirically established, product-market by product-market. If confirmed, they may suggest why most new products fail. But, more hopefully, research may indicate how new product marketing appeals might be made simultaneously to the segments of new markets.

CONCLUSION

The study of consumer initiation has been dogged for too long by loose terminology and simplistic reasoning. As a field that has prided itself on its scientific approach to the acquisition of knowledge, consumer research ought now to reject those hypothetical constructs and tenuous relationships among variables that are no longer relevant to a field in which knowledge, rather than speculation, is demonstrably possible. This chapter has not only suggested a resolution of the problem of inexact and misleading terminology; it has also shown a way forward through the incorporation of operational variables – rather than abstract conjecture – into our models of consumer initiation.

ACKNOWLEDGEMENTS

This chapter first appeared in *The British Journal of Management* (1994) **5**(2), S3–S12, and is reproduced by permission.

REFERENCES

Baker, M.J. (1983). *Market Development*, Penguin, Harmondsworth.

Foxall, G.R. (1984). *Corporate Innovation*, Routledge, London.

Foxall, G.R. (1988). Consumer innovativeness: Creativity, novelty-seeking, and cognitive style, in Hirschman, E.C. and Sheth, J.N. (eds), *Research in Consumer Behaviour*, Vol. 3, JAI Press, Greenwich, CT, pp. 79–113.

Foxall, G.R. (1989). Adaptive–innovative cognitive styles of market initiators, in Kirton, M.J. (ed.), *Adaptors and Innovators: Styles of Creativity and Problem-Solving*, Routledge, London, pp. 125–157.

Foxall, G.R. and Bhate, S. (1991). Cognitive style, personal involvement and situation as determinants of computer use, *TechnoVation*, **11**, 183–200.

Foxall, G.R. and Bhate, S. (1993a). Cognitive styles and personal involvement of market initiators, *Journal of Economic Psychology*, **14**, 33–56.

Foxall, G.R. and Bhate, S. (1993b). Cognitive styles of use-innovators for home computing software applications: Implications for new product strategy, *TechnoVation*, **13**, 311–323.

Foxall, G.R. and Bhate, S. (1993c). Cognitive style and personal involvement as explicators of innovative purchasing of 'healthy' food brands, *European Journal of Marketing*, **27**(2), 5–16.

Foxall, G.R. and Goldsmith, R.E. (1988). Personality and consumer choice: Another look, *Journal of the Market Research Society*, **30**, 111–129.

Foxall, G.R. and Hackett, P. (1992). The factor structure and construct validity of the Kirton adaption–innovation inventory, *Personality and Individual Differences*, **13**, 967–975.

Foxall, G.R. and Haskins, C.G. (1986). Cognitive style and consumer innovativeness: An empirical test of Kirton's adaption–innovation theory in the context of food purchasing, *European Journal of Marketing*, **20**(3/4), 63–80.

Foxall, G.R. and Haskins, C.G. (1987). Cognitive style and discontinuous consumption: The case of 'healthy eating', *Food Marketing*, **3**(2), 19–32.

Gatignon, H. and Robertson, T.S. (1991). Innovative decision processes, in Robertson, T.S. and Kassarjian, H.H. (eds), *Handbook of Consumer Behaviour*, Prentice Hall, Englewood Cliffs, NJ, pp. 316–346.

Goldsmith, R.E. (1989). Creative style and personality theory, in Kirton, M.J. (ed.), *Adaptors and Innovators: Styles of Creativity and Problem-Solving*, Routledge, London, pp. 37–55.

Gryskiewicz, S.S. (1982). The Kirton adaption–innovation inventory in creative leadership development, presented at the British Psychological Society, University of Sussex, Brighton.

Guildford, J.P. (1980). Cognitive styles: What are they? *Educational and Psychological Measurement*, **40**, 715–735.

Hirschman, E.C. (1980). Innovativeness, novelty seeking and consumer creativity, *Journal of Consumer Research*, **7**, 283–295.

Hirschman, E.C. (1984). Experience seeking: A subjectivist perspective of consumption, *Journal of Business Research*, **12**, 115–136.

Horton, R.L. (1979). Some relationships between personality and consumer decision making, *Journal of Marketing Research*, **16**, 233–246.

Howard, J.A. (1977). *Consumer Behaviour: Application of Theory*, McGraw-Hill, New York.

Kirton, M.J. (1976). Adaptors and innovators: A description and measure, *Journal of Applied Psychology*, **61**, 622–629.

Kirton, M.J. (1989). A theory of cognitive style, in Kirton, M.J. (ed.), *Adaptors and Innovators: Styles of Creativity and Problem-Solving*, Routledge, London, pp. 1–36.

Midgley, D.F. (1977). *Innovation and New Product Marketing*, Routledge, London.

Midgley, D.F. and Dowling, G.R. (1978). Innovativeness: The Concept and its Measurement, *Journal of Consumer Research*, **4**, 229–240.

Mudd, S.A. (1990). The place of innovativeness in models of the adoption process: An integrative review, *TechnoVation*, **10**, 119–136.

Mudd, S.A. and McGrath, K. (1988). Correlates of the adoption of curriculum-integrated computing in higher education, *Computers and Education*, **8**, 17–19.

Robertson, T.S. (1967). The process of innovation and the diffusion of innovation, *Journal of Marketing*, **31**, 14–19.

Rogers, E.M. (1983). *The Diffusion of Innovations*, Free Press, New York.

Schiffman, L.G. and Kanuk, L.L. (1987). *Consumer Behaviour*, Prentice Hall, Englewood Cliffs, NJ.

Wind, Y. (1981). *Product Policy: Concepts, Methods, and Strategy*, Addison-Wesley, Reading, MA.

Wind, Y., Mahajan, V. and Cardozo, R.N. (eds) (1981). *New-Product Forecasting*, D.C. Heath, Lexington, MA.

Zaichkowsky, J.L. (1987). The personal involvement inventory: Reduction, revision and application to advertising, discussion paper No. 87-08-08, Faculty of Business Administration, Simon Fraser University.

CONTEMPORARY ISSUES

INTRODUCTION

Margaret Bruce

Major concerns affecting product development include environmental issues and product liability. Environmental issues have begun to challenge the materialism of the 1980s. Many companies are grappling with 'green' issues in response to both legal and consumer demands. Dermody and Hanmer-Lloyd review the different approaches that UK companies are adopting in their attempts to integrate environmental issues into their product development processes. Various techniques exist to support the design of environmentally friendly products, such as life cycle analysis, environmental auditing, total quality management and eco-labelling, and these are all discussed. The main barriers to developing environmentally responsible new products, according to Dermody and Hanmer-Lloyd's research, is a lack of vision, limited idea generation and few guidelines for environmental product design. They argue that an effective approach would be based on a 'cradle-to-grave' philosophy, in which environmental concerns were integrated into the product development process from inception to product disposal. Attaining this requires a great deal of awareness, training, top level commitment and a shift from purely financial to environmental evaluations of product success.

Risks of product development are highlighted by Ritsema, in Chapter 15, in particular those appertaining to product liability. This issue is acute for those companies trading in different countries where different laws exist relating to product liability. Ritsema outlines the main general concerns of product liability and then suggests that these need to be taken account of by marketing and production activities in the product development process. For example, advertising and promotion may suggest that users may use the product in ways that were not considered by the manufacturer, and so on. The reputation of a company can be severely affected if a product is faulty or unsafe and has to be recalled. Currently, product development activities are directed towards the satisfaction of customer needs, rather than towards the prevention of product liability claims. A proactive attitude to product liability, Ritsema argues, needs to be built into the product development process.

CHAPTER FOURTEEN

DEVELOPING ENVIRONMENTALLY RESPONSIBLE NEW PRODUCTS: THE CHALLENGE FOR THE 1990S

Janine Dermody and
Stuart Hanmer-Lloyd

Why does business need to take account of environmental issues in its policies, strategies and operations? Is there really a need to develop products to minimise negative environmental impact? Business certainly appears to be a major contributor in causing environmental damage; consider, for example, the track record of pollution caused by the chemical and petrochemical industries. However, it is also the case that business has a major role to play in environmental protection. This chapter explores some of the strategic and management issues of product development from an environmental perspective. It begins with a review of the literature relating to environmental responsibility within new product development (NPD). It then describes and reports on qualitative research into issues surrounding the integration of environmental responsibility into the NPD process. Results suggest that the integration of environmental issues into the NPD process pose considerable difficulties for managers, and highlight a real need for 'best practice' guidelines.

Product Development: Meeting the Challenge of the Design–Marketing Interface.
Edited by M. Bruce and W.G. Biemans.   © 1995 John Wiley & Sons Ltd.

INTRODUCTION

Environmentalists maintain that business, in response to a rapidly growing world population and increase in lifestyle expectations, is responsible for a wide variety of environmental problems, including an unprecedented consumption of natural resources, an increase in pollution, desertification, ozone depletion, acid precipitation, global warming, and loss of habitats and species diversity. The track record of companies' responses to environmental protection suggests that such charges are merited. The following example reflects attitudes and practices that were very much the norm prior to the media hype of the 1980s:

> A set of aerial photographs of the US chemical company W.R. Grace & Co.'s Curtis Bay plant, Maryland were taken to decorate a senior vice president's office. The photographs revealed a two-square mile red blotch produced by the chemical Grace had been dumping into Chesapeake Bay. When the senior vice president asked a subordinate to do something about the pollution, a new set of prints were developed with the red block neatly airbrushed out! That was the solution; it was 1970, and as the vice president explained, they didn't think about these things.
>
> (adapted from Elkington and Burke 1989)

Twenty-four years later, has anything changed?

Certainly, the past twenty-four years has seen a relentless intensification of environmental pressures on business and a proliferation of environmental concerns taken on board by environmental pressure groups. Environmental concerns and regulations have reshaped the business market, resulting in new practices, technologies, policies and product ranges that minimise environmental impact.

While the environmental commitment of business is somewhat controversial, it must be recognised that business does have a major role to play in managing and protecting the environment. Even committed environmentalists have realised this role, and forged partnerships rather than conflicts with business (Charter 1990; Elkington and Burke 1989). For example, Dr David Bellamy, the British naturalist and conservationist, decided to work closely with the Nuclear Industry Radioactive Waste Executive (NIREX) to find an environmentally acceptable site to dump nuclear waste. Bryn Jones, the founder of Ark (a UK environmental pressure group and manufacturer of 'green' cleaners and detergents), commenting on this need for a new vision, maintained that:

> Because our problems are caused by industry and the solutions must be found by industry, environmentalists have got to roll their sleeves up and get stuck into working with industry.
>
> (Elkington and Burke 1989)

Throughout Europe, governments have translated the environmental role of business into market-led environmental policy. In the UK, the Prime Minister, John Major (1991), in support of his government's market-led environmental strategy, argued that business can advance environmental protection to a much greater extent than regulation ever could. He stated that:

> the principal task of delivering sustainable development will fall to business . . . It is wrong to see modern business as the enemy of the environment. A recent study by Touche Ross shows that over two thirds of companies now have environmental strategies, compared to less than one-third just a year ago. These companies are building the environment into their calculations and into their success. Our leading firms, collectively, are now shaping the necessary new approaches to environmental management . . . Commercial instincts could do as much, if not more, to advance the cause of the environment as government regulation.

Companies can minimise environmental impact by reviewing and adapting their corporate and marketing operations, policies and strategies, and their management styles and training to integrate environmental expertise. A corporate environmental policy can help to achieve this by 'building in' environmental objectives into the ethos of the company and enabling them to filter down through all of the company's operations (Elkington and Burke 1989; Hunt and Auster 1990; Speth 1987). The outcome of all of this is that the environment becomes a fundamental part of business decision making and practice, thereby combining economic growth with sound environmental practice (Holdgate 1987).

It is probably true to say that the attitudes of business to the environmental agenda have changed. During the early to mid-1980s environmental issues were typically regarded as a threat, green consumerism was regarded as a fad and environmentalists as 'embittered, scruffy, anti-business street-fighters' (Kirkpatrick 1990). Since the mid-1980s companies have been cleaning up their environmental record, rather than continuing to ignore the issues and face possible isolation or extinction as a result (Charter 1990). In the 1990s companies will increasingly be required to meet the needs of the environment and its advocates as an integral part of business operations and strategy. As Tony Cleaver, chairman and chief executive of IBM UK Ltd, comments, 'Everyone of us will have to face the challenges of the environment in some way during the decade of the 90s' (Charter 1990).

So, with respect to product development, business is at the leading edge in providing realistic and effective solutions to minimise the environmental impact of their products during development, use and disposal. In reality, however, how many companies are really considering the environmental issues involved in developing new products? The evidence to date suggests a minority, and that integration is being hampered by a lack of vision, experience and expertise (Armstrong 1992).

THE RESPONSE OF BUSINESS TO DEVELOPING ENVIRONMENTALLY RESPONSIBLE NEW PRODUCTS

A call for more environmentally responsible product development was made in the early 1970s (Varble 1972), but such activity was minimal until environmental issues hit the media headlines in the mid- to late 1980s and consumers began questioning business practices. Even then, much of the activity was simply tokenism or cases of consumer misinformation. This typically involved meaningless claims; for example, McDonald's cartons made from recyclable card, BP's claim that their lead-free petrol caused 'no pollution to the environment', phosphate-free washing-up liquids, etc. 'Dolphin friendly cornflakes', launched in the United States in 1990, was considered to be a particularly misleading environmental claim. The manufacturers maintained that, because the production of their cornflakes did not endanger dolphins, it was an environmentally friendly product. The Consumer Protection Agency decided otherwise, so preventing the company from using this slogan to promote the product. In 1990, Friends of the Earth launched their 'Green Con' awards to further prevent deceptive environmental claims being used to attempt to sell products in the UK (Armstrong and Hanmer-Lloyd 1993).

In the 1990s the value of developing environmentally responsible products is increasingly being appreciated. Varble (1972) maintained that 'although environmental changes potentially affect all phases of a business operation, they have particular impact on new product development'. For example, when the British television programme *World in Action* (1990) featured dioxins in chlorine-bleached paper products, Tesco, a major UK retailer, received so many enquiries from customers about their own-brand paper products that they dispensed with their traditional approach to new product development (NPD) and decided to launch non-chlorine bleached nappies immediately. These nappies were still in the early stages of development, but launch was justified by the impact that the *World in Action* programme had on Tesco's customers. This serves to illustrate the power of the media and concerned customer segments – in this case, mothers with young children, who are increasingly being regarded as a 'green consumer' segment in the UK (Armstrong and Hanmer-Lloyd 1993).

In 1991 car manufacturers operating in or exporting to Germany were given two years by the German government in which to develop plans for a 'recyclable car'. They were told to 'clean-up or close down' (Freeman 1990). In July

1992, Honda president Nobuhiko Kawamoto stated that making cars more environmentally friendly was the most important challenge facing manufacturers. In August 1992, Honda withdrew from motor racing to focus more on environmental aspects of development (Lamming 1993).

The Aerosol Connection, published by Friends of the Earth in 1989, resulted in the eight largest aerosol manufacturers announcing that they would phase out CFCs by the end of 1989. These companies accounted for 65% of the UK toiletries market. At the same time, Tesco refused to stock any branded products containing CFCs after July 1989, having eliminated CFCs from their own-label products by September 1988 (Armstrong and Hanmer-Lloyd 1993).

In recognising that companies operate within a commercial world where profit, market share and market position are paramount, what are the key influences on a company to adopt an environmental stance and so develop environmentally responsible products? Companies are increasingly recognising the major influence of all of their stakeholders on policies, strategies and operations (Hanmer-Lloyd and Armstrong 1993).

STAKEHOLDER PRESSURES ON ENVIRONMENTALLY RESPONSIBLE NEW PRODUCT DEVELOPMENT

The examples in the previous section illustrate that environmental pressures on NPD can originate from a variety of stakeholder groups, including consumers, customers, retailers, environmental pressure groups and international governments (Hanmer-Lloyd and Armstrong 1993). Table 14.1 illustrates the range and influence of stakeholder groups on the environmental positioning of a car manufacturer. It provides some insight into the increasingly complex environmental role of marketeers, particularly given the view that environmentally responsible NPD will be a major marketing challenge of the 1990s (Foster 1989). Two areas of stakeholder pressure are discussed below, legislation and green consumerism.

ENVIRONMENTAL LEGISLATION

Welford and Gouldson (1993) maintain that environmental legislation is the most important factor in influencing business to adopt an environmental orientation. They also argue that many proactive approaches to environmental problems also evolve through environmental legislation. A survey by PA

Table 14.1   Stakeholders and their potential interest in the environmental positioning of a car manufacturer

Stakeholder groups	Why do they need to know about the company's environmental impact?
Parent company	Corporate environmental performance, profitability
The board of directors	Corporate environmental performance, profitability
Senior management	Personnel issues, training
Employees	Long-term security: life and well-being the local environment
Customers	Buy company's approach, not just its products
The community	Impact on: life and well-being the local environment
Legislators	Legislative compliance
Investors	Long-term profitability
Suppliers	Cradle-to-grave analysis
Dealers	Sell: products corporate image
Pressure groups	Campaign publicity
Competitors	Edge to marketing/competitive positioning
The media	Corporate image
Trade unions	Protecting employees
Trade associations	Setting industry standards
Professional bodies	Professional standards
Pensioners	Community affairs
Academia	Research

Source: Charter (1992); reproduced by permission of Greenleaf Publishing

Consulting for the Confederation of British Industry (1990) indicated that UK companies regard national and European Community (EC) environmental legislation as playing an important role in encouraging them to adopt an environmental stance in their policies, strategies and processes. Legislation would therefore appear to be a major source of environmental pressure on business.

Prior to the Single European Act (1987), there was no explicit legal provision for Community environmental actions. Environmental initiatives were pursued under Articles 100 or 235 of the Treaty of Rome. The significance of the Single European Act, particularly Articles 100A and 130R, S and T, is that for the first time the need to combine free trade objectives with a high level of environmental protection, or simply to pursue environmental objectives, was recognised. Article 130R, paragraph 1, states:

Action by the Community relating to the environment shall have the following objectives: (i) to preserve, protect and improve the quality of the environment;

(ii) to contribute towards protecting human health; (iii) to ensure a prudent and rational utilization of natural resources.

(European Commission 1990)

Article 130R, paragraph 2, states:

Action by the Community relating to the environment shall be based on the principles that preventative action should be taken, that environmental damage should as a priority be rectified at source, and that the polluter should pay. Environmental protection requirements shall be a component of the Community's other policies.

(European Commission 1990)

Finally, the Act accepts that individual Member States can, if they wish, implement more stringent protective measures compatible with the Treaty of Rome (Article 130T).

While directives have set common standards for environmental quality, their implementation has been left to the responsibility of individual Member States. Consequently, in order for these standards to be translated into effective action, each State must develop appropriate natio.:al legislation, which must be applied and enforced at ground level. For example, in the UK the Environmental Protection Act (1990) builds on both national and EC legislation.

A major problem, however, has been the adoption and implementation of EC legislation into business. The focus of the fifth Environmental Action Programme (1993–2000) is therefore on overcoming many of the problems of previous legislation. It recognises that reform is necessary to improve:

- the preparation of measures
- consultation
- the effectiveness of integrating environmental policy into wider policy frameworks
- follow-ups to legislative measures
- compliance checking and enforcement

Within the fifth Programme, the emphasis has shifted away from controlling and reducing the environmental impact of industry, towards the promotion of industrial competitiveness through proactive approaches based on the adoption of clean technologies and the development of markets for environmentally responsible products. This can be assisted by EC eco-management and auditing, and eco-labelling schemes. The adoption of market-based instruments is perceived to complement the command and control legislation; it does not replace it. Dialogue groups are also proposed within the framework to assist in the design, application and enforcement of environmental legislation.

GREEN CONSUMERISM

A MORI poll published in July 1987 indicated that over the previous twelve months environmental concerns had triggered the biggest change in consumer behaviour since the oil price explosion in the early 1970s (Jackson 1990). The British Social Attitudes Report (Jowel 1991) revealed that changing consumer preferences are resulting in a cultural shift, in which environmental concerns are widely permeating society. Increasingly, consumers will not just be buying a product; they will be buying the company's response to minimising the negative environmental impact of their products and processes (Charter 1992; Welford and Gouldson 1993).

The environmental concern of consumers can therefore influence product design and brand loyalty. A survey of US consumers (June 1991) indicated that consumers had changed brands on environmental grounds at least once. Passingham and Battinson (1990) warned, however, that environmental concern does not always lead to the purchase of a product with environmental attributes; furthermore, purchase of an environmentally responsible product in one market-place does not automatically imply purchase in another. This reflects different rates of adoption for different environmentally responsible products, indicating that environmental attributes are not the only purchasing criteria. For example, while sales of recycled paper products have been very successful, many 'green' cleaners and detergents have been withdrawn from retail sale. This is discussed in more detail later in the chapter.

Consumers concerned about the environmental impact of the products they purchase are classified as 'green consumers'. Holdaway (1989) defines green consumers as 'people who regularly consider the environmental impact of at least some of the products they buy'. According to Holdaway (1989), about 40% of the adult population in the UK are green consumers. It is generally agreed that British green consumers are predominantly upper and middle class (ABC1), well educated, and female (particularly women with young children). With respect to age, the evidence is so contradictory that no reliable conclusions can be drawn as yet, although awareness and activity do appear to be higher among younger generations (Buswell 1991; Coddington 1993; Euromonitor 1990; Holdaway 1989; Passingham and Battinson 1990; Smith 1990).

Green consumers can be segmented into different 'shades' of green. At opposite ends of the spectrum are light and dark greens, with different degrees of 'greenness' between the two.

'Light green' consumers are typically conservationists, preservationists, defenders of public parks and stately homes, and all those people who believe polluted lakes, dying forests, nuclear power, and so on, are 'a bad thing', but do not necessarily go on to conclude that it is therefore necessary to change the whole basis on which society is organised. This is essentially a reformist movement, based on the premise that industrialism can be perfected, or at least improved, to minimise its impact on the environment, and lifestyles do not have to change in any significant way. Probably about 95% of the uses of the term 'green' fit into this category (Porritt and Winner 1988).

'Dark green' consumers are typically radical and visionary, and pose a fundamentalist challenge to the prevailing economic and political world order. At its most ambitious, their green politics regards itself as a global life-saver, an urgent response to a fast-approaching ecological collapse. It demands a totally new ethic, in which plundering mankind abandons its destructive ways, recognises its dependence on Planet Earth, and starts living on a more equal footing with the rest of nature. Such an ideology calls for a dramatic change in lifestyles and consumption (Porritt and Winner 1988).

The Roper Organisation (1990) identified five consumer segments, ranging from dark to light green and non-greens. This classification is presented in

Table 14.2   The Roper Organisation/S.C. Johnson classification of green consumers (incorporating Maslow's hierarchy of needs)

True-Blue Greens:
Active, committed greens whose behaviour is consistent with their environmental beliefs. Typically opinion leaders and innovators in green production adoption. Lifestyle needs and wants reflect self-actualisation (self-development and fulfilment).

Greenback Greens:
Environmental commitment expressed through willingness to pay high prices for green products. Intellectually concerned rather than actively involved. Busy lifestyles focusing on satisfying self-esteem needs and wants (self-esteem, recognition and status).

Sprouts:
Moderate levels of environmental concern and behaviour. They have some environmental tendencies but no clearly established environmentally concerned behaviour patterns. Lifestyle needs and wants reflect social needs (affection, belonging, acceptance).

Grousers:
Limited environmental belief or behaviour of their own but constantly criticise the environmental beliefs and behaviour of others. Lifestyle needs and wants reflect safety, (security, protection, order).

Basic Browns:
Not at all environmentally orientated, do not believe individual actions can contribute to environmental protection. Lifestyle needs based on physiological needs (food, drink, shelter).

Source: Based on the Roper Organisation (1990), Maslow (1954)

Table 14.2. From this classification, it would appear that the first two segments, 'True-Blue Greens' and 'Greenback Greens' are the committed dark greens who, according to Maslow's hierarchy of needs (1954), are higher up the hierarchical pyramid. The 'Sprouts' and 'Grousers' represent the light greens – some environmental concern but no behavioural commitment. The 'Basic Browns' have no environmental commitment. They are a very low income group who are too busy focusing on their own survival to worry about environmental degradation as well. They are at the bottom of Maslow's hierarchical pyramid. This classification scheme reflects the link between education, income and environmental orientation.

Internationally, environmental activities, interests and awareness among green consumers vary. German and Scandinavian consumers, for example, are typically regarded as 'true greens' with respect to their purchasing behaviour and disposal of waste. The differences and similarities among European consumers and the different needs of green segments must be addressed by marketing in developing environmentally responsible products, particularly as business is now in the era of the European Union (EU) and green consumerism reflects underlying value shifts that will influence buyer behaviour and create very volatile market and consumer segments.

DEVELOPING ENVIRONMENTALLY RESPONSIBLE NEW PRODUCTS

A wide variety of questions have emerged regarding the development of environmentally responsible products. For example, what exactly is an environmentally responsible product? How can environmental issues be successfully integrated into the NPD process? Some definitions are given here and suggestions made for effective integration.

CHARACTERISTICS OF ENVIRONMENTALLY RESPONSIBLE NEW PRODUCTS

One of the major recommendations of the Brundtland Report (The World Commission on Environment and Development 1987), 'more from less', can be translated into product development based on the use of minimal resources. The International Chamber of Commerce (1991), in their *Business Charter for Sustainable Development*, agree that products or services must be developed to minimise environmental impact, by being safe to use, efficient in

Table 14.3   Characteristics of environmentally responsible products

Reducing global environmental problems
Energy efficient
Non-polluting
Easily repairable
Designed to last, be reused or recycled
Minimal packaging
Manufactured from renewable resources
Safe disposal
Manufactured from local materials
Designed to satisfy genuine human needs
Sufficient information on product labels
Not harmful to human health
Not containing harmful substances
Not tested on animals

consumption of energy and natural resources, and able to be recycled, reused or disposed of safely. Table 14.3 expands on these environmental attributes. Overall, therefore, environmentally responsible product development is essentially about minimising negative environmental impact throughout the product life cycle. This life cycle involves production, distribution, use and disposal, i.e. from cradle to grave. These issues are discussed in more detail in the section entitled 'Design for the Environment'.

Environmentally responsible products also need to retain the high performance of traditional products and brands, given the limited adoption of totally 'green' products such as detergents and cleaners. The examples of Ark and Ecover, presented below, illustrate the importance of getting the environmental and performance mix of a product right.

In the UK, Ecover and Ark, two 'green' brands of household cleaners and detergents with very little market share, were a catalyst for the introduction of environmental attributes into the cleaners and detergents manufactured by the major multinationals and supermarket chains (ENDS 1990a), for example, Procter & Gamble's ultra range of 'compact' detergents (ENDS 1990d). The cleaning performance of Ark and Ecover products was, however, a major issue among consumers, except for the very committed environmental segments. Consumers, being used to the powerful cleaning capabilities of traditional cleaners and detergents, soon became disillusioned with 'green' cleaners. As a result, demand declined rapidly, retailers withdrew them from their shelves, and in the summer of 1993 both brands were withdrawn from retail sale in the UK. Other cleaning and detergent manufacturers in the UK that focused on developing 'green' brands experienced similar problems. For example, the UK detergent brand 'Greenforce', manufactured by the Robert Mcbride Group, was withdrawn from sale in the UK in the autumn of 1993. These examples emphasise the need for environmental attributes to be integrated as part of product performance – that is, combined excellence in environmental attributes and performance. This is reflected in the environmental quality policy of Procter & Gamble plc (Table 14.4).

Three issues are worth noting from Table 14.4:

- the leading role of the cradle-to-grave concept
- exceeding environmental laws and regulations
- the company's continual assessment to meet environmental goals

Table 14.4   Worldwide environmental quality policy, Procter & Gamble

---

Procter & Gamble is committed to providing products of superior quality and value that best fill the needs of the world's consumers. As a part of this, Procter & Gamble continually strives to improve the environmental quality of its products, packaging and operations around the world.

To carry out this commitment, it is Procter & Gamble's policy to:

- Ensure our products, packaging and operations are safe for our employees, consumers and the environment.

- Reduce or prevent the environmental impact of our products and packaging in their design, manufacture, distribution, use and disposal whenever possible. We take a leading role in developing innovative, practical solutions to environmental issues related to our products, packaging and processes. We support the sustainable use of resources and actively encourage reuse, recycling and composting. We share experiences and expertise and offer assistance to others who may contribute to progress in achieving environmental goals.

- Meet or exceed the requirements of all environmental laws and regulations. We use environmentally sound practices, even in the absence of governmental standards. We co-operate with governments in analysing environmental issues and developing cost-effective, scientifically-based solutions and standards.

- Continually assess our environmental technology and programmes and monitor progress toward environmental goals. We develop and use state-of-the-art science and product life cycle assessment from raw materials through disposal, to assess environmental quality.

- Provide our consumers, customers, employees, communities, public interest groups and others with relevant and appropriate factual information about the environmental quality of P&G products, packaging and operations. We seek to establish and nurture open, honest and timely communications and strive to be responsive to concerns.

- Ensure every employee understands and is responsible and accountable for incorporating environmental quality considerations in daily business activities. We encourage, recognise and reward individual and team leadership efforts to improve environmental quality. We also encourage employees to reflect their commitment to environmental quality outside work.

- Have operating policies, programmes and resources in place to implement our environmental quality policy.

Source: Procter & Gamble (1991)

If this policy is compared against the environmental characteristics presented in Table 14.3, then such multinationals still have some way to go to achieve environmental excellence (if indeed this can ever be attained), but part of being environmentally responsible is to make an environmental commitment in the first place, and then to follow this through with ongoing action, ideas and aspirations.

Table 14.5 Key process and management criteria for NPD success (identified from the literature)

NPD process characteristics

A formal, systematic NPD process will guide and facilitate the new product development project from idea generation to launch (Cooper 1988; Craig and Hart 1991; Johne and Snelson 1988; Moore 1987).

A parallel, rather than sequential, NPD approach will improve success rates (Cooper 1983a). Quinn (1985) and Cooper (1983b) maintained that NPD involves a complex, creative process of convergent and divergent activities characterised by feedback, reworking of stages and multiple approaches. A sequential approach does not allow for this.

Predevelopment activities are critical, and must be built into the NPD process in a systematic and consistent way. While companies tend to minimise their predevelopment activity, success or failure of NPD is directly related to the level of predevelopment input (Cooper 1988).

Evaluation will improve NPD success rates. This essentially involves screening, assessment (market and technical), research and business analysis (Cooper and Kleinschmidt 1990).

Information, particularly information gathered to support evaluation, provides a foundation to NPD and cross-cultural NPD integration (Craig and Hart 1991).

NPD success is dependent on:

1 Interdisciplinary inputs involving R&D, manufacturing, engineering, marketing and sales, which facilitate integrated marketing and technical expertise.
2 Quality marketing and technical inputs to the process.
3 Speed of the process, so enabling first mover advantage, hence competitive advantage.

Managing NPD

Top management has a major role to play in the NPD process, (Boag and Rinholm 1989; Cooper and Kleinschmidt 1987; Johne and Snelson 1989; Maidique and Zirger 1984; Roy et al. 1990).

R&D and marketing managers exert the greatest influence on the NPD process (Hegarty and Hoffman 1990).

Successful NPD requires a teamworking approach, which will involve widespread inter-functional involvement (Barczak and Wilemon 1989; Bingham and Quigley 1990; Johne and Snelson 1990). This inter-functional involvement reflects the range of specialisation and skills required by the team. However, communication barriers, which can sometimes result from this, will need to be overcome (Ginn and Rubenstein 1986; Gupta and Wilemon 1988, 1990; Nystrom 1985; Pinto and Pinto 1990).

INTEGRATING ENVIRONMENTAL RESPONSIBILITY INTO THE NPD PROCESS

Some of the process and management issues critical to successful new product developments have a major impact on the development of environmentally responsible products. These key points are presented in Table 14.5.

The product development literature (see Hart, Chapter 1, this volume) indicates that:

- A formal, systematic and parallel NPD process will improve development success rates.
- Companies need to focus on predevelopment activities.
- NPD needs to be interdisciplinary.
- The process needs to be speed product development to market.
- Top managers must be involved.
- The R&D and marketing managers are key players within NPD.
- A teamworking approach will improve management effectiveness (Armstrong and Hanmer-Lloyd 1994a, 1994b).

Overall, successful NPD is market-led, characterised by ongoing screening and evaluation, involves greater top management control, entails a developed team approach and focuses on the total business concept, not just on the product being developed (Johne and Snelson 1990; see also Johne, Chapter 2, this volume).

NPD, involving the integration of environmental attributes, must therefore take account of the issues identified above, and development should occur in accordance with them. In addition, environmental responsibility should play an active role throughout the process. It needs to be integrated during the initial stages of the NPD process, and filter down through each stage (Armstrong 1992).

Charter (1990) suggests that environmentally responsible NPD essentially involves an active investment policy into R&D and the encouragement of innovation, creativity and collaboration. Where a formal NPD system is in operation, this can be achieved by allocating a percentage of the budget to the development of environmentally responsible products. Where no formal system exists, incentives for green ideas should be encouraged. Active sourcing of 'greener' raw materials and components, constant auditing of suppliers, and recycling should also be integral parts of the 'greener' product development process.

With respect to the product concept, brand new products can have environmental characteristics built in, thereby effectively responding to the need to integrate environmental issues throughout the NPD process. With modified products, however, environmental features are add-ons and as such environmental protection might be reduced. Given that most NPD is a modification of some kind, it is therefore not surprising that the majority of environmentally responsible products being developed are modifications of existing products – range extensions, product revamps, and so on. Recycled or recyclable packaging and packaging reductions are major examples of this. A longer term approach, however, has to be towards complete integration directed by corporate and product strategies, from idea generation to product launch (Armstrong 1992).

DESIGN FOR THE ENVIRONMENT

The importance of design in helping to reduce the environmental impact of products is increasingly being recognised (Potter 1992; Ryan, Hosken and Greene 1992). The term 'design for the environment' (DFE) is frequently used to describe the integration of environmental responsibility into the product design or development process (Coddington 1993; Mackenzie 1991). This essentially involves the integration of the environmental product characteristics and is based on the cradle-to-grave concept identified in Table 14.3. An example is energy efficiency. A design checklist based on cradle-to-grave is presented in Table 14.6, and Figure 14.1 illustrates one company's environmental philosophy based on the cradle-to-grave concept.

Focusing on one aspect of this philosophy – the design process – Figure 14.2 provides an example of AEG's response to integrating environmental concerns into the design process. Their approach incorporates many of the attributes previously listed in Table 14.3.

Table 14.6   A checklist for design for the environment

- Could the product be cleaner?
- Can it be more energy efficient
- Could it be quieter?
- Could it be more intelligent?
- Is it over-designed?
- Is the technology appropriate?
- Is there a risk of product failure?
- How long will it last?
- Have the proposed UK and EC eco-labelling schemes been considered?
- What happens when its useful life ends?
- Can it be designed for re-usability and recycling?
- Can it be easily repaired?
- Can its life be extended through regular maintenance?

Source: Charter (1992); reproduced by permission of Greenleaf Publishing

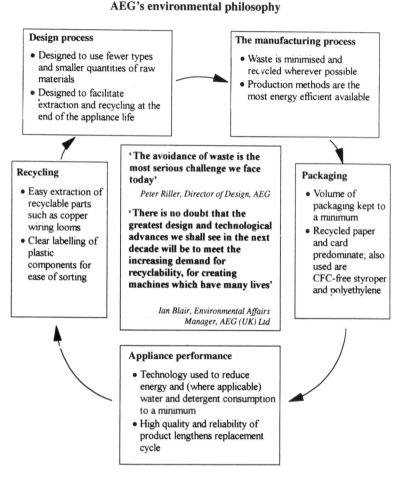

Figure 14.1   Using cradle-to-grave in environmental design (Charter 1992); reproduced by permission of Greenleaf Publishing

A variety of techniques and concepts can be applied to assist the design of environmentally responsible products. Possible approaches include life cycle analysis (LCA), environmental auditing and total quality management (TQM). These are reviewed in brief below.

LIFE CYCLE ANALYSIS

LCA is a relatively new discipline, developed in the 1970s and first used in the packaging industry. It is essentially a diagnostic tool used to judge the total

---

AEG washing machines

Design criteria: Intelligent features and reduced energy and water consumption

The Lavamat was developed to reduce energy and water consumption through a sophisticated microprocessor and sensor system. The accumulation of soap suds in the machine is monitored and excess soap suds reduced by partially slowing the spin speed. This also reduces the quantities of rinsing water required. Energy and water consumption are reduced by the load sensor which automatically determines the water quantity required for the washing load. An extensive range of programmes are provided including energy saving and low temperature programmes. Its microprocessor allows greater flexibility and control. It is fitted with a special valve (Eco-lock) in the sump which prevents undissolved powder entering the drainage system. This helps reduce water pollution and saves around 20% of the recommended washing powder dosage. Sensors redistribute unbalanced loads, so reducing wear to the drum and bearings during the spin cycles. This prolongs its lifespan and reliability. Its shell, tub and drive are all protected against corrosion. The electronically controlled transmission system and insulation ensure minimal noise during use.

AEG

WASHING MACHINES FOR CLEANER FISH

(Slogan used for AEG advertising campaign for Lavamat automatic washing machines.)

Figure 14.2   AEG washing machines

environmental impact of a product or production process from cradle-to-grave (ENDS 1990c; Hunt 1991). Analysis is based on:

- Life cycle inventory: defining what is and what is not to be analysed.
- Environmental evaluation: interpreting the environmental problems associated with the product or process and the nature of their environmental impact.
- Environmental improvement plan: developing a strategy to improve the environmental performance of a company's products and/or production processes and any other area of concern, e.g. energy conservation.

According to Charter (1992), LCA is currently used to:

- Define the present environmental burden of a product or package.
- Support environmental claims and eco-labelling schemes.
- Identify where improvements might be made.
- Guide environmental improvement and development work.

The major benefit of LCA is its ability to expand the debate on the environmental impact of products, processes and packaging away from single-issue

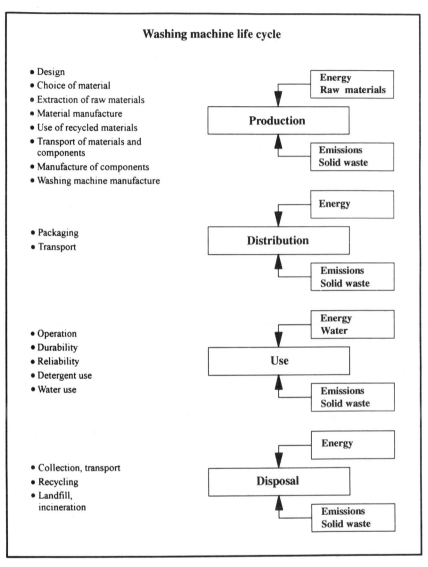

Washing machine life cycle

- Design
- Choice of material
- Extraction of raw materials
- Material manufacture
- Use of recycled materials
- Transport of materials and components
- Manufacture of components
- Washing machine manufacture

Energy
Raw materials

Production

Emissions
Solid waste

- Packaging
- Transport

Energy

Distribution

Emissions
Solid waste

- Operation
- Durability
- Reliability
- Detergent use
- Water use

Energy
Water

Use

Emissions
Solid waste

- Collection, transport
- Recycling
- Landfill, incineration

Energy

Disposal

Emissions
Solid waste

Figure 14.3   Eco-labelling criteria using cradle to grave (PA Consulting 1992); reproduced by permission of the Controller of Her Majesty's Stationery Office

criteria, towards a broader, more holistic perspective. Its use will be driven by increasing regulation and product scrutiny. IBM, for example requests that LCA is carried out on each of its products to determine whether fewer or smaller quantities of toxic materials can be used (Charter 1992).

Eco-labelling schemes also focus on LCA. These schemes will require companies to examine inputs and outputs from cradle to grave. This is illustrated in Figure 14.3, which shows the life cycle of a washing machine and the typical issues and areas that need to be considered. Eco-labelling is discussed in more detail below.

The application of LCA is a controversial area of debate among practitioners and academics. It is considered to be an incomplete tool because of the confusion resulting from methods and assumptions, and the difficulties of practical application (Simon et al. 1992). However, the system of 'environmental priority strategies' (EPS) proposed by Ryding (1991) may go some way towards overcoming some of these difficulties. EPS assists life cycle assessments through its environmental indices, which facilitate evaluation of the environmental impact of product development.

ENVIRONMENTAL AUDITING

Environmental auditing can assist designers by indicating ways of reducing environmental impact throughout the product life cycle. The Confederation of British Industry (CBI) maintains that environmental auditing should be based on cradle-to-grave auditing of all aspects of business operations. This would provide managers with the information needed to set environmental targets to keep ahead of environmental legislation (ENDS 1990b). The aims of the audit are to ascertain what the organisation has done, is doing, and will need to do in the future in relation to the environment. Essentially, the overall aim of the audit is to provide the company with a profile of itself from an environmental perspective; that is, an analysis of its environmental internal strengths and weaknesses, and external opportunities and threats. For example, Fort Sterling conducted a very thorough audit of itself to ensure that the environmental positioning of its products and processes were closely coordinated. The company created an audit team to identify areas that would have the greatest environmental impact, including effluent control, raw materials, transport, internal waste, neighbourhood relations, packaging and employee relations. Significant changes to operations, particularly the production process, occurred as a direct result of Fort Sterling's more environmentally responsible product requirements. This reflects a proactive approach to environmental integration.

TOTAL QUALITY MANAGEMENT

Environmental design can also be enhanced through the application of British Standard BS7750, which is attempting to improve standards in environmental management, marketing and product development by focusing on TQM via environmental quality and product performance. TQM influences product development through guiding principles that assist management decision making (Charter 1992). For companies such as IBM and 3M, environmental excellence has become an integral part of their TQM programmes. For both companies, this includes commitment to prevention rather than cure; that is, commitment to the '3Ps' – 'Pollution Prevention Pays'. 3M launched its 3P programme in 1975 after realising the direct link between environmental excellence, TQM and competitive advantage. The benefits have included reduction in waste, thus generating higher raw material yields, tighter management of suppliers, higher levels of customer satisfaction through improved product quality and a strong market position. The company does admit, though, that quality improvements are becoming more difficult to achieve as the 'easy options' for pollution prevention diminish. This has, however, served to strengthen their resolve for environmental excellence through product innovation by designing-in pollution prevention (Charter 1992).

Rhone-Poulenc have also adopted a 'total quality' approach to environmental protection through their 'environmental index'. The company recognises, however, that the index is geared more towards the implementation of its corporate environmental policy (CEP) rather than an explicit measure of the environmental impact of its operations (Salamitou 1991).

EUROPEAN ENVIRONMENTAL REGULATION: ECO-LABELLING

One area of environmental regulation impacting on environmental design, albeit voluntary at present, is eco-labelling (ENDS 1989). The preceding discussion on environmental design indicates that DFE is likely to be partially dependent on eco-labelling accreditation.

According to the National Advisory Group on Eco-Labelling (NAGEL) (1991), the scheme aims to:

- Provide consumers with authoritative guidelines for assessing environmental product characteristics.
- Encourage the development of environmentally benign products.
- Facilitate trade in these products.

Products being considered for an eco-label will be subjected to rigorous assessment of their environmental impact via LCA (*Financial Times* 1990;

Product life cycle / Environmental fields	Pre-production	Production	Distribution (including packaging)	Utilisation	Disposal
Waste relevance					
Soil pollution and degradation					
Water contamination					
Air contamination					
Noise					
Consumption of energy					
Consumption of natural resources					
Effects on eco-systems					

Figure 14.4 LCA framework for eco-labelling assessment (National Advisory Group on Eco-Labelling 1991)

Department of Trade and Industry 1990). The specific criteria that will be used to assess products applying for the European Eco-Label are listed in Figure 14.4, and include waste, pollution, consumption of resources, and impact on ecosystems across the life cycle of the product being assessed.

In practical terms, however, in the UK the scheme is proving to be extremely difficult to develop, with delays and disagreements among interested parties. Anita Roddick, founder and managing director of The Body Shop (a pioneer environmentally conscious company producing natural cosmetics and toiletries with no animal testing, minimal packaging, etc.), is concerned by the UK Eco-Labelling Board's recent decision to award eco-labels to products that have no regard for endangered species or indigenous people, do not use recycled packaging and whose ingredients are tested on animals.

While these characteristics are increasingly being recognised as important elements of environmentally responsible products, the Eco-Labelling Board is operating within a much narrower context, thereby further complicating environmental integration into NPD. Paulette Dupree, the UK Board's communications manager, is adamant that:

> The ecolabel is purely an environmental label. Although animal testing is a valid issue, it is not an issue relating to the burden on the environment.
>
> (Porritt 1993)

Anita Roddick commented in response that:

> We are astounded that anyone could propose an Eco-Label for cosmetic products which have been tested on animals, or which might use ingredients with unacceptable impacts on Third World cultures or environments. If these issues are not 'ecological' nothing is. Our evidence from consumer surveys show unequivocally that issues like animal testing must be taken into account. If they are not, The Body Shop will campaign vigorously against the scheme.
>
> (Porritt 1993)

While the conflicts resulting from this debate continue, eco-labelling proposals are resulting in increasing confusion among UK companies, rather than easing the development of environmentally responsible products. Jonathan Porritt (1993) a UK writer, broadcaster and environmentalist, described the conflict between The Body Shop and the Eco-labelling Board as 'hairsprays at dawn'! Commenting on it, he maintained that:

> That such weighty issues should be fought out with hairsprays is just one of life's little jokes. Here we all are struggling to save the world from the Four Horsemen of the Ecological Apocalypse, and it all comes down to defining just what a

'green hairspray' might be. Some of us can't help thinking it would be better to do away with hairsprays altogether, green or ungreen. But who are we to precipitate the collapse of western civilisation?

It is against this background of complexities that the research was set. There can be little doubt of the need to integrate environmental responsibility into NPD. The preceding discussion has, however, attempted to highlight the nature and context of the problem, and provide a more informed approach to the issues involved.

THE RESEARCH STUDY

RESEARCH AIMS

The aims of the research were to explore the parameters of the research area, and to provide insight, understanding and direction for further research. This involved researching:

- the nature of the NPD process adopted by UK companies
- the major environmental issues impacting on business
- the impact of these environmental issues on NPD
- definitions and characteristics of environmentally responsible products and new products

The overall aim of the research study was to develop an NPD framework to effectively integrate environmental responsibility into the NPD process.

METHODOLOGY

The research was based on an inductive research paradigm using a qualitative, exploratory research methodology. This approach was adopted because of its strengths in providing understanding and insight into the research area.

Twelve depth interviews were carried out in ten organisations, which included UK manufacturers and retailers, professional bodies and design agencies. Judgement sampling was used; respondents were either recommended, or identified from the secondary research and literature review. Respondents were selected for their NPD and/or environmental experience and expertise, and were typically at senior levels within the organisation. A respondent profile is presented in Table 14.7.

Table 14.7   Respondent profiles

Organisations	Respondents	Expertise/responsibility
Government department (1)	Civil servant	Environmental: policy department responsible for eco-auditing policy
Trade/professional associations (3)	Head of environmental management unit Project manager (environmental projects in business) Special adviser (environment)	Environmental: Associations involved in developing environmental policy and environmental guidelines for business, and EC directives Advising members/business on addressing environmental issues in business
Manufacturers; industrial and consumer products (4)	Health and safety director Business executive Marketing manager (2) NPD manager	Environmental and NPD Two of the four manufacturers had integrated environmental responsibility into their operations and policy Of the remaining two, one had recently revised its NPD approach, providing valuable information for the research The heath and safety director was responsible for implementing environmental quality across country (industrial) Environmental knowledge/roles of business executive and marking manager (high) industrial Environmental knowledge of respondents in consumer companies limited, focus on NPD
Retailer (1)	Marketing manager Packaging design and development controller	Environmental and NPD Environmental policy being translated into product development specifications Very active in NPD
Design agency (1)	Managing director	Recognised for its expertise in designing environmentally responsible products Involved in policy development, e.g. eco-labelling

RESEARCH FINDINGS

Key Stakeholders Impacting on the Development of Environmentally Responsible New Products

Legislation, and customer and consumer demand were identified by respondents as major sources of environmental pressure on the NPD function. Respondents stressed that firstly, managers need to keep abreast – or preferably just ahead – of current environmental legislation. Secondly, business must not move ahead of customer and consumer demands. Companies could arrive at the market-place 'ahead' of their customers and consumers, but experience has indicated that sales levels would be disappointing because current needs and wants would not be addressed.

Respondents indicated that, in terms of purchasing behaviour, consumer demand in particular was limited, making it difficult for marketing managers to justify developing environmentally responsible products in the first place. What is likely to be the case is that environmental pressure is originating from 'medium' and 'dark green' consumers who, as a potential target market for environmentally responsible products, do not have the substantial financial attraction and market growth of more traditional consumer segments.

Respondents maintained that while consumers tend to agree with the need for environmental protection, this is not necessarily translated into their buyer behaviour. Respondents believed that this is because environmental attributes are not considered a priority. Typically, for consumer durables, environmental attributes would be rated sixth or seventh after price, performance, features, service, and so on. Respondents maintained that consumers are interested in environmental issues but are not necessarily prepared to change their lifestyles to consume less. However, environmentalists generally hold that a change in lifestyle to reduce consumption is a critical factor in environmental protection. Thus, there appears to be a gap between consumer knowledge, attitudes and action. While this is a common occurrence in consumer behaviour, it does little to ease the integration of environmental issues into NPD.

Definitions and Characteristics of Environmentally Responsible New Products

While respondents had difficulty in defining 'environmental responsibility', they felt that existing definitions were inadequate. They maintained that no products were 'environmentally friendly'; definitions really need to focus around the concepts of responsibility and environmental impacts. Products

Table 14.8   Characteristics of environmentally responsible products, as identified in the study

- Waste minimisation
- Energy efficiency
- Recyclability
- Emission reductions
- Improved product lifespan
- Improved product information from manufacturers
- Level of usefulness: serving a real need
- Minimal use of non-renewable resources: 'more from less'
- High performance
- Full integration of the cradle-to-grave concept

were perceived to be environmentally responsible if they had minimal negative environmental impact. The specific characteristics identified are presented in Table 14.8.

Respondents also stated that performance must not be diluted because of environmental characteristics. Products that do not provide high performance cannot be truly green, Ark and Ecover being cited as examples. Respondents perceived products with diluted performance as still causing environmental damage through their production and disposal. It was therefore maintained that environmental characteristics should be integrated into existing or new products or brands like any other product attribute, rather than developing separate 'eco' ranges. These characteristics reflect the environmental attributes presented in Table 14.3 and are supported by the literature.

Integrating Environmental Responsibility into the NPD Process

Overall, respondents stressed that environmental integration is complex and difficult (see the section entitled 'Barriers to developing environmentally responsible products', p. 316). However, they identified a number of process characteristics that provide a context for environmentally responsible NPD.

Firstly, the idea generation process needs to be controlled. Consequently, ideas are typically generated in-house rather than referring to external sources such as stakeholder groups. Secondly, the idea screening process can be very subjective; models designed to improve objectivity are not well understood, and so are rarely used. Thirdly, the need to bring new products on stream faster has meant that organisations often miss out or 'gloss over' relevant stages in the process. This is likely to increase the probability of NPD failure and a lack of built-in environmental checks during the NPD process.

Respondents maintained that, overall, environmental responsibility needs to be integrated at the very start of the NPD process, which will enable the cradle-to-grave concept to be built in. They stressed that there was little value in thinking about environmental performance near completion because it is unlikely that it would be an integral part of the product. For some companies this involves looking 10–15 years ahead.

Managing the Integration of Environmental Responsibility into the NPD Process

With respect to the management of the NPD process, respondents maintained that there is limited corporate expertise in NPD, which creates problems for environmental integration. The cross-functional, teamworking approach adopted by the NPD decision making unit and project teams can, however, help to build-in environmental expertise where it does exist, so facilitating the integration of environmental expertise into the NPD function. Teams were represented by R&D, marketing, sales, technical, international, quality (BS5750), design and manufacturing. Unfortunately, while a cross-functional approach is advocated in the literature, respondents maintained that its complexity results in communications problems, which are further aggravated by departmental politics.

Respondents maintained that the links between the product development unit and environmental affairs is very tenuous and, as such, inhibits environmental product development. It was suggested that this lack of communication and integration was partially the result of limited consumer demand, making the commercial viability of environmentally responsible products more difficult to justify.

Respondents stressed that a fully integrated environmental management system is critical to the effective integration of environmental issues, not only into NPD, but within all business functions. This involves top management responsibility: clear targets and objectives, review procedures, and actions. Approaches vary to include combinations of the following:

- the development of an environmental policy
- environmental auditing
- environmental monitoring
- cost–benefit analysis
- life cycle analysis
- developing specialised environmental teams
- environmental information
- voluntary guidelines

However, respondents acknowledged that few environmental management systems have as yet been developed or operationalised.

Table 14.9   Management styles for environmentally responsible NPD

1. Internal environmentally skilled managers or technical experts are integrated into the NPD decision making unit. Their responsibilities include communicating, developing and integrating environmental responsibility at all levels and functions, company-wide, e.g. environmental affairs director.
2. Existing members of the decision making unit are expected to be aware of and integrate environmental issues into NPD, e.g. quality manager, marketing manager, R&D manager, etc.
3. External consultants, specialists, designers, etc., are used to assist the decision making unit in developing environmentally responsible products.

Environmental Expertise within the NPD Function

Respondents identified three different management styles reflecting varying levels of environmental expertise within the NPD decision making unit and project team (Table 14.9).

Respondents claimed that in many cases the NPD decision making unit or team lacked the necessary skills, perception (vision) and training to effectively integrate environmental responsibility into the NPD process. Environmental knowledge of marketing managers was generally regarded as inadequate. Consequently, their ability to develop environmentally responsible products is likely to be very limited, consisting of tokenism at best. Limited knowledge and skills were perceived to be the result of a lack of training and education, conflicting information, the difficulty of the subject area, and a gap between policy and action.

Respondents maintained that in situations where companies wanted to integrate environmental responsibility into their NPD, but had limited skills to do so, reliance was placed on specialist organisations such as environmental design consultancies. These specialists were perceived to spend a lot of time submerged in the issues and therefore to be better informed about them.

Barriers to Developing Environmentally Responsible New Products

The integration of environmental responsibility into NPD was regarded as a very difficult and complicated task. Respondents highlighted the following issues:

- There is limited idea generation for environmental improvement. Companies are looking for ways to improve the environmental performance of their products, but there are not enough 'brilliant ideas' to do so.
- There are no set guidelines for environmental product design. Environmental design features will be dependent on the product, product category

and existing infrastructure; for example, it is no good making a recyclable product if the infrastructure to recycle it does not exist. Alternative materials are not always readily available or safe. Respondents were concerned that new developments or alternatives were being used that were unsafe and the environmental impact was unknown. This point was highlighted by one respondent from a manufacturing company, who explained that:

> We needed to eliminate the use of CFCs in our product. We decided to use butane, which was already being used in fly sprays. We had walls blown down, the cans were getting warm and exploding. We ended up with a very flammable product. It's a balancing act between safety and the environment.

As a result, the design and development team can become embroiled in a very complex and involved debate while trying to maintain the commercial reality of product development.

■ While respondents acknowledged the value of the cradle-to-grave concept in the development process, respondents who actually used it maintained that it was difficult, costly and time consuming to implement.

■ The environmental impact of products needs to be assessed in order to identify areas for improvement. The difficulty in achieving this, however, was stressed. Few NPD teams even attempt it because existing measurement techniques are so limited. A starting point is to look at current environmental performance in order to identify the 'best' environmental performance attributes, for example energy, waste disposal etc. LCA can help by setting a framework of potential environmental impacts underpinned by a quantitative measurement system. Whatever the approach, it needs to be built into the product development brief to become an integral part of the NPD process.

■ Eco-labelling accreditation is causing some concern to respondents. The proposed UK and EC schemes were perceived to be complicated and expensive to implement, and still very much in the developmental stages with respect to classification of product types and definitions. The packaging design and development controller (UK retailer), commenting on the eco-labelling concept, argued that:

> Somewhere along the line someone is going to have to develop some standard definitions. The only people who can do this are the government and they seem to be backing away from the issues, saying 'it's up to industry to do it'. But there are too many vested interests to do this. Everyone is trying to protect their own industry segment. So what is needed are some definitions.

■ Environmental integration into the NPD process is being hampered by a lack of communication between cross-functional members of the NPD team.

■ A lack of environmental experience and expertise also circumvents integration into the NPD process.

■ The development of environmentally responsible products is being impaired by limited market demand. Respondents were concerned about what it is that consumers really want and what they are prepared to pay for. This reflects the conflict between consumers' environmental beliefs and environmental action, discussed above. According to one marketing manager retailer:

> Companies are facing a dilemma, the conflict between improving the environmental performance of a product and giving consumers what they want. It is very frustrating because of the huge gaps in consumer behaviour, saying one thing, doing another.

DEVELOPING ENVIRONMENTALLY RESPONSIBLE NEW PRODUCTS: TOWARDS A FRAMEWORK FOR SUCCESS

Successful environmentally responsible product development essentially revolves around building standards of excellence into NPD to minimise environmental impact while retaining product performance. This can be conceptualised as a 'best practice' approach. It should be recognised, however, that 'best practice' is constantly evolving as knowledge, expertise, science and technology improve.

The research highlights the need for guidelines and referral frameworks to ease and improve environmental integration into NPD. Both the research and the literature have identified a multiplicity of issues which need to be addressed and emphasised. While business is beginning to appreciate the importance of both NPD and environmental integration, in terms of best practice or standards of excellence, related operations and strategies are still in their infancy. This research can, however, begin to identify guidelines towards developing best practice for the development of environmentally responsible products. These are discussed below.

DEFINITIONS

It is not clear that the terms 'green', 'environmentally responsible', 'environmentally friendly', 'environmentally sensitive', etc., are synonymous and are interpreted in the same way among and between business and environmental academics and practitioners. Hence, meanings need to be defined and standardised, with any differences being explained clearly. Likewise, definitions of what constitutes an environmentally responsible product need to be standardised by an independent body with relevant expertise, knowledge and experience of the issues involved. Eco-labelling can begin to address some of these issues, but serious flaws in the scheme must be overcome initially.

INTEGRATING ENVIRONMENTAL RESPONSIBILITY INTO THE NPD PROCESS

Environmental responsibility should play an active role throughout the NPD process. It needs to be integrated during the initial stages of the process and filter down through all stages of development, reflecting the cradle-to-grave concept. This is equally applicable to brand new and modified products, and environmental and non-environmental product ranges.

Environmentally responsible NPD practices should encompass the concepts of a systematic approach, involving parallel processing and completion of all stages of development (simple modifications being excepted). An ongoing evaluation system should be built into the process. Assessment of commercial viability needs to be made more objective and should include non-financial measures such as environmental performance indicators. Such indicators are still in the early stages of development.

ENVIRONMENTALLY RESPONSIBLE PRODUCT DESIGN

A well-designed, environmentally responsible product must balance traditional design criteria, such as performance, efficient manufacture, ease of use, attractive design, etc., with environmental characteristics. These characteristics must aim to reduce environmental impact during the product life cycle by using minimum resources to achieve maximum output – the cradle-to-grave principle. Cradle-to-grave can therefore underpin a best practice approach in environmental design. Performance quality of products must also be sustained or enhanced if the product is to be commercially viable.

Environmental performance indicators need to be applied to assess the environmental impacts of potential designs, i.e. going beyond traditional financial measures. BS7750 accreditation can also provide a framework for environmental quality within NPD via TQM.

MANAGING ENVIRONMENTAL INTEGRATION

Top management support can facilitate the successful commercialisation of environmentally responsible products, and a teamworking approach will help to provide a rich mix of skills and experiences to integrate environmental concerns in the NPD process. Otherwise, environmental concerns will be marginalised and carried out by personnel with limited skills and expertise.

Through the numerous examples and research reported here, it can be seen that while some companies are making significant efforts in the integration of environmental issues within NPD, others are not. Raising awareness of the important issues involved in successfully developing environmentally responsible products and developing guidelines to assist implementation are very much needed.

REFERENCES

Armstrong, J. (1992). Developing environmentally responsible products: A marketing framework. Unpublished work.

Armstrong, J. and Hanmer-Lloyd, S. (1993). Integrating environmental responsibility into the new product development process: Towards a best practice approach, in Groningen–UMIST Workshop: Meeting the Challenges of Product Development, University of Groningen, The Netherlands, May.

Armstrong, J. and Hanmer-Lloyd, S. (1994a). Successfully developing environmentally responsible products: The response of UK manufacturers of detergents and household cleaning products, in Groningen–UMIST Workshop: Meeting the Challenges of Product Development, UMIST, Manchester, May.

Armstrong, J. and Hanmer-Lloyd, S. (1994b). Developing environmentally responsible detergents and household cleaning products: Towards a framework for success, in Marketing Education Group (MEG) Annual Conference, University of Ulster, Coleraine, July.

Barczak, G. and Wilemon, D. (1989). Leadership differences in new product development teams, *Journal of Product Innovation Management*, **6**(4), 259–267.

Bingham, F. and Quigley, C. (1990). A team approach to new product development, *Journal of Marketing Management*, **6**(1), 47–58.

Boag, D. and Rinholm, B. (1989). New product management practices of small high technology firms, *Journal of Product Innovation Management*, **6**(2), 109–122.

Buswell, D. (1991). Consumers and the environment: British infants or rainbow warriors? in *Research 2000: Market Research Society Conference Papers*, pp. 195–205.

Charter, M. (1990). *Greener Marketing: A Responsible Approach to Business*, KPH Marketing.

Charter, M. (ed.) (1992). *Greener Marketing: A Responsible Approach to Business*, Greenleaf Publishing.

Coddington, W. (1993). *Environmental Marketing: Positive Strategies for Reaching the Green Consumer*, McGraw-Hill, New York.

Confederation of British Industry (1990). *Waking Up to a Better Environment*, CBI, London.

Cooper, R.G. (1983a). The new product process: An empirically based classification scheme, *R&D Management*, **13**(1), 1–13.

Cooper, R.G. (1983b). A process model for industrial new product development, *IEEE Transactions on Engineering Management*, **30**(1), 2–11.

Cooper, R.G. (1988). The new product process: A decision guide for management, *Journal of Marketing Management*, **3**(3), 238–255.

Cooper, R.G. and Kleinschmidt, E.J. (1987). New products: What separates winners from losers? *Journal of Product Innovation Management*, **4**(3), 169–184.

Cooper, R.G. and Kleinschmidt, E.J. (1990). New product success factors: A comparison of 'kills' versus successes and failures, *R&D Management*, **20**(1), 169–184.

Craig, A. and Hart, S. (1991). Determinants of new product development success, in Marketing Education Group (MEG) Annual Conference, Cardiff Business School.

Department of Trade and Industry (1990). *Environmental Labelling of Consumer Goods*, HMSO, London.

Elkington, J. and Burke, T. (1989). *The Green Capitalists*, Victor Gollancz, London.

ENDS (1989). Eco-labels: Product management in a greener Europe, *ENDS Report*, **178**, November.

ENDS (1990a). Ecover raises the stakes in fresh challenge to detergent majors, *ENDS Report*, **184**, May.

ENDS (1990b). Emerging issues in environmental auditing, *ENDS Report*, **185**, June, 11–13.

ENDS (1990c). Life-cycle analysis: An environmental management tool for the 1990s, *ENDS Report*, **188**, September, 19–21.

ENDS (1990d). Success of compact powders positions detergent majors for phosphate curbs, *ENDS Report*, **191**, December, 24–25.

Euromonitor (1990). *Environmental Business Handbook*, Euromonitor.

European Commission (1990). *Environmental Policy in the European Community*, edn 4, periodical 5, Office for the Official Publications of the European Communities, Luxembourg.

Financial Times (1990). Brussels plan 'green' label to grade consumer products, 30 November.

Foster, A. (1989). Decent, clean and true, *Management Today*, February, 56–60.

Freeman, L. (1990). Lever and P&G green plans differ, *Advertising Age*, 23 July, 46.

Friends of the Earth (1989). *The Aerosol Connection*, FoE, London.

Ginn, M.E. and Rubenstein, A.H. (1986). The R&D/production interface: A case study of new product commercialisation, *Journal of Product Innovation Management*, **3**, 158–170.

Gupta, A.K. and Wilemon, D. (1988). The credibility–cooperation connection at the R&D–marketing interface, *Journal of Product Innovation Management*, **5**, 20–31.

Gupta, A.K. and Wilemon, D. (1990). Improving R&D/marketing relations: R&D's perspective, *R&D Management*, **20**(4), 277–290.

Hanmer-Lloyd, S. and Armstrong, J. (1993). Environmental stakeholder groups, in Confederation of British Industry Breakfast Club Seminar, Bristol Business School, University of the West of England.

Hegarty, W. and Hoffman, R. (1990). Product/market innovations: A study of top management involvement among four cultures, *Journal of Product Innovation Management*, **7**, 186–199.

Holdaway, R. (1989). The significance of the green consumer, in *Green Consumer – Green Business*, CBI conference report, Rooster Books, London.

Holdgate, M. (1987). Industry: Caring for the environment, *Journal of the Royal Society of Arts*, February, 195–224.

Hunt, C.B. and Auster, E.R. (1990). Proactive environmental management: Avoiding the toxic trap, *Sloan Management Review*, Winter, 7–18.

Hunt, R.G. (1991). LCA of soft drink containers, *Integrated Environmental Management*, No. 4.

International Chamber of Commerce (1991). *Business Charter for Sustainable Development*, ICC.
Jackson, S. (1990). Screaming green murder? *Director*, May, 56–61.
Johne, F.A. and Snelson, P.A. (1988). Success factors in product innovation: A selective review of the literature, *Journal of Product Innovation Management*, **5**(2), 114–128.
Johne, F.A. and Snelson, P.A. (1989). Product development approaches in established firms, *Industrial Marketing Management*, **8**(2), 113–124.
Johne, F.A. and Snelson, P.A. (1990). *Successful Product Development and Management Practices in American and British Firms*, Basil Blackwell, Oxford.
Jowel, R. (1991). *British Social Attitudes Report*, 8th report, Gower, London.
Kirkpatrick, D. (1990). Environmentalism, *Fortune*, 12 February, 44–51.
Lamming, R. (1993). *Beyond Partnership Strategies for Innovations and Lean Supply*, Prentice Hall, Englewood Cliffs, NJ.
Mackenzie, D. (1991). *Green Design, Design for the Environment*, Laurence King.
Maidique, M.A. and Zirger, B.J. (1984). A study of success and failure in product innovation: The case of the US electronics industry, *IEEE Transactions on Engineering Management*, **31**(4), 192–203.
Major, J. (1991). Global problems: Global solutions, address to *The Sunday Times* international conference on the environment, London, July.
Maslow, A. (1954). *Motivation and Personality*, Harper & Row, New York.
Moore, W.L. (1987). New product development practices of industrial marketers, *Journal of Product Innovation Management*, **4**, 6–19.
National Advisory Group on Eco-Labelling (NAGEL) (1991). *Environmental Labelling*, No. 1, Spring (published by the Department of Trade and Industry and the Department of the Environment).
Nystrom, H. (1985). Product development strategy: An integration of technology and marketing, *Journal of Product Innovation Management*, **2**, 25–33.
PA Consulting (1992). Washing machine criteria, study for the Department of Trade and Industry/Department of the Environment.
Passingham, J. and Battinson, N. (1990). The green consumer revolution: How the availability of environmentally friendly products has really affected household purchasing patterns, in Market Research Society conference papers, pp. 75–85.
Pinto, M.B. and Pinto, J.K. (1990). Project team communication and cross functional cooperation in new program development, *Journal of Product Innovation Management*, **7**, 200–212.
Porritt, J. (1993). *Green Magazine*, March.
Porritt, J. and Winner, D. (1988). *The Coming of the Greens*, Fontana, London.
Potter, S. (1992). The design and commercial success of 'green' products in small firms, in the greening of design seminar, Institute of Advanced Studies, Manchester Metropolitan University, 29 February.
Procter & Gamble (1991). Company literature, Environmental Affairs Department.
Quinn, J.B. (1985). Managing innovation, controlled chaos, *Harvard Business Review*, **53**, 73–84.
Roper Organisation and S.C. Johnson & Son Inc. (1990). The environment: Public attitudes and behaviour, report, New York.
Roy, R. *et al.* (1990). *Design and the Economy*, The Design Council, London.
Ryan, C.J., Hosken, M. and Greene, D. (1992). EcoDesign: Design and the Response to the Greening of the International Market, in *Design Studies*, Butterworth-Heinemann, London.
Ryding, S.O. (1991). Environmental priority strategies in product design, *Integrated Environmental Management*, No. 4, Nov, 18–19.

Salamitou, J. (1991). The environmental index: An environmental management tool for Rhone-Poulenc, *Integrated Environmental Management*, No. 4, Nov, 7–9.
Simon, M., Hinnells, M., Leeming, N. and Harrison, R. (1992). Life cycle analysis; methodology and problems, in the greening of design seminar, Institute of Advanced Studies, Manchester Metropolitan University, 29 February.
Smith, G. (1990). How green is my valley? *Marketing and Research Today*, June, 76–82.
Speth, G.S. (1987). An environmental agenda for world business, *Across the Board*, March, 21–26.
Varble, D.L. (1972). Social and environmental considerations in new product development, *Journal of Marketing*, **36**, 11–15.
Welford, R. and Gouldson, A. (1993). *Environmental Management and Business Strategy*, Pitman, London.
World Commission on Environment and Development (1987). *Our Common Future* (the Brundtland report), Oxford University Press, Oxford.

CHAPTER FIFTEEN

PRODUCT LIABILITY ISSUES IN PRODUCT DEVELOPMENT

Henk Ritsema

In this chapter the focus is on the relationship between product development, marketing and product liability. Based on the European Communities' Directive, it is argued that product liability is an issue to be taken seriously in each of the stages of developing, manufacturing and marketing a product. On no account should matters of product liability be solely of interest to a company's legal department.

INTRODUCTION

Developing and marketing new products is, of course, of great importance to any company. New products help to keep the company healthy. There are also, however, many risks associated with the development, production and marketing of new products. It is worth noting that such risks are not limited to those traditionally listed in marketing literature; there are also sources of risks that lie beyond the scope of what is normally considered to be the marketer's principal domain. These risks can nevertheless have a profound impact on the performance and reputation of a product, as they can on the performance and reputation of the company marketing these products. Such sources of risks can be found in a company's legal environment. This chapter seeks to address one of the risks that a company will have to challenge in the process of

Product Development: Meeting the Challenge of the Design–Marketing Interface.
Edited by M. Bruce and W.G. Biemans.   © 1995 John Wiley & Sons Ltd.

developing, producing and marketing new products – the risk of product liability. This risk may change tremendously, in both nature and magnitude, once a company is no longer confined to its home market, but enters one or more foreign markets. This is the case because each country has its own specific laws and regulations relating to product liability.

Over the past decade both product liability and product safety have been given considerable attention by the regulatory authorities of the European Union (EU) (the former EC or European Community). *Product liability* is concerned mainly with the financial compensation for damage caused to private persons by defective products. Damage may refer to both personal injury and damage to property, and liability for defective products is a civil liability. The objective of *product safety regulation*, on the other hand, is to prevent dangerous products from being marketed and to ensure that they are recalled from the market, should they at any time be identified as dangerous. Product safety regulation, therefore, is mainly within the domain of criminal law. Product liability regulations and product safety regulations can be seen as complementary issues. In 1985, a Product Liability Directive (Directive 85/374 (1985) OJ L210/29; 'the Directive') was adopted by the Council of Ministers of the European Community. A Product Safety Directive (Directive 92/59 (1992) OJ L228/24) was adopted in 1992. The discussion in this chapter focuses on the first Directive and its implications for the process of product development and the marketing of products.

A Directive is an instruction addressed to the Member States. It is binding as to the result to be achieved, but leaves Member States a free choice with regard to the form and the method of implementation in their national legislation. Member States were allowed a period of three years to provide for the necessary changes. Not all countries were able to meet the deadline set in the Directive; in fact, only two actually did so, Italy in 1988 and the UK in 1987. Extensive delays occurred in France and Spain. This chapter focuses on the implications of this 'common' product liability regime for companies operating within the EU. To achieve this, the key issues of the Directive are identified first of all. They relate to such issues as the nature of the concept of liability underlying the Directive, as well as its scope in terms of products and producers that fall under the Directive. In order to consider the relationship between product development, marketing and product liability, use is made of a simple and basic model of product development (Urban, Hauser and Dholakia 1987) to structure the discussion. For an in-depth discussion of the various aspects of the Directive, see also Albanese and Del Duca (1987), Campbell and Campbell (1993), Clark (1989), Greer (1989), Hodges (1993) and Wright (1989). On the basis of the discussion of the aforementioned, the relationships between the various elements of the process of formulating and implementing a marketing strategy are considered. Having identified these links, the possibilities for preventing product liability claims, as far as possible, are examined. The relevant issue in this respect is: how can one incorporate product liability issues when developing new products, formulating a marketing strategy and consecutive marketing plans, etc. in order to minimise the risks of product liability claims? Claims, of course, need not necessarily lead to court proceedings. They may be settled out of court, and such settlements may be advantageous to the various parties involved.

Normally, product liability legislation is primarily associated with consumer protection. The Directive under discussion, however, does not focus on consumer protection alone. One of its declared objectives is to harmonise the rules and regulations of the twelve individual Member States with regard to product liability. Differences in product liability regimes may result in distortions in international competition. This, in turn, may result in a non-optimal flow of products within the Community. Of course, product liability rules can have a restrictive effect on business activities. A harmonisation of these rules, however, clearly reduces the degree of uncertainty facing internationally operating companies. Eventually, more similar product liability rules will apply to all consumers and producers in the Common Market. This Directive, therefore, fits in with the plans for the European Internal Market. It provides a good example of the interdisciplinary approach that is needed with respect to many legal aspects in a national as well as an international setting. What is needed is not just an in-depth discussion of the various legal aspects of laws and other legal instruments that are related to business activities; understanding these aspects can only be a first step. It is essential to take things further and (to try to) incorporate these aspects in the functional activities within a company, such as production and marketing.

STRICT LIABILITY

The liability under the Directive is a so-called strict liability. From this it follows that two elements need to be discussed: (i) the concept of product liability as such will have to be clarified, and (ii) the meaning of the adjective 'strict' in conjunction with product liability will have to be considered. As stated in the introduction, product liability refers to the civil liability of a producer for damage or injury caused by a defective product. Basically, there are two options open to the victims of defective products, under which they can sue for compensation.

The first option is to sue for breach of contract. This option, however, is only open to the buyer of the product. To be more precise, the claim needs to be based on a contractual relationship (such as, for instance, sale, lease or hire purchase). Under the concept, which is known as 'privity of contract', only the parties to the contract can sue and be sued. Thus, the buyer of a defective product will normally only be able to sue the dealer or the shop from which he or she acquired the product in question. Only in specific circumstances will there be a contractual relationship between the manufacturer and the consumer.

The second option is to base a claim under the law of tort. A tort is a civil wrong other than a breach of contract. This is the only option open to a victim of a defective product who was not party to a contract. Such victims may, for instance, be innocent bystanders or users of the product other than the buyer. The circumstances under which such a victim could sue for damages varied from one Member State to another before the adoption of the Directive. Prior to 1987 – the year in which the Directive was implemented in the UK – the most important tort in product liability cases under English law was negligence (Wright 1989). This means breach of a duty to take reasonable care, resulting in damage or injury. Victims were able to sue anyone whom they considered responsible; their claim was not limited to the immediate supplier. The main problem with negligence, however, was in proving that there actually was lack of reasonable care: victims had to prove that the defendant had failed to take reasonable care. This may be difficult. Defendants might argue that they had done their best and that, for instance, the risk could not be foreseen. Issues relating to the burden of proof as well as issues of causation can involve highly technical scientific matters, and victims may consequently find it impossible to satisfy the court that the defendant had failed to take reasonable care. Apart from that, the cost and time involved in pursuing a claim may be very substantial. Furthermore, there may be problems in actually identifying the manufacturer of the defective product, let alone the added problems of having to deal with a manufacturer located in another jurisdiction. As a result of these various issues, victims of defective products could easily be denied compensation. The adoption of the Directive created a special regime based on strict liability for personal injury or damage to personal property.

It is essential to understand that product liability refers to a situation in which a defective product has caused personal damage to a private person (a 'consumer') or to the property of a private person. Damages to the defective product itself or to the property of others than a private person, such as, for example, a wholesaler, are therefore not included in the concept of product liability. With regard to the Directive, it is of no importance whether or not the defective product is primarily intended for industrial use or for use by consumers. What matters is that the product in question has inflicted damage to a consumer (a private person), or to his or her property.

As stated, the Directive imposes a regime of 'strict liability' upon producers, meaning that no fault or negligence on the part of the producer is required for the liability to come into effect. Common as this may be in the USA, for some of the Member States of the European Communities this meant a more severe product liability regime than they used to have. For a description of the various national systems 'before' and 'after' the Directive, see Association Européenne d'Etudes Juridiques et Fiscales (1975), Campbell and Campbell (1993), Hodges (1993) and Posch (1984).

Some crucial aspects that will have to be considered by individual companies are:

- the scope of the liability
- requirements with respect to testing
- possible effects of service on liability
- available defences in the case of a law suit (Manley 1987)

In the following, it is shown that whereas 'strict liability' is at the basis of the Directive, there are still certain circumstances in which the liability of the producer can be lifted (exclusion of liability). In other words, the liability under the Directive is not an 'absolute liability'. In case of absolute liability, no defences whatsoever would be allowed. To prevent claims and to be able to take advantage of the possibilities for exclusion, producers will have to take into account the various aspects of the Directive in developing and marketing products. Of course, this holds for new products as well as for existing products: the Directive does not differentiate between these two categories.

PRODUCERS

According to the Directive, producers of defective products can be held liable for the damages caused by their products. The definition of a producer in the Directive, however, is rather broad. The various participants in the chain of production and distribution who can be held liable as 'a producer' are listed in Table 15.1.

Table 15.1   Producers under the Directive

Manufacturer of a finished product
Manufacturer of a component part
Producer of a raw material
Quasi-producer
EU importer
Supplier

The principal person who can be held liable is the manufacturer of a finished product or a component part, as well as the producer of raw materials. These can be called 'real' producers. Systematically, they are indeed the producers who should actually be held liable in the case of a defective product. Restricting liability to the real producer, however, can easily result in a situation in which no one can be held accountable for damage caused by a defective product. For instance, in cases where the real producer is a foreign (non-EU) company without an establishment within one of the Member States, it may be extremely difficult to sue for damages. In order to guarantee the victim maximum protection, the definition of a producer also includes the importer of a product into the EU and the person presenting the product as his or her own by putting a trade mark, name or any other kind of distinctive sign on it (quasi-producer). In case none of these producers can be identified, the supplier of the product can be looked upon as the producer by the victim, and thus be held liable under the Directive. This effectively means that there will always be at least one person in one of the Member States whom the victim can sue for damages.

In this chapter the focus is on the 'real' producers, i.e. the manufacturers of finished products and component parts. Focusing on this category of producers does not mean that the issue of product liability is of no interest to the other producers as defined by the Directive. Several of the issues that are relevant to the 'real' producer might also prove to be relevant to these other producers. It is, however, the 'real' producer who will face the whole range of possible consequences of the product liability regime for the company and its performance in the market-place.

It is important to note that the provisions laid down in the Directive do not only influence the relationship between producers and consumers of their products. The Directive may also have repercussions on the relationships between one producer and other companies involved in the production and distribution of the product. Since the Directive forbids any exclusion of liability as far as the consumer is concerned, the various 'producers' may very well turn to drafting contractual provisions, in which the burden of product liability claims is eventually shifted up or down the channel of production and distribution. Furthermore, the Directive may be of considerable importance to producers located outside the EU as well. As was stated earlier, a company that imports products into the EU would be regarded as a producer and can consequently be held liable. Bearing this in mind, importing companies are likely to negotiate contracts in which some kind of reimbursement by the 'real producer' is arranged, in case the importer is sued for damages.

DEFECTIVE PRODUCTS

In the process of developing new products the following steps have to be made (Urban, Hauser and Dholakia 1987):

- opportunity identification
- designing new products
- testing and improving products
- managing the life cycle

The opportunity identification phase deals with identifying market opportunities and generating ideas for new products. In the designing phase the producer tries to find out how consumers will perceive the product, thus enabling him or her to create a product that is best suited to meet consumers' preferences. In the next phase, what the producer is concerned with is actually testing the product and the marketing strategy. In the final phase, managing the life cycle, the product is being sold in the market-place, and attention will focus on introducing the product and managing it throughout its life cycle.

If problems concerning product liability are to be prevented, or if, at least, damages resulting from defective products are to be minimised, attention will have to be paid to adequate measures in each of the steps. This, however, does not mean that product liability issues will be of the same importance in all stages of the product development process.

In order to be able to establish a clear link between the different phases of the product development process and product liability, it will first be necessary to see how products can turn into defective products, thus creating a potential threat to consumers. In product liability cases a distinction is sometimes made between various categories of faults a producer can make in the process of developing, manufacturing and marketing a product. Distinctions can be drawn between (Prag 1975):

- defective construction
- defective production
- faulty or inadequate instructions
- development defects

In the case of a construction defect the situation is that there is a basic fault in the design or construction of a product, resulting in a series of products with a defect. Defective production refers to the situation where the defect only has influence on the quality of a limited number of items (maybe even just one product), and not on a whole series of products. In cases where the producer has omitted instructions that are necessary to make the product suitable for ordinary use an instruction defect can arise. Finally, a development defect refers to the situation where later research shows that a product that was considered safe at the time of production proved not to be safe after all. From this it also follows that, in principle, a construction defect can be the result of a development defect. Normally a construction defect will refer to a situation where the defect could have been prevented or detected when the product was put into circulation.

From this classification it becomes evident that, for a company that is seriously trying to prevent putting defective products onto the market-place, it will not be sufficient to concentrate only on the production phase. Preventing product liability claims can only be done successfully if due attention is paid to it in all stages of the product development process. In doing this, it has to be realised that there is no such thing as 100% safety. This means that even when all possible precautions and measures are taken by a producer, some form of defective products will inevitably be sold in the market at some time or another, thus possibly causing damage to consumers.

The above classification – useful as it may be to give a better understanding of the origins of defects in products – is not used in the Directive, which does not classify defects. According to the Directive, a product is considered to be defective when it does not provide the safety that a person is entitled to expect, taking all circumstances into account. These circumstances include, in the Directive's terms, the presentation of the product, the use to which it could reasonably be expected that the product would be put and the time when the product was put into circulation. It has to be stressed that in a specific case other circumstances can also be taken into account. The definition of defectiveness and the possibilities for the exclusion of liability are of great importance when reviewing the process of developing and marketing new products from a product liability point of view, as is discussed below.

The key question, then, is what actions need to be taken in the various phases in the process of developing and marketing new products? Actions should be focused on creating a situation that guarantee minimal risks of liability for the producer.

THE DESIGNING PHASE

INTRODUCTION

Important elements in the designing phase are the mapping of the product perceptions of consumers, product positioning, forecasting of sales potential, and, finally, product engineering and the marketing mix to complete the design (Urban, Hauser and Dholakia 1987). Taking product liability considerations explicitly into account when reviewing these aspects can be a major step towards preventing products from becoming defective. In this section the relevant elements are discussed.

CONSUMERS' PERCEPTIONS

Information on consumers' perceptions of the product is necessary to be able to ensure a good positioning of the product. This information can, however, also reveal relevant product liability information. As stated before, a critical factor in judging the defectiveness of a product is the use to which a product can be expected to be put. This means that the safety of a product should not just be determined on the basis of its fitness for use but, more importantly, by the degree of safety that the public at large is entitled to expect from the product. In developing core benefits for a product, and consequently positioning them correctly against competitive products, the producer should be very much aware of the possible use his product might actually be put to by the public at large. To do this, a product manager will first of all need to identify the dimensions that describe the market in question (such as, for instance, ease of use). Next, the existing products have to be positioned along these dimensions. Furthermore, the physical features corresponding to the perceptual positioning have to be identified, and, finally, it has to be established where consumers prefer the product to be on the dimensions just identified. All of this information is vital to reveal useful information about the manner in which the consumer intends to use this particular product. On the basis of consumers' preferences, a product manager can evaluate whether or not there is a real chance that the product will be put to a use for which it was not intended in the first place. If this way of using the product can be looked upon as a reasonable use of the product, the question arises as to whether any action should be taken with respect to this kind of use of the product. This, of course, will depend on the product manager's perception of whether or not this particular way of using the product might easily lead to defectiveness.

POSITIONING THE PRODUCT

Whereas mapping consumers' product perceptions can reveal relevant information about the manner in which a consumer *intends* to use a product, the actual positioning of the product can be a major factor in influencing the use to which a product is *actually* put once it becomes available to the consumer, thus possibly influencing the degree of safety the public at large is entitled to expect. It is important to understand that 'the public at large' refers to those consumers who do not have specific expertise with regard to the product in question. Even consumers without specific knowledge will, of course, have to take into account that using a product always includes a certain degree of risk. The circumstances referred to in the Directive, which were mentioned in the section entitled 'Defective Products', are therefore of great importance. Where the Directive refers to the use to which a product can reasonably be expected to be put, this has to be read in conjunction with the recitals to the Directive, where it is stated that in no way shall a producer be liable in case of misuse of the product not reasonable under the circumstances. The borderline between 'use' and 'misuse' can be influenced by the producers. For instance when designing the product, the producer can take into account, bearing in mind the function of the product, possible detrimental side effects. Using consumer preferences to position the product will therefore also have to take account of the fact that this may influence the use of the product, and thus its safety. A good understanding of how the product may be used in the future is therefore important in trying to avoid possible claims.

ENGINEERING AND MARKETING MIX

In the final stage of the designing phase in the product development process, the core benefit proposition(s) will need to be implemented by the final engineering of the physical product and the creation of the advertising copy. The engineering task is to take the core benefit proposition requirements and design the best physical product to meet them. Of course, designing the physical product is also a key issue when trying to prevent future product liability claims. Development faults, as well as construction faults, can easily arise at this stage. Under the Directive a producer will not be liable for development faults, yet the definition of development faults is fairly strict. A producer can only successfully plead a development fault if he or she is able to prove that the state of scientific and technical knowledge at the time when the product was put into circulation was not such as to enable the defect to be discovered. It is important to note that the ability of the individual producer to discover the defect is of no importance, nor is the 'state of the art' in the sector in which the producer is operating. The only issue that actually matters is the scientific and technical knowledge available to the producer at the moment when the product was put into circulation. Producers will have to see to it that this information is indeed available to them, and that, if/when it becomes necessary, they actually use it in designing products. Otherwise, the so-called 'state-of-the-art' defence will not be available to them. Each of the Member States of the EU can, by way of derogation of this provision, provide in its national legislation that the producer shall be liable even if he or she proves that the state of scientific and technical knowledge at the time when the product was put into circulation was not such as to enable the existence of a defect to be discovered. Most Member States, however, have opted to include this defence in their national legislation.

As far as the engineering of a component part is concerned a special defence holds for the producer of such a part. The producer is excluded from liability in such cases where a defect can be attributed to the design of the product in which the component has been fitted or to the instructions given by the manufacturer of the finished product to the producer of the component part. In cases where the producer of the product gave only general instructions to the producer of the component, a fault in designing the component part by its producer is still possible. It is evident that this exception will mainly be applied in the case of a faulty construction.

Advertising and promotion can also be of great importance where product liability is concerned. First of all, incorrect or incomplete advertising or promotional activities can cause an instruction fault. On the other hand, a good advertising campaign in combination with other promotional activities can also make the consumer more aware of the things that the product can do and, more importantly, the things it cannot do. In this way the consciousness of the public in general towards potential dangers of the product may be raised, thus causing consumers to be more careful when using the product.

The same holds for the presentation of the product. Promotion, for instance, can make the public more aware of the difference between 'use' and 'misuse' of the product. Here, the link with product engineering and the marketing mix elements becomes evident.

TESTING AND IMPROVING THE PRODUCT

The main goals in the phase of testing and improving the product are reducing risks and maximising profits. As far as product liability is concerned, testing of the physical product is extremely important. It can help to detect and correct construction faults and even development faults. By definition, testing the physical product cannot be very helpful where production faults are concerned, since they can occur only once production of the products has actually started. Testing the advertising may help in preventing instruction faults.

As far as the testing includes test marketing or the use of pre-test markets, it has to be realised that, in general, the product liability rules will also apply in these situations. The producer can only be excused from liability if the product was neither manufactured for sale or any other form of distribution for economic purposes, nor manufactured or distributed in the course of business. This will, however, not apply in the case of test-marketing a product.

Since the terms associated with the defences to strict product liability are normally rather difficult to meet, it is important to safeguard against claims as far as possible. Therefore, when testing the product physically, it is advisable to simulate the toughest conditions that a product is likely to encounter (Manley 1987). Since the Directive does allow for certain defences, a company will be well advised to keep records of the information relating to this phase.

INTRODUCING AND MANAGING THE PRODUCT

INTRODUCTION

Once it has been decided to introduce the product, it will become clear how successful the producer has been and will be in managing product liability risks. As far as development defects are concerned, they can not, by definition, be prevented, since the producer did not, and more importantly could not, have any knowledge about the faults made in developing the products. The producer will, however, have to take good care in continually reviewing the new technical and scientific knowledge relating to the product or production process. Once this knowledge becomes available, the producer is no longer excused if products that still have the same defect continue to be put into circulation.

CONSTRUCTION DEFECTS

With regard to construction failures, it can be concluded that the foundations for avoiding this type of failure will have to be laid during the process of designing, testing and improving the product. Over the life cycle of the product, the producer should, however, be aware of the fact that the group of people using the product can change over time. Consequently, the safety requirements regarding the product may also shift as time goes by. For instance, various types of products that are now used by consumers when working on their own houses were only used by professionals some 10–15 years ago. It is evident that those professionals cannot be compared to the public at large when it comes to actually handling the product and judging its safety. Therefore, it may be necessary to redesign the product for this nonprofessional use by, for example, adding or omitting certain features. It may also be necessary to change the instructions that go with the product in order to educate the new group of users.

PRODUCTION DEFECTS

The category of faults that is most difficult to prevent is that of production faults. Since these are more or less 'individual' faults in one product (or a limited number of products), they may be very difficult to detect. This does not mean, however, that production faults have to be accepted as a fact of life. Indeed, most attention is actually given to the prevention of this category of defects. Since these faults are so closely linked to the production process itself, this is only to be expected. A well-organised production process and a good quality control system may help to prevent and detect this type of failure. Moreover, a quality control system can also be a very effective means of detecting construction faults at an early stage.

PUTTING PRODUCTS INTO CIRCULATION

When producing, the producer becomes liable for defects in products at the moment when they are put into circulation. The basic liability extends for a certain period of time from that moment on. From this it becomes evident that it is necessary for a producer to be able to track when, in fact, a certain series of products were actually put into circulation. If a registration system does not exist, it may be difficult to counter consumers' claims. As was indicated before, it is important to know the date when the products were put into circulation when the matter of the 'state-of-the-art' defence arises. It becomes even more important if one considers that the Directive states that a producer shall not be liable if it is probable that the defect causing the damage did not exist at the time when the product was put into circulation by the producer, or that the defect only came into being afterwards.

RECALL

If the worst comes to the worst, a company should be prepared to take immediate action. In other words, it should have a 'script' on how to react when defective products show up in the market. The appropriate action may be to recall the (potentially) defective products. Product recall has been compared to driving a car backwards at speed with little warning, which is a difficult thing to do, especially if one has no previous experience (Abbot 1991). Being able to manage a product recall requires advance planning.

CONCLUDING REMARKS

From the above discussion it is evident that product liability issues can be linked to practically every phase in the process of developing and marketing products. Product liability is not just an issue that becomes important once a product has been launched. During the whole process of developing, producing, marketing and selling products, it has to be kept in mind that it is worth undertaking the necessary measures in order to prevent future product liability claims. This, however, is easier said than done. The process of developing, producing and marketing products is not primarily directed towards preventing product liability claims; it is – first and foremost – directed towards satisfying customers' needs. In the long run, however, these needs will be best satisfied with good and safe products.

Product liability issues are by no means a key issue when developing, producing and marketing products. They should not, however, be neglected. Paying due attention to these matters may prevent later claims. Therefore, the idea of preventing products from becoming defective should be incorporated into the entire process of developing and marketing new products. In other words, the attitude of companies towards product liability should be *proactive*, rather than *reactive*. Incorporating these issues into the process of developing and marketing means that product liability matters should not be of interest merely to the legal department. Changes in liability regulations, such as the changes brought about by the Directive, can be a good starting point for integrating these aspects into the overall strategy of a company.

REFERENCES

Abbot, H. (1991). *Managing Product Recall*, Pitman, London.
Albanese, F. and Del Duca, L.F. (1987). Developments in European product liability, *Dickinson Journal of International Law*, 5(2), 193.
Association Européenne d'Etudes Juridiques et Fiscales (1975). *Product Liability in Europe*, Kluwer/Harrap, Deventer/London.
Campbell, D. and Campbell, C. (1993). *International Product Liability*, Lloyd's of London Press Ltd, London.
Clark, A. (1989). *Product Liability*, Sweet and Maxwell, London.
Greer, T.V. (1989). Product liability in the European Economic Community: The new situation, *Journal of International Business Studies*, XX(2), 337.
Hodges, C.J.S. (ed.) (1993). *Product Liability – European Laws and Practice*, Sweet and Maxwell, London.

Manley, M. (1987). Product liability: You are more exposed than you think, *Harvard Business Review*, September/October, 28.

Posch, W. (1984). Recent developments of product liability law in Europe and nearby, in Campbell, D. and Rohwer, C. (eds), *Legal Aspects of International Business Transactions*, North-Holland, Amsterdam, p. 141.

Prag, P. (1975). A comparative study of the concept and development of product liability in the USA, Germany and Scandinavia, *Legal Issues of European Integration*, **1**, 67.

Urban, G.L., Hauser, J.R. and Dholakia, M. (1987). *Essentials of New Product Management*, Prentice-Hall, Englewood Cliffs, NJ.

Wright, C.J. (1989). *Product Liability*, Blackstone Press, London.

INDEX